The Spectacle of the Real:
From Hollywood to 'Reality' TV and Beyond

Edited by Geoff King

intellect™
Bristol, UK
Portland, OR, USA

First Published in the UK in 2005 by
Intellect Books, PO Box 862, Bristol BS99 1DE, UK
First Published in the USA in 2005 by
Intellect Books, ISBS, 920 NE 58th Ave. Suite 300, Portland, Oregon 97213-3786, USA
Copyright ©2005 Intellect Ltd

A catalogue record for this book is available from the British Library

ISBN 1-84150-120-4
Cover Design: Gabriel Solomons
Copy Editor: Holly Spradling

Printed and bound in Great Britain by Antony Rowe Ltd.

Contents

Leon Hunt

Notes on Contributors

Michele Aaron lectures on film int he department of American and Canadian Studies at the University of Birmingham. She is editor of *The Body's Perilous Pleasures* (1999) and *New Queer Cinema: A Critical Reader* (2003) and has published a number of articles, most recently on Jewishness and gender, and queer film and cinematic fiction. She is currently completing a book entitled *Spectatorship: the Power of Looking On*. Email: michele.aaron@brunel.ac.uk

Peg Aloi teaches creative writing and film studies at Emerson College in Boston, Massachusetts. She is also a freelance film critic for the *Boston Phoenix*. Recent publications include essays in the anthologies *Seven Seasons of Buffy* from BenBella Books, and *The Last Pentacle of the Sun: Writings to Benefit the West Memphis Three* from Arsenal Pulp Press. She is also co-editing(with Hannah Sanders) a collection of academic essays on contemporary paganism in the US and UK. Email: Amberapple@aol.com

Jay David Bolter is Director of the Wesley New Media Center and Wesley Chair of New Media at the Georgia Institute of Technology. He is the author of *Turing's Man: Western Culture in the Computer Age* (1984); *Writing Space: The Computer, Hypertext, and the History of Writing*, (1991; second edition 2001); and *Remediation* (1999), written in collaboration with Richard Grusin. In addition to writing about new media, Bolter collaborates to construct new digital media forms. With Michael Joyce, he created Storyspace, a hypertext authoring system. With Blair Macintyre, he is building an Augmented Reality (AR) system to create dramatic and narrative experiences for entertainment and informal educational settings. Email: jay.bolter@lcc.gatech.edu

Frances Bonner lectures in film and television in the School of English, Media Studies and Art History at the University of Queensland, Australia. She is the author of *Ordinary Television* (2003) and one of the authors of *Fame Games: The Production of Celebrity in Australia* (2000). Her principal research areas are non-fiction television and magazine coverage of health issues. Email: F.Bonner@mailbox.uq.oz.au

Bernadette Flynn is a lecturer in screen production and digital media in The School of Film, Media and Cultural Studies at Griffith University, Australia. Her research focuses on the areas of computer games, digital aesthetics, documentary and spatiality. With a background in video art and production, she has been engaged in new media research practice since 1993. Her current project is an exploration of dynamic spatialization in the Neolithic temples of Malta. Her writing

can be found online and in journals including Media Information Australia, M/C and Information, Communication and Society.
Email: B.Flynn@mail box .gu.edu.au

Leon Hunt is a senior lecturer in Film and TV Studies at Brunel University. He is the author of *British Low Culture: From Safari Suits to Sexploitation* (1998) and *Kung Fu Cult Masters: From Bruce Lee to Crouching Tiger* (2003).Email: leon.hunt@brunel.ac.uk

Misha Kavka is a lecturer in Film, Television and Media Studies at the University of Auckland. She has published articles on feminism, camp, gothic cinema, and New Zealand television, as well as co-editing a book on feminist theory, *Feminist Consequences: Theory for the New Century*. She is currently writing a book about the global manifestations and media impact of reality television. Email: m.kavka@auckland.ac.nz

Douglas Kellner is George Kneller Chair in the Philosophy of Education at UCLA and is author of many books on social theory, politics, history, and culture, including *Camera Politica: The Politics and Ideology of Contemporary Hollywood Film*, co-authored with Michael Ryan; *Critical Theory, Marxism, and Modernity*; *Jean Baudrillard: From Marxism to Postmodernism and Beyond; Postmodern Theory: Critical Interrogations* (with Steven Best); *Television and the Crisis of Democracy*; *The Persian Gulf TV War*; *Media Culture*; and *The Postmodern Turn* (with Steven Best). Recent publications include: *Media Spectacle*; *Grand Theft 2000: Media Spectacle and the Theft of an Election*; *The Postmodern Adventure: Science, Technology, and Cultural Studies at the Third Millennium* (co-authored with Steve Best); and *September 11, Terror War, and the Bush Presidency*. Email: kellner@ucla.edu

Geoff King is a senior lecturer in Film and TV Studies at Brunel University and author of books including *New Hollywood Cinema: An Introduction* (2002), *Spectacular Narratives: Hollywood in the Age of the Blockbuster* (2000), *American Independent Cinema* (2005), *Film Comedy* (2002) and *Mapping Reality: An Exploration of Cultural Cartographies* (1996). He is currently completing a study of videogames co-authored with Tanya Krzywinska. Email: geoff.king@brunel.ac.uk

Tanya Krzywinska is a reader in Film and TV Studies at Brunel University. She is the author of *A Skin For Dancing In: Possession, Witchcraft and Voodoo in Film* (2000), co-author with Geoff King of *Science Fiction Cinema: From Outerspace to Cyberspace* (2000) and co-editor with Geoff King of *ScreenPlay: Cinema/ Videogames/ Interfaces* (2002). She has published a number of articles on subjects ranging from hard-core pornography to *Buffy the Vampire Slayer*. Forthcoming publications include *Sex in the Cinema* (2005) and a co-authored book with Geoff King on videogames. Email: tanya.krzywinska@brunel.ac.uk

Dean Lockwood is a lecturer in Media Theory in the Department of Media Production at the University of Lincoln. His approach to media theory is informed by his earlier doctoral studies in modern social and cultural theory. He is currently interested in the reflexive consequences of media and how media facilitate or inhibit new ways of constructing and envisioning social reality. Email: dlockwood@lincoln.ac.uk

Julian Petley is a professor in Film and TV Studies at Brunel University. He is the co-editor of *Ill Effects* (Routledge 2001) and *British Horror Cinema* (Routledge 2002). He is currently co-editing a collection on contemporary horror cinema for Verso and writing a monograph on *Witchfinder General* for I.B. Tauris. Email: julian.petley@brunel.ac.uk

Michele Pierson is a lecturer in film and television studies at the University of Queensland and is the author of *Special Effects: Still in Search of Wonder* (2002). She is currently researching the cultural and institutional history of experimental film and new media in Australia, Britain and the United States. Email: m.pierson@mailbox.uq.edu.au

Lisa Purse holds a degree in English and an MA in Film and Drama from the University of Reading. She is currently researching her PhD in film at Reading, and also teaches film in the Department of Film, Theatre and Television at the University. The subject of her thesis is gendered representation and spectatorship in contemporary mainstream American action cinema. Email: lisapurse@hotmail.com

Lee Rodney is Assistant Professor in the School of Visual Arts, University of Windsor (Canada). She is completing a PhD in Visual Culture at Goldsmiths College, London (UK). Her research focuses on the articulation of real time in experimental film, video and performance from 1965 to the present. Email: lrodney@uwindsor.ca

Kathy Smith is a senior lecturer in Theatre Studies at London Metropolitan University. She has published articles on various subjects. Her research interests include theories of identity, spectatorship and representation, with particular reference to psychoanalysis, feminism, modern theatre/performance practices, and the theatre of Samuel Beckett. Email: k.smith@londonnet.ac.uk

Paul Ward is a lecturer in Film and Television Studies at Brunel University. His main research interests are exploring the interface between fiction and non-fiction forms in TV and film, and the convergence/dialectic between animation and live action. His doctoral research investigates animation as a cultural form in relation to film and media studies. His publications include 'Videogames as remediated animation', in King and Krzywinska (eds.) *ScreenPlay: Cinema/Videogames/ Interfaces* (2002) and *Defining Documentary* (forthcoming 2005). Email: paul.ward@brunel.ac.uk

Mike Wayne is a senior lecturer in Film and Television at Brunel University. He is the author of *Political Film: the dialectics of Third Cinema* (Pluto Press) and *The Politics of Contemporary European Cinema: Histories, Borders, Diasporas* (Intellect Books) and *Marxism and the Media: Key Concepts and Contemporary Trends* (Pluto Press). Email: michael.wayne@brunel.ac.uk

Amy West is currently enrolled in the doctoral programme of the Department of Film, Television and Media Studies at the University of Auckland. She is in the process of writing a thesis on reality television. Email: awes001@ec.auckland.ac.nz

Preface

Jay David Bolter

The first years of the twenty-first century constitute the right occasion to revisit the notion of spectacle. Our culture's desire for spectacle has gained in intensity, just as our ability to stage spectacle has increased in technical sophistication. It is no longer only analog film and television that mediate spectacle for us. Film and television remain important, but these media are now hybrid forms that combine the digital with the analog. Computer graphics and digital signal transmission and processing have extended the reach of conventional television and film, while the new media technologies of the Internet, above all the World Wide Web, are supplementing and remediating earlier forms.

Ever since McLuhan coined the phrase 'global village,' it has been claimed that communications technologies have annihilated the distance that separates the viewer from the event. Until recently, however, that claim was an exaggeration of what the technology could reliably and consistently achieve. Only on special occasions and under the best circumstances could the communications network be configured to present the world as spectacle to an audience of viewers in North America, Europe and a few other developed countries. McLuhan was writing about the global village in the late 1960s, when the coverage of the Vietnam War was being cited as the example of the televisual networks' ability to bring violence from halfway around the world into American living rooms. It is worth remembering, then, that at the time the images of the war were recorded on film, the film flown to the United States, processed, and then shown on the nightly news a day or more later. We need only compare this lengthy procedure to the coverage of the Persian Gulf War in the early 1990s and the Iraq War in 2003 to appreciate the difference that fully developed global communications can make in fulfillling their McLuhanesque promise or Virilian threat.

Today, it really does seem as if television cameras can be put anywhere on earth in a matter of days, hours, or minutes. Televisual coverage of the world as spectacle is now possible, at least for the audiences in the industrialized nations. We can see the world in so-called 'real time.' As Lee Rodney and others explicitly recognize, one might even have called this volume the 'Spectacle of the Real-Time,' because in the current hybrid (analog/digital) media world, the concept of real-time delivery now plays a key role in defining the real or the authentic for our culture. Real-time is televisual 'liveness' as refined by digital processing.

Instead of 'real time,' however, we should call it 'near-real time.' We can see distant events almost as they happen, where the gap between the occurrence and our consumption of the images may be measured in seconds, minutes, or hours. In that gap, the communications system (both as a technology and as a cultural and economic force) 'processes' the signal: in other words, those in control of the technology both manufacture and constrain the spectacle for us. Sometimes a matter of seconds is enough to reshape the image. A seemingly harmless example is the yellow stripe on the (American) football field. To indicate where the first-down line is, a computer graphics company, Princeton Video Image, has combined software and hardware to place a virtual yellow stripe across the field. The players appear to walk over the stripe, because the computer employs a carefully calibrated map of the surface of the field to separate the players from the grass. The processing happens within the few seconds between the time the image is recorded and the time it is broadcast. Ostensibly, the processing is to enhance the viewer's enjoyment of the spectacle. However, once the gap has been opened, economic opportunity, which abhors a vacuum, pours in. The same company offers to paint digital advertising, company logos, on the field at the same time. In sport broadcasting and elsewhere, digital processing routinely inserts virtual advertising on walls and fences.

Other cultural forces can also intervene to contain and constrain the viewer's reading of the spectacle. In fact, the gap becomes contested territory, reflecting our culture's ambivalence over what should and should not be seen. The desire for total coverage suggests that nothing should be left out: the experience should be immediate, and the media technology should be effaced. The gap should be as short and unobtrusive as possible. On the other hand, the culture, particularly American culture, refuses to see everything. For example, in their 'total coverage' of the collapse of the World Trade Center, the networks soon began editing out the images and sounds of falling bodies (those who had jumped from upper stories), which they deemed too brutal. In the age of near-real time spectacle, coverage acquires two meanings: to report the event completely and at the same time to cover over and refuse to acknowledge the gaps.

At the technical level, the gaps are covered by making the representation appear seamless for the viewer. On the football field, computer compositing makes the first-down stripe appear to be painted on the grass. Likewise, in the coverage of September 11 (as Geoff King shows in his chapter of this volume), the techniques of traditional continuity editing were gradually applied to the raw video footage. In the first hours after the attack, the networks had to make do with fragmentary shots of the crashing planes. Their problem was the absence of what Hollywood cinematographers would call 'coverage' of the event: they did not have a range of shots from various angles of the planes hitting the two towers. As they found and assembled footage during the first couple of days, continuity editing became possible. By the second or third day, viewers brought up on the technique of Hollywood disaster movies were able to watch a sequence of images that made dramatic sense. Continuity editing itself is, of course, the techinque of eliding the gaps, which the original film theorists of spectacle called 'suture.'

By editing the fragmentary shots into a continuous sequence, the networks were helping to provide an interpretation of the events and thus to cover over the sense of dislocation that their audience felt. The endless, running commentary from the various news anchors served the same purpose, providing coverage in both senses: the commentary appeared to offer a complete and unmediated experience while covering over the gaps. The news networks had long realized that their coverage of a disaster needed to be turned into a story. The technique of narrativization was used extensively throughout the September 11 coverage, as vignettes of sacrifice and heroism served to build a larger story. The technique was used again in the coverage of the American mobilization against and invasion of Iraq. Each phase in that conflict was given a dramatic title by each of the networks, exactly as if it was an episode in a larger drama. To call the run-up to the war something like 'Showdown in Iraq' precludes other interpretations that American viewers might have. The Pentagon, too, mastered the technique of coverage. 'Embedding' reporters with the troops guaranteed that seemingly 'total coverage' would include its own intepretation: the reporters would almost necessarily see the troops' battle as their own. When commandos were sent in to rescue Jessia Lynch, the team brought its own video equipment, again guaranteeing coverage in both senses.

Total real-time coverage demands that everything must be fitted into the larger narrative. An event that has not been narrativized constitutes a source of anxiety. When in January 2002, a 15-year-old boy crashed a small plane into a building in downtown Tampa, there was palpable anxiety: did this act belong to the terrorism story? After it was announced that authorities had ruled out terrorism, the national media reflected the nation's relief. The story had been moved out of one narrative into a safer one (it was merely the desperate act of a suicidal youth).

Although the desire to contain the ambiguities of 'real events' by fashioning them into a story is not peculiar to our contemporary media culture, our current cultural moment does seem to be obsessed with this practice. The popularity of reality TV, discussed in this volume, clearly reflects the desire of its viewing audience to see the 'real' in dramatic terms. The non-actors in reality programming cannot help but participate in the drama that is scripted for them. The presentation is so carefully orchestrated that gaps are hardly permitted to form before they are closed. Ambiguity of intepretation is always the first player to be 'voted off the island.' Reality TV could almost be seen as a dry run, in which the audience learns to accept the controlled narrativization of televisual events. Viewers will then be prepared to accept the narrative structures offered in the less well-scripted, real-time coverage of wars and disasters.

As I read the remarkable essays in this volume, I find many insights into the manifestations of coverage in contemporary media: the desire for immediacy and real-time representation, the need to cover up the emerging gaps, and the techniques developed for seamless, narrative interpretation. The events of September 11 provide a paradigm here, but a range of other spectacles and representational practices are also examined. They include pornography and sex in films (always about both coverage and covering the gap); horror films and the representation of disease and death; reality TV; and closed-circuit and surveillance video. Taken together, the authors in this volume give me hope that the gap cannot be covered over indefinitely. Their essays reveal the ambiguities and inconsistencies in our culture's desire for the seamless spectacle of the real-time.

Introduction: The Spectacle of the Real

Geoff King

Hollywood special effects offer spectacular creations or re-creations that make claims to our attention on the grounds of their 'incredible-seeming reality'. They can appear both 'incredible' and 'real', their appeal based on their ability to 'convince' – to appear real in terms such as detail and texture – and on their status *as* fabricated spectacle, to be admired as such. At a seemingly very different end of the audio-visual media spectrum, 'reality' television offers the spectacle of, supposedly, the 'real' itself, a 'reality' that ranges from the banality of the quotidian to intense interpersonal engagements (two extremes experienced in series such as *Big Brother*, for example). The two also overlap in many instances, however, nowhere more clearly and jarringly in recent years than in the ultimate 'spectacle of the real' constituted by the destruction of the World Trade Center in New York, live-reality television coverage of which evoked constant comparison with big-screen fictional images.

Impressions of the 'real' or the 'authentic' (or the authentic-seeming) are valued as forms of media spectacle in a number of other contemporary media forms. Examples in film range from the Dogme 95 movement, in its association with grainy image quality and unsteady hand-held camerawork, to the 'uncanny' verisimilitude of the latest developments in computer-generated animation displayed in features such as *Final Fantasy: The Spirits Within* (2001) and *Shrek* (2001). Spectacle and notions of the authentic – skill, competition – are conjoined in television productions such as live or recorded coverage of sporting events, as well as in recently proliferating reality TV/game-show hybrids. Videogames, using computer-generated animation techniques similar to those of film, also offer a blend of images that are spectacular and that often stake claims to authenticity, the latter especially the case in the highly detailed simulations offered by many flying and driving games.

This collection seeks to explore some of the issues emerging from this fascination with both the impression of 'reality' and the fact that it is often presented and experienced as a form of spectacle; or, alternatively, the fascination with the spectacular and the fact that it is often considered in terms of its apparent 'realism'. Broad questions considered through the examination of a wide range of textual material concern the nature and different forms of both 'spectacle' and of 'the real' (along with 'reality', 'realism' and 'authenticity'); and, especially, the points of conjuncture between the two.

The genesis of this project pre-dates by some months the spectacularly real events of September 11, 2001, its beginnings lying in an effort to bring together strands of research being pursued by a number of members of staff in Film and TV Studies at Brunel University. The attacks on the World Trade Center and the Pentagon, and their aftermath, created a heightened context for work in this area, however, and have been a constant presence during the germination process that resulted in the production of this book. *The Spectacle of the Real* started as a conference at Brunel in January 2003. The call for papers for the conference was being drafted at the time of September 11, producing a number of contributions in which the coverage of 9/11 was directly addressed. The conference itself came as the US and British administrations were preparing an attack on Iraq, a largely opportunistic endeavour pursued under the cloak of the outraged reaction to the events of 9/11/01. The process of converting conference programme and papers to book occurred both during and in the aftermath of that attack, which produced its own blend of images that claimed the status of both the spectacular-real (the blazing Baghdad skyline after US-led bomb and missile attacks) and a 'real' defined through reduced visual quality as a marker of authenticity (indistinct green-and-white night-vision images of conflict).

The contributions to this collection are organized into three parts. The first revolves around broad issues of spectacle, ideology and catastrophe, with a particular emphasis by some writers on the events of 9/11/01. The second part is focused on reality TV, the third on different manifestations of spectacle, the real and the conjunction of the two, in film. As important as the divisions, however, are the many overlaps that occur across the breadth of specific issues covered by the book. One of the strengths of the 'Spectacle of the Real' conference was the readiness of participants to make cross references from one paper to another, in the case of both those giving papers and those contributing from the floor in the discussions that followed each panel. The aim of this book has been to maintain this spirit as far as is practical in the more fixed format of a collection of separate essays, either explicitly, in references from one chapter to another, or implicitly, in crossovers that range from considerations of the use of similar formal devices in different media contexts (unsteady camerawork as a signifier of authenticity in coverage of 9/11, other forms of reality TV and horror movies, for example) and to links based on the analysis of different aspects of a single social-historical-media conjuncture, over which the shadow of 9/11 and its aftermath has loomed large.

All of the contributions to Part One contain reference to the events of September 11, 2001, but these take a range of different forms, from close focus on the coverage of 9/11 to consideration of that particular spectacle-of-the-real as part of broader engagements with questions relating to the conjuncture of spectacle, the spectacular and that which claims the status of the real. The opening chapter, 'Media Culture and the Triumph of the Spectacle', by Douglas Kellner, a prolific critic of the American culture of spectacle, offers a wide-ranging survey of the extent to which spectacle has entered the domains of economy, politics, society, entertainment and everyday life. 'Megaspectacles' such as those constituted by 9/11 and by coverage of events ranging from the O.J. Simpson trial to the funeral of Diana, Princess of Wales, and the attempted impeachment of President Bill Clinton, are, Kellner suggests, phenomena that dramatize the controversies and struggles of media culture. Drawing on Guy Debord's seminal work, *Society of the Spectacle*, Kellner combines an compressive account of the realms of life into which a spectacle-oriented approach has intruded with a critical edge. He suggests that the world of global media-saturated spectacle is far from all-conquering, citing as examples the recent backlash against McDonald's and the failure of the right-wing Republican effort to unseat Clinton.

After the broad survey offered by Kellner, the following two chapters approach the coverage of 9/11 more directly. The second chapter, 'Real Time, Catastrophe, Spectacle: Reality as Fantasy in Live Media', by Lee Rodney, situates 9/11 in the context of real-time media images, the surveillance-oriented coverage of the era of the ubiquitous web-cam, numerous examples of which were unblinking witness to the destruction of the World Trade Center. The equation of views of Manhattan skyscrapers and real-time footage is used by Rodney as a point from which to move from 9/11 to Andy Warhol's extended-duration film of the Empire State Building, the two linked directly by an homage to Warhol in which the collapse of the twin towers was captured. Further connections are traced between the dynamics of real time, of television 'liveness', of reality TV, the principal subject of Part Two, and coverage of the American foreign policy initiatives – the attacks on Afghanistan and Iraq – that followed in the wake of 9/11. My own chapter, '"Just Like a Movie"? 9/11 and Hollywood Spectacle', looks more closely at the footage of the destruction of the World Trade Center itself. A number of much-cited similarities are sketched between the images that dominated global TV screens and those of recent Hollywood blockbuster films, but also differences that acted as markers of modality, clearly establishing the status of the coverage as that of real-spectacle rather than the big-screen fictional variety. This chapter then analyses the way some footage was redeployed during 9/11 and in its aftermath in a manner that more closely resembled the kind of assemblage associated with fictional convention, a process that, it is suggested, can be understood as one of seeking to heal the rift of discontinuity created by such instances of disruptive spectacular intrusion.

Possible sources of reframing or containment of the breach constituted by coverage of 9/11 are also considered by Kathy Smith in chapter 4, 'Reframing Fantasy: September 11 and the Global Audience'. For Smith, the witnessing of the first moments, the collision of the planes with the twin towers, created a moment of rupture that cut across the usual frameworks that determine the impact of three forms of representation: the 'presence' of theatre, the more distanced images of cinema and the familiar and domesticated arena of television. A number of psychoanalytically based models are explored in an effort to account for the pleasure experienced in the viewing of fictional representations of the disastrous and the impact that resulted when such images became all-too real. A more abstract and theoretically oriented perspective is taken in chapter 5, 'Teratology of the Spectacle', by Dean Lockwood, an account that moves through the work of prominent commentators on the conjunction of spectacle and real, such as Jean Baudrillard, Jacques Derrida and Slavoj Zizek, although a number of threads of continuity with the preceding chapters are maintained. The presence of Debord, a figure difficult to avoid in this arena, marks a connection with Kellner, while Paul Virilio is cited both here and by Rodney. Lockwood also shares with Kellner a spirit of critical optimism – absent, often, from the work of theorists writing in this area – a belief that 'ideology as spectacle' might contain the seeds of its own downfall. Historical context is provided in this case in the suggestion of parallels between the present situation and anxieties about the 'virtualization' of life in the era of pre-cinematic visual entertainments dating back to the late eighteenth century.

Part Two begins with an account of the form of reality TV that makes the strongest claim to the status of producing 'authenticity', the caught-on-tape format explored in Amy West's 'Caught on Tape: A legacy of low-tech reality'. The caught-on-tape variety of reality TV, comprised of spontaneous hand-held camcorder footage and imagery from closed-circuit television systems, stakes its claim to 'the real' on the combination of two qualities, West suggests: its essentially amateur, low-grade quality and the accidental nature of what it captures. In its hand-held manifestation, authenticity is asserted through testimony to the experience of a subjective real, that of the inexpert and unrehearsed motions of the camera in the hands of its operator. In its fixed, CCTV-type incarnation, a claim to authenticity is staked through precisely the opposite: the objectivity of an entirely disinterested perspective. For West, caught-on-tape is the forerunner of the later generation reality TV, but one whose legacy continues to be felt, in the shape of devices such as 'amateur' or diary-type inserts used as guarantors of authenticity within more professionalized and narrative-oriented formats.

If impressions of authenticity are often created by formal means – the low-grade, unsteady images of caught-on-tape footage, from the examples cited by West to much of the coverage of 9/11 – a different perspective is taken by Misha Kavka in chapter 7, 'Love 'n the Real; or, How I learned to love Reality TV'. In what she describes as real-love TV, reality shows based explicitly around the process of dating and seeking a partner, and in broader reality/game-show hybrids such as *Big Brother*, Kavka suggests that a key dimension in which 'reality' is asserted is at the level of affect. The sense of unmediation created formally may be a careful construct, and the setting is simulated, but this, Kavka argues, can still result in the *stimulation* of real feeling, for both participant and viewer. The connection holds up, ultimately, Kavka suggests, because the manner in which such shows construct forms of intimacy have much in common with the ways in which 'real love' works in the outside world.

The possibility that too much reality, in its more spectacular forms, can generate *excess* affect is considered in the following chapter, Frances Bonner's 'Looking Inside: Showing Medical Operations on Ordinary Television'. Hence the warnings that appear at the start of programmes of the kind Bonner examines, in which the spectacle is, indeed, very real: that of the insides of the human body exposed during medical operations. The spectacle, in these cases, is relatively small scale, not that of the extended coverage of special events such as royal funerals or collapsing skyscrapers, but that which is found in the more humdrum arena of what Bonner terms 'ordinary' television. In both cases, Bonner suggests, spectacular impact requires compensation for the low audio-visual quality of television in the form of the intensity that results from the basis of images in actuality – another conjunction, that is, between spectacle and real. The danger of viewers 'falling into the spectacle', deemed problematical in the reproduction of imagery that has human reality at its heart, is warded off by containing devices; in this case, principally, the constant presence of the narrative that grounds the spectacle in the experiences of concrete individuals.

In sequences showing real-life operations on television, the ultimate reality-spectacle is that constituted by the sight of the exposed interior of the body. The corporeal also plays a major part, although far more hedged by ambiguity, in the assertions of authenticity found amid the spectacular display of professional wrestling explored by Leon Hunt in 'Hell in a Cell and Other Stories: Violence, Endangerment and Authenticity in Professional Wresting'. The sight of blood is an index of authenticity in wresting as in medical operations. In professional wrestling, however, the blood may be real but its appearance is often faked, self-inflicted by the use of concealed blades. It remains real, however, as does other bodily damage. In this arena, Hunt suggests, what is sought by the viewer is corporeal evidence of the real within a frame acknowledged to be fictional, staged and inauthentic. In some cases, the carefully staged is displaced by moments of greater reality, when stunts do not go to plan or real conflict intrudes on the theatrical. Separating out the two, however, is extremely difficult, Hunt suggests, the fake spectacle and that of the real remaining tightly bound up one within the other. A conjunction of signifiers of the real and the simulated is also at the centre of the following chapter, 'Docobricolage in the Age of Simulation', by Bernadette Flynn, which draws parallels between the reality TV of *Big Brother* and the computer game, *The Sims*. Both draw on documentary conventions, Flynn suggests, specifically those of Direct Cinema and *cinéma vérité*, but in a manner that is mixed with a more playful exploration of the stuff of everyday domestic life. The result, for Flynn, is not the 'crisis' in documentary suggested by some commentators, but a new way of exploring the manner in which truth and identity are constructed on-screen.

That claims to the status of authenticity remain rooted in the conventional, in the qualities of other forms of representation more than any external reality, is the argument of the chapter that begins Part Three, in which the focus turns to film. In 'A Production Designer's Cinema: Historical Authenticity in Popular Films Set in the Past', Michele Pierson examines a range of strategies used to give historical spectacle a flavour of the authentic, many of which are based on the simulation of past representations, from films that draw on paintings of the times in which they are set to those that borrow from past conventions of photography and of cinema itself. The importance of production design is emphasized, sometimes in competition, perhaps, with the role of the director, the stakes being especially high, Pierson suggests, in cases in which significant aspects of mise-en-scéne are added in post-production, rather than being actually present at any level of 'reality' at the time of shooting. In the case of historical reconstruction, the viewer is invited to admire both the spectacle itself, as something impressively spectacular, and the claims it makes to the status of authenticity, however much that is based on a recycling of previous representational forms. A similar dynamic is often found in the consumption of the special effects sequences characteristic of contemporary science fiction or fantasy cinema, as suggested both by Pierson and in chapter 12, 'The New Spatial Dynamics of the Bullet-Time Effect', by Lisa Purse. The bullet-time effect, the principal special effects novelty offered by *The Matrix* (1999), is designed, as Purse suggests, to flaunt both the supposed verisimilitude of the image, seen in seamless three-dimensionality, and to impress as constructed spectacular effect, a key selling point of Hollywood science fiction. The defining quality of this particular effect, Purse argues, is the manner in which it draws the spectator into the fictional space of the film independently of character-alignment, creating an impression of immersion in the diegetic universe, a movement *into* the spectacle that mirrors that experienced by the characters within the computer-generated Matrix of the film.

Form and content are closely aligned in the bullet-time effect, as is the conjunction between spectacle and assertion of reality. The same can be said of the effects created by the rotoscoped animation of *Waking Life* (2001), explored by Paul Ward in the following chapter, '"I was dreaming I was awake and then I woke up and found myself asleep": Dreaming, spectacle and reality in *Waking Life*'. The distinguishing characteristic of rotoscoped animation is its peculiar relationship with the real, or at least the conventional cinematic 'real' constituted by 'live action' footage, its images being the result of an animated tracing over of 'real' imagery. The spectacle of the particular image quality created by the form of rotoscoping used in *Waking Life*, a 'shimmering, wobbling' impression, as described by Ward, creates a sense of unease and uncertainty, drawing attention to its status as both clearly animated, and thereby conventionally understood as 'less real', and identifiably grounded in the greater reality of the live-action footage on which it is based. The result, for Ward, is the ideal vehicle for the mediation offered by the film on the problems of distinguishing between waking and dreaming states of existence.

Tangled assertions of the real and the unreal, or fake, are also traced in chapter 14, 'Cannibal Holocaust and the Pornography of Death', by Julian Petley. In the context of contemporary debates about 'mock-documentary', Petley examines Cannibal Holocaust (1979), an Italian fiction feature mistaken on some occasions for an example of the 'snuff' movie, in which people are really killed on screen. The film uses numerous devices to create an impression of verisimilitude but, as Petley suggests, some of these also draw attention to the process of representation while others serve to disguise the fabricated nature of much of the action that unfolds before the camera. At the same time, Cannibal Holocaust also features sequences in which animals really are killed on screen, shot in a style similar to that used for the fake killing and mutilation of humans, a device used to intensify the 'realistic' impression of the latter, and a film-within-the-film in which what are probably real sequences of human death are declared to be fake. The result, Petley suggests, is a violation of carefully sanctioned conventions through which distinctions are usually made between the representation of death in factual and fictional modes.

Assertions of the more 'real' or 'authentic' are often used by film-makers seeking to revitalize overly familiar genre frameworks, a dimension of the horror film considered by Peg Aloi in chapter 15, 'Beyond the Blair Witch: A New Horror Aesthetic'. Impressions of authenticity are often the product of more practical factors, however, as Aloi suggests in the case of The Blair Witch Project, its American independent horror contemporaries Session 9 (2001) and Wendigo (2001) and precursors such as George Romero's Night of the Living Dead (1968), each of which creates a happy marriage of low-budget necessity and novel reality-aesthetic. The horror-specific context, for Aloi, is a reaction against more spectacular, gore-effects-based mainstream production, a renewal of horror via lessons learned from the work of the Dogme collective in Scandinavia.

A more politicized reading of horror films is offered by Mike Wayne in chapter 16, 'Spectres and Capitalism, Spectacle and the Horror Film', in which connections are traced between the concepts of spectacle and the spectre. Wayne reads the spectacle of the spectre, in the ghost-oriented horror film, as one of a number of figurations of aspects of the social sphere that are repressed in the broader (Debordian) spectacle of commodity capitalism. Spectres in films such as The Eye (2002), Candyman (1992) and The Ring (1999) are interpreted as traces of repressed sociality or repressed social groups while those of possession narratives such as Fallen (1998) are read, symptomatically, as (dis)embodiments of the abstraction and homogenization worked by capitalism on the human body. Critical approaches to the horror genre have, as Wayne suggests, been dominated by psychoanalytical explanations, with horror often understood not through the Marxist frame used in his readings but in terms of what a combination of Freudian and Lacanian theory sees as the constitutive 'lack' of the subject, and the fetish-substitutions put in its place. It is precisely this nexus that is taken up, at the specific point of intersection between spectacle and the real, in the following chapter, 'Looking On: Troubling Spectacles and the Complicitous Spectator', by Michele Aaron. From the perspective of psychoanalytical theory, Aaron suggests, cinematic spectacle, making its own claims to authenticity, stands in for a necessarily absent reality, a contract of disavowal into which the spectator willingly buys as a defensive mechanism. The question explored by Aaron, however, is what happens in particular cases in which the contract is broken by the film, in examples such as *Peeping Tom* (1960), *The Eyes of Laura Mars* (1978) and *Strange Days* (1996), in which self-reflexive devices call the attention of viewers to the fictional status of the representation and implicate them in the extreme violence of the on-screen events. Self-reflexivity in cases such as these has the potential to throw into question the safe distance at which viewers remains from such material, Aaron concludes, including the possibility of implication in the production of real-life spectacles such as those of 9/11.

A similar point is made in the final chapter, 'The Enigma of the Real: The qualifications for real sex in contemporary art cinema', by Tanya Krzywinska. In her study of the spectacle of the real constituted by the use of sequences of real sexual activity in examples of recent European 'art' cinema such as *Romance* (1999), *Intimacy* (2000) and *The Piano Teacher* (2000), Krzywinska considers a number of strategies through which such material is legitimated and made acceptable to both censors and the prospective audience. One of these is the existence of a reflexive dimension, in which sex is not just depicted on screen but in which its darker conflicts and contradictions are foregrounded, refusing the viewer the option of untroubled enjoyment of erotic spectacle. A number of formal devices are used to strengthen an impression of unmediated reality, including many of the signifiers of authenticity explored in previous chapters, and associated specifically in this case with the hand-held aesthetic of raw, low-budget hard-core productions. A modal slippage exists, as Krzywinska argues, between the reality of the sexual activities of performers – they are 'really' doing this, producing a marketable spectacle of actual sex – and the fictional frame within which it is meant to be contained. The latter plays a far stronger part than is the case in conventional hardcore, however. The narrative dimension, with its exploration of psychological complexities and character conflicts, is one of the most important signifiers of the 'art' status through which such films stake their claims to legitimacy, a process located by Krzywinska as part of a longer history of the strategies through which sexually charged material has secured its place on screen.

No effort has been made in this collection to enforce a common line on contributors, as is evident from the use of a number of different methodologies and a variety of points of theoretical focus. The same goes for this introduction, which has sought to give a flavour of each of the contributions rather than to engage them critically in debate, or to reduce them to any single synthesis. What emerges, though, is a clear sense that the 'spectacle of the real' is a powerful presence in many aspects of contemporary audio-visual media culture, and that its two components often exist in a state of mutual implication, as this formulation suggests. The value of a thematically oriented collection such as this is its ability to trace such phenomenon across media, rather than being limited to a focus on any one particular terrain. The production of spectacle is closely tied up with assertions of authenticity, just as the 'authentically real' is often displayed as a form of spectacle in its own right, a relationship that extends from the seemingly most 'real' to the most fantastically spectacular articulations of contemporary film, television and related media.

Part I Spectacle, Ideology, Catastophe

1. Media Culture and the Triumph of the Spectacle

Douglas Kellner

During the past decades, the culture industries have multiplied media spectacles in novel spaces and sites, and spectacle itself is becoming one of the organizing principles of the economy, polity, society, and everyday life. The Internet-based economy has been developing hi-tech spectacle as a means of promotion, reproduction, and the circulation and selling of commodities, using multimedia and ever-more sophisticated technology to dazzle consumers. Media culture itself proliferates ever more technologically sophisticated spectacles to seize audiences and increase their power and profit. The forms of entertainment permeate news and information, and a tabloidized infotainment culture is increasingly popular. New multimedia that synthesize forms of radio, film, TV news and entertainment, and the mushrooming domain of cyberspace, become spectacles of technoculture, generating expanding sites of information and entertainment, while intensifying the spectacle-form of media culture.

Political and social life is also shaped more and more by media spectacle. Social and political conflicts are increasingly played out on the screens of media culture, which display spectacles such as sensational murder cases, terrorist bombings, celebrity and political sex scandals, and the explosive violence of everyday life. Media culture not only takes up expanding moments of contemporary experience, but also provides ever more material for fantasy, dreaming, modeling thought and behavior, and constructing identities.

Of course, there have been spectacles since premodern times. Classical Greece had its Olympics, thespian and poetry festivals, its public rhetorical battles, and bloody and violent wars. Ancient Rome had its orgies, its public offerings of bread and circuses, its titanic political battles, and the spectacle of Empire with parades and monuments for triumphant Caesars and their armies, extravaganzas put on display in the 2000 film *Gladiator*. And as Dutch cultural historian Johan Huizinga (1986 and 1997) reminds us, medieval life too had its important moments of display and spectacle.

In the early modern period, Machiavelli advised his modern prince of the productive use of spectacle for government and social control, and the emperors and kings of the modern states cultivated spectacles as part of their rituals of governance and power. Popular entertainment long had its roots in spectacle, while war, religion, sports, and other domains of public life were fertile fields for the propagation of spectacle for centuries. Yet with the development of new multimedia and information technologies, technospectacles have been decisively shaping the contours and trajectories of present-day societies and cultures, at least in the advanced capitalist countries, while media spectacle also becomes a defining feature of globalization.

In this chapter, I will provide an overview of the dissemination of media spectacle throughout the major domains of the economy, polity, society, culture and everyday life in the contemporary era and indicate the theoretical approach that I deploy. This requires a brief presentation of the influential analysis of spectacle by Guy Debord and the Situationist International, and how I build upon this approach, followed by an overview of contemporary spectacle culture and then analysis of how my approach differs from that of Debord.

Guy Debord and the Society of the Spectacle

The concept of the 'society of the spectacle' developed by French theorist Guy Debord and his comrades in the Situationist International has had major impact on a variety of contemporary theories of society and culture.[1] For Debord, spectacle 'unifies and explains a great diversity of apparent phenomena' (Debord 1967: #10). Debord's conception, first developed in the 1960s, continues to circulate through the Internet and other academic and subcultural sites today. It describes a media and consumer society, organized around the production and consumption of images, commodities, and staged events.

For Debord, spectacle constituted the overarching concept to describe the media and consumer society, including the packaging, promotion, and display of commodities and the production and effects of all media. Using the term 'media spectacle', I am largely focusing on various forms of technologically constructed media productions that are produced and disseminated through the so-called mass media, ranging from radio and television to the Internet and latest wireless gadgets. Every medium, from music to television, from news to advertising, has its multitudinous forms of spectacle, involving such things in the realm of music as the classical music spectacle, the opera spectacle, the rock spectacle, and the hip hop spectacle. Spectacle forms evolve over time and multiply with new technological developments.

My major interest in *Media Spectacle* (Kellner 2003), however, is in the megaspectacle form whereby certain spectacles become defining events of their era. These range from commodity spectacles such as the McDonald's or Nike spectacle to megaspectacle political extravaganzas that characterize a certain period, involving such things as the O.J. Simpson trials, the Clinton sex and impeachment scandals, or the Terror War that is defining the current era.

There are, therefore, many levels and categories of spectacle. Megaspectacles are defined both quantitively and qualitatively. The major media spectacles of the era dominate news, journalism, and Internet buzz, and are highlighted and framed as the major events of the age, as were, for instance, the Princess Diana wedding and funeral, the extremely close 2000 election and 36 day 'Battle for the White House', or the September 11 terror attacks and their violent aftermath. Megaspectacles are those phenomena of media culture that dramatize its controversies and struggles, as well as its modes of conflict resolution. They include media extravaganzas, sports events, political happenings, and those attention-grabbing occurrences that we call news – a phenomena that itself has been subjected to the logic of spectacle and tabloidization in the era of media sensationalism, political scandal and contestation, seemingly unending cultural war, and the new phenomenon of Terror War. Megaspectacles such as the O.J. Simpson trials, the Clinton sex and impeachment scandals or the ongoing Terror War dominate entire eras and encapsulate their basic conflicts and contradictions, while taking over media culture.

More generally, my conception of media spectacle involves those media and artifacts which embody contemporary society's basic values and serve to enculturate individuals into its way of life (Kellner 1995, 2003). Thus, while Debord presents a rather generalized and abstract notion of spectacle, I engage specific examples of media spectacle and how they are produced, constructed, circulated, and function in the present era. As we proceed into a new millennium, the media are becoming more technologically dazzling and are playing an ever-escalating role in everyday life. Under the influence of a multimedia image culture, seductive spectacles fascinate the denizens of the media and consumer society and involve them in the semiotics of an ever-expanding world of entertainment, information, and consumption, which deeply influence thought and action. In Debord's words: 'When the real world changes into simple images, simple images become real beings and effective motivations of a hypnotic behavior. The spectacle, as a tendency *to make one see the world* by means of various specialized mediations (it can no longer be grasped directly), naturally finds vision to be the privileged human sense which the sense of touch was for other epochs' (#18). According to Debord, sight, 'the most abstract, the most mystified sense corresponds to the generalized abstraction of present day society' (*ibid*).

Experience and everyday life are thus shaped and mediated by the spectacles of media culture and the consumer society. For Debord, the spectacle is a tool of pacification and depoliticization; it is a 'permanent opium war' (#44) which stupefies social subjects and distracts them from the most urgent task of real life – recovering the full range of their human powers through creative practice. Debord's concept of the spectacle is integrally connected to the concept of separation and passivity, for in submissively consuming spectacles, one is estranged from actively producing one's life. Capitalist society separates workers from the products of their labour, art from life, and consumption from human needs and self-directing activity, as individuals inertly observe the spectacles of social life from within the privacy of their homes (#25 and #26). The Situationist project, by contrast, involved an overcoming of all forms of separation, in which individuals would directly produce their own life and modes of self-activity and collective practice.

The correlative to the spectacle for Debord is thus the spectator, the reactive viewer and consumer of a social system predicated on submission, conformity, and the cultivation of marketable difference. The concept of the spectacle therefore involves a distinction between passivity and activity and consumption and production, condemning lifeless consumption of spectacle as an alienation from human potentiality for creativity and imagination. The spectacular society spreads its wares mainly through the cultural mechanisms of leisure and consumption, services and entertainment, ruled by the dictates of advertising and a commercialized media culture. This structural shift to a society of the spectacle involves a commodification of previously non-colonized sectors of social life and the extension of bureaucratic control to the realms of leisure, desire, and everyday life. Parallel to the Frankfurt School conception of a 'totally administered,' or 'one-dimensional,' society (Horkheimer and Adorno 1972; Marcuse 1964), Debord states that 'The spectacle is the moment when the consumption has attained the *total occupation* of social life' (#42). Here exploitation is raised to a psychological level; basic physical privation is augmented by 'enriched privation' of pseudo-needs; alienation is generalized, made comfortable, and alienated consumption becomes 'a duty supplementary to alienated production' (#42).

Spectacle Economy

Since Debord's theorization of the society of the spectacle in the 1960s and 1970s, spectacle culture has expanded in every area of life. In the culture of the spectacle, commercial enterprises have to be entertaining to prosper and as Michael J. Wolf (1999) argues, in an 'entertainment economy,' business and fun fuse, so that the E-factor is becoming a major aspect of business. Via the 'entertainmentization' of the economy, television, film, theme parks, video games, casinos, and so forth become major sectors of the national economy. In the U.S., the entertainment industry is now a $480 billion industry, and consumers spend more on having fun than on clothes or health care (Wolf 1999: 4).

To succeed in the ultracompetitive global marketplace, corporations need to circulate their image and brand name, so business and advertising combine in the promotion of corporations as media spectacles. Endless promotion circulates the McDonald's Golden Arches, Nike's Swoosh, or the logos of Apple, Intel, or Microsoft. In the brand wars between commodities, corporations need to make their corporate logos familiar signposts in contemporary culture. Corporations place their logos on their products, in ads, in the spaces of everyday life, and in the midst of media spectacles such as important sports events, TV shows, movie product placement, and wherever they can catch consumer eyeballs, to impress their brand name on a potential buyer. Consequently, advertising, marketing, public relations and promotion are an essential part of commodity spectacle in the global marketplace.

Celebrity too is manufactured and managed in the world of media spectacle. Celebrities are the icons of media culture, the gods and goddesses of everyday life. To become a celebrity requires recognition as a star player in the field of media spectacle, be it sports, entertainment, business, or politics. Celebrities have their handlers and image managers to make sure that they continue to be seen and positively perceived by publics. Just as with corporate brand names, celebrities become brands to sell their Madonna, Michael Jordan, Tom Cruise, or Jennifer Lopez product and image. In a media culture, however, celebrities are always prey to scandal and thus must have at their disposal an entire public relations apparatus to manage their spectacle fortunes, to make sure their clients not only maintain high visibility but also keep projecting a positive image. Of course, within limits, 'bad' behaviour and transgressions can also sell and so media spectacle always contains celebrity dramas that attract public attention and can even define an entire period, as when the O.J. Simpson murder trials and Bill Clinton sex scandals dominated the media in the mid and late 1990s.

Entertainment has always been a prime field of the spectacle, but in today's infotainment society, entertainment and spectacle have entered into the domains of the economy, politics, society, and everyday life in important new ways. Building on the tradition of spectacle, contemporary forms of entertainment from television to the stage are incorporating spectacle culture into their enterprises, transforming film, television, music, drama, and other domains of culture, as well as producing spectacular new forms of culture such as cyberspace, multimedia, and virtual reality.

The Culture of the Spectacle
Sports has long been a domain of the spectacle with events such as the Olympics, World Series, Super Bowl, soccer World Cup, and NBA championships attracting massive audiences, while generating sky-high advertising rates. These cultural

rituals celebrate their society's deepest values (i.e. competition, winning, success, and money), and corporations are willing to pay top dollar to get their products associated with such events. Indeed, it appears that the logic of the commodity spectacle is inexorably permeating professional sports which can no longer be played without the accompaniment of cheerleaders, giant mascots who clown with players and spectators, and raffles, promotions, and contests that feature the products of various sponsors. Sports stadiums themselves, often named after their corporate sponsors, contain electronic reproduction of the action, as well as giant advertisements for various products that rotate for maximum saturation – previewing environmental advertising in which entire urban sites are becoming scenes to boost consumption spectacles.

Film has long been a fertile field of the spectacle, with 'Hollywood' connoting a world of glamour, publicity, fashion, and excess. Hollywood film has exhibited grand movie palaces, spectacular openings with searchlights and camera-popping paparazzi, glamorous Oscars, and stylish hi-tech film. While epic spectacle became a dominant genre of Hollywood film from early versions of *The Ten Commandments* through *Cleopatra* and *2001* in the 1960s, contemporary film has incorporated the mechanics of spectacle into its form, style, and special effects. Films are hyped into spectacle through advertising and trailers which are ever louder, more glitzy, and razzle-dazzle. Some of the most popular films of the late 1990s were spectacle films, including *Titanic*, *Star Wars: Episode One - The Phantom Menace*, *Three Kings*, and *Austin Powers*, a spoof of spectacle that became one of the most successful films of summer 1999. In 2002-2003, a series of comic book hero spectacles were among the most popular films. *Spiderman* (2002) was one of the most popular films ever and has spawned planned sequels and a cycle of films presenting comic book heroes such as *The Hulk*, another of the *X-Men* series, and the comic book-like *Matrix Reloaded*, *Terminator 3*, and *Charlie's Angels: Full Throttle*. These films embody fantasies of attained spectacular powers that enable the protagonists to conquer enemies and prevail in hi-tech environments. These cinematic spectacles are an expression of a culture that generates ever-more fantastic visions as technology and the society of the spectacle continue to evolve in novel and surprising, sometimes frightening, forms.

Television has been from its introduction in the 1940s a promoter of consumption spectacle, selling cars, fashion, home appliances, and other commodities along with consumer lifestyles and values. It is also the home of sports spectacle such as the Super Bowl or World Series, political spectacles such as elections (or more recently, scandals), entertainment spectacle such as the Oscars or Grammies, and its own events including breaking news or other special events. Following the logic of spectacle entertainment, contemporary television exhibits more hi-tech glitter, faster and glitzier editing, computer simulations, and with cable and satellite television, a fantastic array of every conceivable type of show and genre.

TV is today a medium of spectacular programmes such as *The X-Files* or *Buffy, the Vampire Slayer*, and spectacles of everyday life such as MTV's *The Real World* and *Road Rules*, or the globally popular *Survivor* and *Big Brother* series. In 2002-3, there was a proliferation of competitive reality shows in the U.S. involving sex, dating, and marriage including *The Bachelor*, *The Bachelorette*, *Cupid*, and the short-lived *Are You Hot?* In these shows, men and women humiliate themselves, facing scorn and rejection, as they compete for the favors of sexual competitors and their few moments of media glory and reward. And entertainment and spectacle are apotheosized in *American Idol*, the breakaway hit of summer 2002 that rewards young wanna-be entertainers who perform well-known pop songs, while humiliating those judged to be losers.

Real-life events, however, took over TV spectacle during 2000-2001 in, first, an intense battle for the White House in a dead-heat election, that arguably constitutes the greatest political crime and scandal in U.S. history (see Kellner 2001). After months of the Bush administration pushing the most hard-right political agenda in memory and then deadlocking as the Democrats took control of the Senate in a dramatic party re-affiliation of Vermont's Jim Jeffords, the world was treated to the most horrifying spectacle of the new millennium, the September 11 terror attacks and unfolding Terror War. These events promise an unending series of deadly spectacle for the foreseeable future and have so far unleashed Terror War in Afghanistan and Iraq, as well as Jihadist terrorist attacks throughout the world (see Kellner, 2003).

Theatre and fashion are additional fertile fields of the spectacle, which has also been brought into the world of high art in phenomena such as the Guggenheim Museum's retrospective on Giorgio Armani, the Italian fashion designer, and plans to open a Guggenheim gallery in the Venetian Resort Hotel Casino in Las Vegas, with a seven-story art museum next door. Contemporary architecture is also ruled by the logic of the spectacle and critics have noticed how art museums are coming to trump the art collection by making the building and setting more spectacular than the collections.[2] The Frank Gehry Guggenheim Museum in Bilbao, Spain, the Richard Meier Getty Center in Los Angeles, the retrofitted power plant that became the Tate Modern in London, Tadao Ando's Pulitzer Foundation building in Saint Louis, and Santiago Calatrava's addition to the Milwaukee Museum of Art, all provide superspectacle environments to display their artwork and museum fare. Major architectural projects for corporations and cities often provide postmodern spectacle whereby the glass and steel structures of high modernism are replaced by buildings and spaces adorned with signs of the consumer society and complex structures that attest to the growing power of commerce and technocapitalism.

Popular music is also colonized by the spectacle with music-video television (MTV) becoming a major purveyor of music, bringing spectacle into the core of musical production and distribution. Madonna and Michael Jackson would have never become global superstars of popular music without the spectacular production values of their music videos and concert extravaganzas. Both also performed their lives as media spectacle, generating maximum publicity and attention (not always positive!). Musical concert extravaganzas are more and more spectacular (and expensive) and younger female pop music stars and groups such as Mariah Carey, Britney Spears, Jennifer Lopez, or Destiny's Child deploy the tools of the glamour industry and media spectacle to make themselves spectacular icons of fashion, beauty, style, and sexuality, as well as purveyors of music. Pop male singers such as Ricky Martin could double as fashion models and male groups such as 'N Sync use hi-tech stage shows, music videos and PR to sell their wares. Moreover, hip-hop culture has cultivated a whole range of spectacle, ranging from musical extravaganzas, to lifestyle cultivation and real-life crime wars among its stars.

Eroticism has frequently permeated the spectacles of Western culture, and is prominently on display in Hollywood film, as well as popular forms such as burlesque, vaudeville, and pornography. Long a major component of advertising, eroticized sexuality has been used to sell every conceivable product. The spectacle of sex is also one of the staples of media culture, permeating all cultural forms and creating its own genres in pornography, one of the highest grossing domains of media spectacle. In the culture of the spectacle, sex becomes shockingly exotic and diverse, through the media of porno videos, DVDs, and Internet sites which make available everything from teen-animal sex to orgies of the most extravagant sort. Technologies of cultural reproduction such as home video recorders (VCRs) and computers bring sex more readily into the private recesses of the home. And today the sex spectacle attains more and more exotic forms with multimedia and multisensory sex, as envisaged in Huxley's *Brave New World*, on the horizon.

The spectacle of video and computer games has been a major source of youth entertainment and industry profit. In 2001, the U.S. video game industry hit a record $9 billion in sales and expects to do even better in the next couple of years (*Los Angeles Times*, Jan. 1, 2002: C1). For decades now, video and computer games have obsessed sectors of youth and provided skills needed for the hi-tech dot.com economy, as well as fighting postmodern war. These games are highly competitive, violent, and provide allegories for life under corporate capitalism and Terror War militarism. In the game *Pac-man*, as in the corporate jungle, it is eat or be eaten, just as in air and ground war games, it is kill or be killed. *Grand Theft Auto 3* and *State of Emergency* were two of the most popular games in 2002, with the former involving high-speed races through urban jungles and the latter involving political riots and state repression! While some game producers have tried to cultivate kinder, gentler, and more intelligent gaming, most of the best-selling corporate games are spectacles for predatory capitalism and macho militarism and not a more peaceful, playful, and cooperative world.

The examples just provided suggest media spectacle is invading every field of experience from the economy, to culture and everyday life, to politics and war. Moreover, spectacle culture is moving into new domains of cyberspace that will help to generate future multimedia spectacle and networked infotainment societies. My studies of media spectacle strive to contribute to illuminating these developments and to developing a critical theory of the contemporary moment.

Debord and the Spectacle: A Critical Engagement

In using the concept of spectacle, I am obviously indebted to Guy Debord's *Society of the Spectacle* and the ideas of the Situationist International; so acknowledging the debt, I might also say that there are three major differences between my engagement of the concept of the spectacle and Debord's model. First, while Debord develops a rather totalizing and monolithic concept of the society of the spectacle, I engage specific spectacles, like McDonald's and the commodity spectacle, the Clinton sex scandals and impeachment spectacle, or the 9/11 terrorist attacks and Terror War spectacle (Kellner 2003a and 2003b).

I should also acknowledge the obvious point that I am reading the production, text and effects of various media spectacles from the standpoint of U.S. society, and in an attempt to theorize contemporary U.S. society and culture and, more broadly, globalization and global culture, whereas Debord is analyzing a specific stage of capitalist society, that of the media and consumer society organized around spectacle. Moreover, Debord exhibits a French radical intellectual and neo-Marxian perspective while I have specific class, race, gender, and regional standpoints and deploy a multiperspectivist model, using Marxism, British cultural studies, French postmodern theory, and many other perspectives (Kellner 1995, 2003a and 2003b).

Secondly, my approach to these specific spectacles is interpretive and interrogatory. That is, I try to interrogate what major media spectacles tell us of contemporary U.S. and global society. For example, what McDonald's tells us about consumption and the consumer society, or globalization; what Michael Jordan and the Nike spectacle tells us about the sports spectacle and the intersection of sports, entertainment, advertising, and commodification in contemporary societies; what the O.J. Simpson affair tells us about race, class, celebrity, the media, sports, gender, the police and legal system and so on in the U.S., and what the obsessive focus on this event for months on end tells us about American media and consumer society.

In my studies of media spectacle, I deploy cultural studies as diagnostic critique; reading and interpreting various spectacles to see what they tell us about the present age, whereas Debord is more interested in a critique of capitalism and revolutionary alternatives. The 'popular' often puts on display major emotions, ideas, experiences, and conflicts of the era, as well as indicating what corporations are marketing. A critical form of cultural studies can thus help decipher dominant trends of the era and contribute to developing critical theories of the contemporary era (Kellner 1995 and 2003a; Best and Kellner 2001).

Thirdly, I analyze the contradictions and reversals of the spectacle, whereas Debord has a fairly triumphant notion of the society of the spectacle, although he and his comrades sketched out various models of opposition and struggle and in fact inspired in part the rather spectacular May '68 events in France. For an example of the reversal of the spectacle, or at least its contradictions and contestation, take McDonald's. When I began my studies of media spectacle, McDonald's was a figure for a triumphant global capitalism. McDonald's was constantly expanding in the U.S. and globally; its profits were high and it was taken as a paradigm of a successful American and then global capitalism. George Ritzer's book *The McDonaldization of Society* (1993, 1996) used McDonald's as a model to analyze contemporary production and consumption, while books such as *Golden Arches East* (Watson et al. 1997) valorized McDonald's as bringing modernity itself to vast sectors of the world including Russia and China, and McDonald's was praised for its efficient production methods, its cleanliness and orderliness, and for bringing food value and fast, convenient food to the masses.

Suddenly, however, McDonald's became the poster corporation for protest in the anti-corporate globalization movement. The McDonald's corporation had sued two British Greenpeace activists who produced a pamphlet attacking McDonald's unhealthy food, its labour practices, its negative environmental impact, and called for protests and boycotts. McDonald's countered with a lawsuit and an anti-McDonald's campaign emerged with a web-site, McSpotlight, that became the most accessed in history; global and local protests emerged; and whenever there was an anticorporate globalization demonstration, somewhere a McDonald's was trashed. Suddenly, therefore, McDonald's expansion was halted, profits were down almost everywhere for the first time, and new McDonald's were blocked by local struggles. Moreover, in the U.S. and elsewhere, there were lawsuits for false advertising, for promoting addictive substances and junk food, and a lot of bad publicity and falling profits that continue to haunt McDonald's through the present.

Finally, I am aware how Debord's conception of the society of the spectacle trumps my own analysis of the contradictions of the spectacle, their reversal and overturning. A Debordian could argue that despite the vicissitudes of the

McDonald's spectacle, or criticism of the labour practices of Nike, and other contradictions and contestations of spectacles within contemporary capitalist societies, that capitalism itself still exists more powerfully than ever, that the media and consumer society continues to reproduce itself through spectacle, and that a market society thrives upon the vicissitudes of spectacle, the ups and downs of various corporations, personalities and celebrities.

While this argument is hard to answer in the face of the continued global hegemony of capital, I think it is useful to analyze the contradictions and contestations of media spectacle within specific societies and to counter the notion that political spectacles are all-powerful and overwhelming. For instance, I have a study in *Media Spectacle* of how the efforts of the U.S. Republican Party to use negative media politics to remove Clinton from the presidency through the spectacle of sex scandals and impeachment backfired.

There are, I believe, several reasons why Clinton survived the spectacle of the sex scandal and impeachment. British cultural studies has long affirmed the existence of an active audience that is not totally manipulated by the media and it appears that there is residual respect for the president, or was at the time, and that people did not like and resisted the attacks on Clinton and the national media exposure of his personal life. The Republican strategy was also seen by many, correctly I believe, as an illicit right-wing attack on an elected president, part of a culture war in the U.S. that dates back to the 1960s.

There were, to be sure, highly contradictory effects from the Clinton spectacles. The Republican assault on the president won sympathy and support for the beleaguered Clinton, but enabled the Republicans to focus attention on the failings of the president. They were also able to block his political agenda, and then to highlight negatives of the Clinton/Gore presidency in the 2000 election that made it difficult for Gore to emphasize the unparalleled peace and prosperity of the past eight years, positives that quickly turned to negatives with the highly destructive and incompetent economic and foreign policy disasters of the Bush administration.

Most of the examples given above are U.S. based, although with global impact, but the spectacle itself is becoming increasingly global, from the Princess Diana spectacle – probably the most interrogated event in global cultural studies – to 2003 spectacles such as the SARS-related fear of a global epidemic and the global literary and cinematic spectacle of Pottermania. In terms of global spectacle, more distressingly, there is also the al Qaeda global terrorism spectacle that is the topic of my recent book *From September 11 to Terror War: The Dangers of the Bush Legacy* (Kellner 2003b). The terror spectacle of fall 2001 revealed that familiar items of everyday life such as planes or mail could be transformed into instruments of spectacular terror. The al Qaeda network hijacking of airplanes turned ordinary instruments of transportation into weapons as they crashed into the World Trade Center towers and Pentagon on September 11. Mail became the delivery of disease, terror, and death in the anthrax scare of fall and winter 2001. And rumours spread that the terror network was seeking instruments of mass destruction such as chemical, biological, and nuclear weapons to create spectacles of terror on a hitherto unforeseen scale.

Globalization, Technological Revolution, and the Restructuring of Capitalism

Behind the genesis and ascendancy of the expansion of media spectacle, the rise of megaspectacle and of the new virtual spectacle of cyberspace and an emerging Virtual Reality (VR), are the twin phenomena of the global restructuring of capitalism and the technological revolution resulting from the explosion of new forms of media and communication technology, computer and information technology, and, on the horizon, biotechnology. In earlier writings, I introduced the concept of *technocapitalism* to describe a configuration of capitalist society in which technical and scientific knowledge, computerization, automation of labour and intelligent technology play a role in the process of production analogous to the function of human labour power and the mechanization of the labour process in an earlier era of capitalism (Kellner 1989). The technological revolution and global restructuring of capital continues to generate new modes of societal organization, polity, sovereignty, forms of culture and everyday life, and new types of contestation.

Thus, as developing countries move into the new millennium, their inhabitants, and others throughout the globe, find themselves in an ever-proliferating infotainment society, a globally networked economy, and an Internet technoculture. Contemporary theorists find themselves in a situation, I would suggest, parallel to the Frankfurt school in the 1930s which theorized the emergent configurations of economy, polity, society and culture brought about by the transition from market to state monopoly capitalism. In their now classical texts, they accordingly analyzed the novel forms of social and economic organization, technology, and culture, including the rise of giant corporations and cartels and the capitalist state in 'organized capitalism,' in both its fascist or 'democratic' state capitalist forms. They also engaged the culture industries and mass culture which served as new types of social control, novel forms of ideology and domination, and a potent configuration of culture and everyday life (Kellner 1989).

In terms of political economy, the emerging postindustrial form of technocapitalism is characterized by a decline of the state and increased power of the market, accompanied by the growing strength of globalized transnational corporations and governmental bodies and decreased force of the nation-state and its institutions (Kellner 2002). To paraphrase Max Horkheimer, whoever wants to talk about capitalism, must talk about globalization, and it is impossible to theorize globalization without talking about the restructuring of capitalism.

Globalization involves the flow of goods, information, culture and entertainment, people, and capital across a new networked economy, society, and culture (see the documentation in Castells 1996, 1997, and 1998). Like the new technologies, it is a complex phenomenon which involves positive and negative features, costs and benefits, an upside and a downside. Yet, like theories of new technologies, most theories of globalization are either primarily negative, seeing it as a disaster for the human species, or as positive, bringing new products, ideas, and wealth to a global arena. As with technology, I propose a *critical theory of globalization* that would dialectically appraise its positive and negative features, its contradictions and ambiguities; a theory that is sharply critical of its negative effects, skeptical of legitimating ideological discourse, but that also recognizes the centrality of the phenomenon in the present and that affirms and develops its positive features (see Kellner 2002).

To conclude: developing countries and the globalized world are emerging into a culture of media spectacle that constitutes a novel configuration of economy, society, politics, and everyday life. It involves new cultural forms, social relations, and modes of experience. It is producing an ever-expanding spectacle culture with its proliferating media spectacle, megaspectacles, and interactive spectacles. Critical social theory thus faces compelling challenges in theoretically mapping and analyzing these emergent forms of culture and society and the ways that they may contain novel forms of domination and oppression as well as potential for democratization and social justice.

References

Best, Steven and Douglas Kellner (2001) *The Postmodern Adventure. Science Technology, and Cultural Studies at the Third Millennium*. New York and London: Guilford and Routledge.

Castells, Manuel (1996, 1997, 1998) *The Networked Society*. Malden, Mass. and Oxford UK: Blackwell.

Debord, Guy (1967) *Society of the Spectacle*. Detroit: Black and Red.

Horkheimer, Max and Theodor W. Adorno (1972) *Dialectic of Enlightenment*. New York: Continuum.

Huizinga, Johann (1986) *Homo Ludens: A Study of the Play-Element in Culture*. Boston: Beacon Press.

_____ (1997) *The Autumn of the Middle Ages*. Chicago: University of Chicago Press.

Kellner, Douglas (1989) *Critical Theory, Marxism, and Modernity*. Cambridge and Baltimore, Polity Press and John Hopkins University Press.

_____ (1995) *Media Culture*. London and New York: Routledge.

_____ (2001) *Grand Theft 2000*. Lanham, Md.: Rowman and Littlefield.

_____ (2002) 'Theorizing Globalization,' *Sociological Theory*, Vol. 20, Nr. 3 (November): 285-305.

_____ (2003a) *Media Spectacle*. London and New York: Routledge.

_____ (2003b) *From September 11 to Terror War: The Dangers of the Bush Legacy*. Lanham, Md.: Rowman and Littlefield.

Marcuse, Herbert (1964) *One-Dimensional Man*. Boston: Beacon Press.

Ritzer, George (1993; revised edition 1996) *The McDonaldization of Society*. Thousand Oaks, Ca.: Pine Forge Press.

_____ (1999) *Exchanting a Disenchanted World. Revolutionizing the Means of Consumption*. Thousand Oaks, Ca.: Pine Forge Press.

Watson, James L. (ed) (1997) *Golden Arches East: McDonald's in East Asia*. Palo Alto, California: Stanford University Press.

Wolf, Michael J. (1999) *Entertainment Economy: How Mega-Media Forces are Transforming Our Lives*. New York: Times Books.

Notes

1   Debord's *The Society of the Spectacle* (1967) was published in translation in a pirate edition by Black and Red (Detroit) in 1970 and reprinted many times; another edition appeared in 1983 and a new translation in 1994. Thus, in the following discussion, I cite references to the numbered paragraphs of Debord's text to make it easier for those with different editions to follow my reading. The key texts of the Situationists and many interesting commentaries are found on various Web sites, producing a curious afterlife for Situationist ideas and practices. For further discussion of the Situationists, see Best and Kellner 1997, Chapter 3; see also the discussions of spectacle culture in Best and Kellner 2001 and Kellner 2003a, upon which I draw in this article. Thanks to Geoff King for comments that helped with the revision of this text.

2   See Nicholai Ouroussoff, 'Art for Architecture's Sake,' *Los Angeles Times* (March 31, 2002). I might note that economic downturn in the U.S. in 2003 forced postponement of the expansion of the Los Angeles County Art Museum and other spectacular architectural projects.

2. Real Time, Catastrophe, Spectacle: Reality as Fantasy in Live Media

Lee Rodney

Of the numerous documentary 'vignettes' of Afghan life that flooded American media in October 2001, there was one that focused on the unlikely subject of popular haircuts in Kabul. The picture, posted on the MSNBC news-site, featured a well-groomed Afghan teen admiring his new haircut in the mirror of a barber shop. The picture and story were taken from a news item that ran earlier that year, in January 2001, stating that local barbers had been jailed in Kabul for specializing in a new style dubbed the 'Titanic'-a Leonardo di Caprio-inspired hairdo (really a kind of 1920s pageboy) worn by a small but significant number of young Afghan men.

As a news item, this story made an emotional appeal to the presumed 'universality' of Hollywood sentiment, operating on the conceit that the world basks in the glory of America's image. In this way the haircut represented a gesture of dissent, as haircuts often do. But in this American economy of likeness, the subtle changes of such a translation pass by un-recognized. It had been presumed that the 'Titanic', as a haircut, was a subtle concession to the draw of American popular culture, one that signalled the loosening of regimental Taliban codes. However, the emulation of one of America's most popular screen-angels on the streets of Kabul is far less radical than the style's new name: as the haircut was called the 'Titanic', rather than, the 'di Caprio', the emphasis shifts from teen idol to Hollywood event. In this play of mimicry we are reminded of the naiveté of that early 20th-century romantic disaster, the gigantic and impervious vessel of new technology downed by a stubborn block of ice, as well as the vanity of recreating the tragedy, Hollywood style, at the century's close. The slipperiness of meaning here seems to suggest a battle over the image, one that was confirmed in the words of a Taliban cleric, who bluntly told the American journalist: 'you did not see this haircut' (Mendenhall, 2001: 1).

The cleric's response emphasizes that the lens of Western news media can only render Afghan culture in the realm of 'phantasmatic' projection. MSNBC's portrayal of street life in Kabul aimed to present the 'Other without otherness', to borrow a phrase from Slavoj Zizek. Writing recently on our increasingly convoluted relationship to the real, Zizek notes the number of 'virtualized' products that are marketed by the reduction of their malignant properties; 'coffee without caffeine, cream without fat'. Spinning the list off into the broader cultural sphere, he suggests that the American idea of war without warfare (that is without American casualties) sits at the pinnacle of this process of virtualization. Similarly, virtual reality simply provides reality deprived of its substance, without the 'hard, resistant kernel of the real' (Zizek, 2001: 11).

If the 'Titanic' was misrecognized in its mediated portrayal, a similar complication is found in the reception of 9/11 as a live televised event, as it could not immediately be disentangled from the fictional images of disaster movies by which it had been preceded. The incessant repetition of the crash scene and the gray haze of 'ground zero' ensured that the spectacle remained bloodless. Captured on video by vigilantes and web-cams all over Manhattan (by cameras 'manned' and 'unmanned' alike) the telegenic spectacle seemed crafted for real-time media. It gained its impact through the effects of space-time compression that airplanes and televisions so handily bring about. But now, thanks to the ubiquity of the web-cam, skyjackings take place in real time; thus 9/11 probably had an operational budget that was a fraction of that of the filming of *Titanic* (1997). As it was often remarked after September 11, watching the twin towers fall was like 'watching a movie'; that is to say the event was uncannily recognizable from the outset. But, as Zizek warns, it was not so much that the event shattered our illusory sphere, but rather that 'the fantasmatic screen apparition entered our reality [...] America got what it fantasized about and that was the biggest surprise' (16).

In a different take on the idea of wish-fulfilment, Paul Virilio writes in *Pure War* that 'the riddle of technology is also the riddle of the accident [...] every technology produces, provokes [or] programs a specific accident' (Lotringer and Virilio 1997: 37-8). In these terms it is debatable whether September 11 was incident or accident. Either way, whatever disparity lies between the circumstances that led to the demise of the twin towers and the sinking of the Titanic, both were large scale icons of global capital and modern engineering that symbolized an era. The sunken steamship and the fallen skyscrapers were both thought to be indestructible. And just as the storyline of the Titanic was ready-made for Hollywood film, that of September 11 was ready-made for CNN.

In the coverage of September 11, from its start as a 'breaking news event' to the media frenzy that followed for months afterward, it became clear that real-time footage took on a new status in terms of its relationship to spectacle. What I want to suggest in this chapter is that, while we witnessed a very specific kind of catastrophe in the event of 9/11, the role of real-time media cannot be underestimated in terms of providing the apparatus for an event such as this to take place. This is not the same thing as apportioning blame to specific media entities. Rather, I wish to suggest that real-time technology, as hyped and deployed in the very discourse and imagery of 'liveness', is something that has been building for decades.

Furthermore, I want link the coverage of 9/11 with the news presentation of more recent events. The prevalence of 'amateur' video footage in much of what now stands for 9/11 certainly influenced how the invasion of Iraq was subsequently presented in 2003. The emphasis on 'real life' confusion as conveyed in the jerky, vertiginous sequences, dirty lenses and hysterical commentary that came through in the camcorder tapes of the World Trade Center collapse gave new life to the old form of the eye-witness account. The introduction of embedded journalists in Iraq and the excessive focus on 24/7 coverage also emphasized real-time information and appeared 'unedited'. CNN's web-site, for example, was called 'Baghdad Live' and featured a panoramic view of the aerial bombardment of Baghdad. The similarity between news presentation and reality media in the last few years has led some commentators to pronounce the arrival of a new 'military-entertainment' complex. Just as the military-industrial complex described the gray area between interests of industry and military, or the military *as* industry, there is an increasingly gray area between 'managed combat information, news and entertainment' (Crandall 2003: 2).

'Empire': Skyscrapers, Surveillance, and Spectacle

Tall buildings and web-cameras are partners in the architecture of transparency; the drive for an expanded horizon links both the aspirations of the glass tower and the surveillance image. This connection was made abundantly clear in a video installation by the German artist Wolfgang Staehle that coincided with the events of September 11. Staehle's exhibition included three real-time video projections web-cast from various locations around the world: Berlin's television tower, the Comburg monastery in Germany and a wide, panoramic view of lower Manhattan. Two years prior, Staehle web-cast New York's Empire State Building. *Empire 24/7* was an update and homage to Warhol's languid film of the same subject from the early 1960s. In the new, equally Warholian version, Staehle's panoramic feed of lower Manhattan not surprisingly featured the World Trade Center's collapse – a 'grim coincidence' as it was stated in a somewhat paranoid disclaimer issued by the Postmasters Gallery not long after the event (rhizome.org 2001).

The 'grim coincidence' that supposedly marred Staehle's exhibition linked *Empire 24/7* and subsequent works not only to Warhol's *Empire* of 1964 but also, if inadvertently, to Warhol's disaster series, screen prints such as *White Burning Car* (1963) and *Ambulance Disaster* (1963). What this aberration makes evident is that Warhol's silent films are the formal compliment of the disasters: the freeze-frame punctuality of the disaster-the tragic instant rendered over and over-becomes the absent, yet anticipated moment in the monotonous silent films. *Empire* stands apart from Warhol's other silent films such as *Sleep* (1963), *Eat* (1963), *Drink* (1964) or *Henry Geldzahler* (1964) in so far as these are portraits, whereas the monumentality of *Empire* stands somewhere between landscape and history painting. Warhol's disasters, on the other hand, carried with them a strange sense of intimacy as they were usually individual tragedies rather than large-scale catastrophes. But Staehle's re-make of *Empire* at least suggested that disaster was immanent to the frame of Warhol's film. Although nothing happens in *Empire* one watches as if something might, which is part of the basis of the appeal of surveillance images and web-cam sites .

Empire was filmed as NASA and AT&T were sending their first satellites into orbit. Telstar gave us, among other things, the capacity for live satellite broadcasts in 1962, which on the one hand enhanced the cozy notion of a global village, but also intensified Cold War conflicts through conceptually shrinking the geographical distance between the US and the USSR. *Empire*, it should be recalled, was filmed at the height of the Cold War, after the Cuban missile crisis of 1962 and Kennedy's assassination in 1963. This conjunction of crises signaled the extent to which the speed of telecommunication had altered the shape and intensity of political events, at least in terms of popular reception. As the length of news transmission time was negligible it became increasingly possible to 'see at a distance'. The boundaries of privacy pressed inward as the far became near and television began to live up to its hyped potential as a window on the world.

In the 1960s the status of real time gained ground. It emerged, reconfigured as a discourse of liveness, which placed a premium on capturing events. By the early 1960s, liveness was synonymous with the separate technological lineages of broadcast, communications and cybernetics which all had real-time components that were boosted by satellite transmission. The live was fashioned as a kind of total record, much in the way that early cinema held out a promise of a world picture, answering to the desire to image everything everywhere, a dream of 'representation without loss' (Doane 1999: 78). Television still thrives on this generalized fantasy of 'live broadcasting'; although the vast majority of current broadcasting is not live, the discourse of liveness is shot through television's imaginary. We experience it in the simulated live-the canned laughter or laugh track that is the hallmark of sitcoms, and, of course, in reality television. Writing in the early 1980s, before the onslaught of reality TV programs, television theorist Jane Feuer suggested that 'by postulating an equivalence between time of event, time of television creation and transmission-viewing time, television as an institution identifies all messages emanating from the apparatus as 'live' (Feuer 1983: 14). With the opposition between live and recorded broadcasts, 'live' comes to signify 'real', with its suggestion of being present, or 'being there'.

Empire seems like a perverse response to the increasing prevalence of 'live' culture. 'My time is not your time', Warhol famously said of his silent films. Wary of the false promises of real time (and the presumed universality of the live image of broadcast television), Warhol went against its grain. His films were shot at sound speed (24 frames per second) and projected at silent speed (16 frames per second). Therefore, they are slowed by a third and unwind at a pace that is out of sync with the viewer (Taubin 1994: 21).

In 1964 the Empire State Building was the world's tallest structure, housing the head offices of RCA and NBC. Atop its 1454 feet stood a powerful broadcast tower, an emblem of America's brave new frontier. Warhol and his crew shot *Empire* from the 41st floor of the Time-Life building, filming continuously from dusk until nightfall, a total of six and a half hours (Angell 1994: 16). Thus the Empire State is not seen from the ground up (the everyday perspective of the pedestrian) nor is it seen from the top down (the once in a lifetime view of the suicidal jumper or the tourist); rather what one sees in *Empire* is a view of the headquarters of one media conglomerate viewed from the perspective of another, partners in a new empire of colonization and control.

The Empire State Building held the title of the world's tallest building from 1931 until 1972 when the first of the World Trade Center towers outgrew it by 112 feet. This skyward ascent signaled that the Western frontier in the twentieth century was no longer horizontal: the drive toward colonization was creeping steadily upward toward the stratosphere, rather than terrestrially outward (Virilo 2000: 23). The Empire State Building currently presents itself as a kind of virtual watchtower hosting four live web-cams that continuously run on its site with two northern and two southern views of Manhattan. The live web-cam, in Paul Virilio's terms, is an 'automatic vision machine', yet one more example of a substitute horizon, which 'operates within the space of an entirely virtualized geographical reality' (16). In spite of its poor optical quality, 'live transmission has become a promotional tool directing anyone and everyone's gaze to some privileged vantage-point' (17).

The most strident critics of new technologies seem to mourn the loss of the 'real' as real time steadily erodes distance and space. Paul Virilio cites real time as precisely that which detaches (or disenfranchises) us from temporality and eradicates distance/space. He reminds us of the increasing technological capacity to measure time, from the 'swinging pendulum to the throbbing quartz pulse' and warns with foreboding zeal that currently time is measured by the 'movement of the shutter, as cameras and their monitors become so many precision watches or model light clocks' (Virilio 2000: 60). For Virilio, real time is highly artificial: it is less 'real' than time measured by the rhythmic passing of night and day, for example. More importantly, however, real time is also that which steadily diminishes space. The speed and simultaneity of technologies of transport and telecommunication have reduced distances and compressed time. Space becomes for Virilio the contested 'ground' of the real. Commenting on Virilio's disdain for real time, John Rajchman finds an implicit and constant tension between a 'grounded lived space and an ungrounded live time' (Rajchman 2000:84).

There is an opposition to be noted here between Virilio's take on real time as a constantly accelerating or accelerated effect (or as that which sets the world into a quest for ever increasing speeds) and Warhol's engagement with real time. Virilio revels in the idea that real time is the dystopian outcome of our demand for speed, a kind of onslaught of time that continually bombards us at a steadily increasing rate. Warhol's experiments, both filmic and videographic, however, seem to suggest that real time might work otherwise. While *Empire* was not shot in real time, it suggests that real-time culture, rather than accelerating time, makes it stands still, holding the present in an ever-widening horizon. That Warhol was obsessed with endless duration is evident in some of his most famous films such as *Empire* and his long filmic portraits, *Eat* and *Sleep*. But perhaps it is less well known that in 1969 he proposed the idea for an 'all night' television show suitably called 'Nothing Special' where, according to Warhol, 'we'd just sit there and wait for something to happen and nothing would' (Angell: 3). 'Nothing Special' never happened but as an idea it resonates perhaps more strongly now than it did when it was proposed.

Warhol shot *Empire* not long after *Sleep* (1963) and the two films are conceptual counterparts to one and other, both structurally and formally. Where *Sleep* is voyeuristic, *Empire* is vigilant. The roaming eye in *Sleep* becomes a watchful eye in *Empire*, providing a kind of surveillance image long before live video became the standard of the surveillance industry. Though, unlike contemporary surveillance images, Warhol's *Empire* seems to occupy a kind of dream world, shrouded in its 16mm haziness. *Empire 24/7,* Wolfgang Staehle's more recent 'live' version of the original film, situates the building in a kind of eternal present, in contrast with Warhol's earlier version. Real time has an inextricable relationship with the present, rendering it as a kind of threshold. In this way, *Empire 24/7* should not be thought of as an update or endless extension of Warhol's version. Rather, Staehele's constant and clinical illumination of the building runs counter to Warhol's filmic portrayal.

Unlike the hyper-present of real time, Warhol's work from the late sixties tends to override the present, which is lost in the incongruous gap between his silent films and the screen prints of the disaster series. While the disaster series framed and repeated the dead/past, the films tended to render their subjects as virtual (ghostly), irrevocably othered, and neither living nor dead. *Empire* singularly symbolized that edge between glamour and death much in the same way that the subject of Warhol's screen prints oscillated from the Jackies and Marilyns to the electric chairs and car crashes during this same period. In the disaster series, Warhol focuses on the 'moment when the spectacle cracks'. He uses repetition compulsively in his screen prints: 'I don't want it to be essentially the same – I want it to be exactly the same. Because the more you look at the same exact thing, the more the meaning goes away and the better and emptier you feel' (quoted in Foster 1996: 131).

The disaster series preceded the advent of the porta-pack video camera (the first commercially available video camera, which went on the market in 1965), but the series seems to prefigure the age of instant replay. Warhol's experiments with still and moving image, repetition and continuity, economically summed up the televisual impulse toward repetition. With the advent of videotape, live events no longer happened only once. Instant replay became television's new trick, and the counterpart to liveness. The live image and instant replay are the twin obsessions that emerged from the mid-sixties onward, one feeding off the other in what Mary Ann Doane refers to as 'television's compulsion to repeat.' One anticipates the accident and then watches it over and over once it happens: 'information, crisis, catastrophe', each televisual state generates the next in the economy of liveness, each level feeding into and increasing the intensity of the next (Doane 1990: 231).

While it is true that the image of the planes colliding into the World Trade Center now fails to shock, Warhol's logic of repetition and emptiness seems to be slightly out of step with the representation of the WTC disaster, but only *just* slightly. In the same vein as Warhol, Zizek seems to imply that with instant replay we are beholden to repetition as a means of confirming the real.

> *When in the days after September 11 our gaze was transfixed by the images of the plane hitting one of the WTC towers, we were all forced to experience what the 'compulsion to repeat' and jouissance beyond the pleasure principle are: we wanted to see it again and again; the same shots were repeated ad nauseam, and the uncanny satisfaction we got from it was jouissance at its purest. It was when we watched the two WTC towers collapsing on the TV screen that it became possible to experience the falsity of 'reality TV' shows.*

(Zizek: 12)

If we can understand television as a catastrophe machine, a kind of stage for catastrophe, the live web-cam is now certainly a part of its mechanics. It is this capacity to capture catastrophe (along with banality) that gives the live cam its currency.

The Reality of Representation: from Liveness to Embeddedness

In television's obsession with reality, where ordinary people are showcased as actors, and mundane situations as drama, we are asked increasingly to see ourselves as though on television, or video at least. This is not the same thing as being virtual, but rather occupying a feedback loop-living 'live'. This is a shift in terms of how we understand ideas such as simulation and spectacle: a shift that emphasizes, not the disappearance of reality, but rather a reversal of how the problem is posed. Jordan Crandall puts the situation cogently when he writes: 'the reality of representation is substituted for the representation of reality. That is, authenticity arises less from the authenticity of reality per se than the authenticity of the means by which reality is portrayed' (Crandall 2003: 7).

It may be reductive to suggest parallels between the course of American foreign policy and the format of reality TV. But I would like to trace the influence of entertainment television on the format of television news. The sheer volume of first person narrative accounts of 9/11, and the embedded strategies deployed in the coverage of the invasion of Iraq, suggested an emphasis on witnessing disproportionate to what one might usually associate with international news reporting. The war itself seemed to be contextualized as a reality TV show to put right the wrongs of September 11 (which was swiftly and notably called 'The Attack on America'), and to quell the sense of righteous indignation that reached epic proportion in middle America. The confessional ethos of afternoon talk shows, such as *Oprah*, *Ricky Lake* and most recently *Dr. Phil* establish the idea of victimhood as the only legitimate position from which to speak and be heard. Reality TV on the other hand, operates through a cycle of surveillance, punishment and reward that broadly mimics the drama of justice so dear to the social contract. These two popular genres of television form a dialectical pairing. One plays out the act of confession, while the other images the detainment, control and punishment or reward. The two types of shows symbolically enact the Foucauldian drama of modern institutions: the demonstrative performance of the talk show, followed up by the pseudo-surveillant corrective of reality TV. The chain of events from the aftermath of September 11 to the invasion of Iraq has also followed a similar path in terms of its mediated representation-from the confessional apparatus of the talk show (played out in the drama of 9/11) to the retribution enacted in the nightly coverage of the invasion of Iraq, which has taken on the dimension of surveillance as punishment and ultimately entertainment.

'Reality TV' writes Vincent Pecora, 'elaborates surveillance as a sublime object'.

> *Advanced capitalist society at the dawn of the new millennium is less about truth versus fiction, or authenticity versus simulation. It is instead about a quest for real life that requires surveillance for its-for our-verification.*

(Pecora 2002: 348)

Pecora's suggestion that surveillance functions as both a 'quest for real life' and a 'sublime object' seems to come close to describing the qualitative difference between the discursive field of the virtual and that of the live. Even though Pecora suggests that questions of truth versus fiction, and authenticity versus simulation, are not of central concern to the production and value of surveillance images, an increased contemporary awareness of what is at stake in the virtual provokes this 'quest for the real', which the 'live' image promises, but does not quite provide.

Embedded media seem to up the ante, to promise even more. Indeed much of what constitutes the official memory of September 11, 2001 takes the form of what might be, in retrospect, quite similar to 'embedded' footage we saw during the invasion of Iraq. Here I refer to Paramount's documentary, *9/11* (2001), which is largely shaped around footage shot by an independent French camera crew that followed a New York fire brigade into the eye of the storm on the day that the attack on the twin towers took place. Though many of us saw 9/11 live on television, we can now watch it again, through the eyes of a fireman, just as we watch the conflict in Iraq through the eyes of an American or British solider. The power of embedded media, Crandall argues, lies in its ability to return to the viewer what is purportedly taken away with spectacle – to situate the viewer, as it were 'on the other side of the shield, dropped on to the battlefield of the Real' (Crandall: 7).

References

Angell, Callie (1994) *The Films of Andy Warhol: Part II Andy Warhol Film Project*. New York: Whitney Museum of American Art.

Crandall, J. (2003) 'Unmanned: Embedded Reporters, Predator Drones and Armed Perception'. CTHEORY 4/9/2003, accessed at www.ctheory.net

Doane, M. A. (1999) 'Temporality, Storage, Legibility: Freud, Marey and the Cinema' in J. Bergstrom (ed.) *Endless Night: Cinema and Psychoanalysis, Parallel Histories*. Berkeley: University of California Press.

Doane, M. A. (1990) 'Information, Crisis, Catastrophe' in P. Mellencamp (ed.) *Logics of Television*, London: BFI Publishing.

Feuer, J. (1983) 'The Concept of Live Television: Ontology as Ideology' in E. A. Kaplan (ed.) *Regarding Television: Critical Approaches-An Anthology*. Los Angeles: The American Film Institute.

Foster, H. (1996) *Return of the Real*. Cambridge, Mass: MIT Press.

Lotringer, S., Virilio P. (1997) *Pure War*. New York: Sexiotexte.

Mendenhall, P. (2001) 'Afghanistan tests the Taliban'. Accessed at www.msnbc.com/news/56407, September 22, 2001

Pecora, V. (2002) 'The Culture of Surveillance'. *Qualitative Sociology*, vol. 25, no. 3, fall.

Rajchman, J. (2000) *Constructions*. Cambridge, Mass: MIT Press.

Rhizome.org. "2001" – Wolfgang Staehle at Postmasters, http://rhizome.org accessed September 22, 2001

Taubin, Amy (1994) 'My Time is not your time'. *Sight and Sound*, June

Virilio, P. (2000) *Polar Inertia*. London: Sage Publications.

Virilio, P. (2000) *The Information Bomb*. London: Verso.

Zizek, S. (2002) *Welcome to the Desert of the Real*. London: Verso.

3. "Just Like a Movie"?:9/11 and Hollywood Spectacle

Geoff King

Even while it was still unfolding, the attack on the World Trade Center of 11 September 2001 was described on numerous occasions as like something 'from a movie'. The tone used by commentators at the time and later in the day was usually one that sought to capture the extraordinary and 'unbelievable' nature of the scenes they were witnessing: the aircraft hitting the twin towers, the fireball impact, and the eventual collapse of two such familiar landmarks on the Manhattan skyline. The images were, in some respects, uncannily similar to those offered by a number of Hollywood blockbusters produced in the previous decade. The spectacle of high-profile American buildings being severely damaged or entirely blown to bits became a familiar one in the 1990s, especially in action-disaster-sci-fi hybrids such as *Independence Day* (1996) and *Armageddon* (1998). More generally, the sight of buildings or aircraft exploding into fireballs has been common currency in Hollywood action films.

On September 11, then, what seemed to be happening was that some of these familiar kinds of images were being witnessed – but for real, rather than as part of Hollywood fantasy. A very real event was experienced – at least in part – through a frame provided by Hollywood spectacle. What should we make of this? One answer is to leap to the kinds of conclusions that come from some versions of 'postmodern' theory, which talk about a blurring of boundaries between the world of reality and that of media spectacle: arguments to the effect that the whole of reality has been swallowed up by media spectacle, or that even the most real events have been preceded by their equivalent in the world of images. Such claims are often made in a rather sweeping manner, however, that gives little if any sense of the specific qualities of such images and the more subtle nuances of the relationship between fictional spectacle and the spectacle of the real.

My aim in this chapter is to look more closely at the images themselves, and the ways they were deployed. My argument is that there are some overlaps between 'real' images in a case such as this and fictional images, specifically those from a particular kind of Hollywood cinema, and there are broader points to make about the role of spectacular images within the realm of the real. But it is important not to get carried away; if there are points of similarity between the images of 9/11 and those from Hollywood movies, there are also a number of important differences. This chapter will start by outlining some similarities, the nature of which are relatively obvious. It will then suggest some major differences, before moving on to examine, perhaps most significantly, some ways in which real images were redeployed during the coverage on September 11th and afterwards in a manner that made them more movie or fiction-like than they were in their original 'live' manifestation.

Similarities

The main points that led to the evocation of movie images in relation to the attack on the World Trade Centre are quite straightforward, along the lines already indicated. The fireball that erupted when the second tower was hit was reminiscent of the ubiquitous fireball-explosion images of recent and contemporary Hollywood action-disaster movies, including images of exploding aircraft and exploding buildings. This is true in general (fireball explosions wrecking buildings and destroying aircraft, respectively, in each of the first two films of the *Die Hard* series, for example, among many others), and for some images that more closely resemble different aspects of those of September 11. The meteor storm that hits Manhattan in *Armageddon* is one obvious example: a panoramic shot of the aftermath includes the image of one of the World Trade Center towers with its cap missing and the upper reaches in tatters and, like its real-world equivalent, belching smoke and flame. Manhattan is also widely trashed in *Godzilla* (1998), a film the destructive images of which include aircraft (in this case military helicopters) coming to grief among the concrete canyons of the city. A helicopter disappears uncannily into the structure of an office block in *The Matrix* (1999), before bursting explosively outwards, an image similar to a number of shots of the second plane impact of 9/11, in which the aircraft vanishes from sight, momentarily, before exploding through the building. The explosive collapse or severe damage of skyscrapers has featured in numerous Hollywood spectacular extravaganzas, ranging from *Armageddon* and *Independence Day* to the closing sequence of *Fight Club* (1999), the latter being attributed to a deliberate human act of destruction. Images of the huge dust cloud that followed the collapse of the World Trade Center towers had also been foreshadowed in varying ways in the disaster cycle of the latter years of the 20th century. An actual dust cloud is manifested, although only seen briefly, after the toppling of the distinctive peak of the Chrysler building in *Armageddon*. Structures of shape and scale similar to that of the real-world dust cloud, from which people flee in terror, are also manifested by fireballs in *Independence Day* and the tidal wave-front that sweeps up Manhattan in *Deep Impact* (1998). Some of those who told their stories afterwards likened the experience of trying to escape the dust and debris specifically to being inside a movie scenario. It is certainly a strange and somewhat uncanny experience to review any of these scenes after September the 11th, or after reviewing recorded images of the latter.

Elements of similarity between the real and fictional spectacles seem to have caused a great deal of discomfort for many commentators at the time, for reasons that are not hard to understand. The Hollywood versions offer enjoyable fantasies of destruction: enjoyable precisely because they can safely be indulged in the arena of fantasy. I have argued elsewhere that this might be appealing in at least two respects (King 2000). Firstly, as sheer spectacle: the dramatic audio-visual intensity of the images, as rendered by Hollywood with the latest in special effects technologies. Secondly, as something that can be understood in terms of long-standing American myths and ideologies: specifically, the notion of a cleansing destruction of centres of government and urban decadence, against which certain powerful notions of American-ness have often been defined. To have this imagined fantasy of destruction realized in actuality was potentially very unsettling for those who might have enjoyed the fictional version. There was also, perhaps, a guilty thrill in witnessing the spectacle of the live-actuality version and its constant repetition on the day. And also, perhaps, a post-hoc guilt about previous enjoyment of the Hollywood version. For some on the extreme right, the lesson to be learned from the real version was in fact much the same as that which could be read into the fiction. Christian fundamentalists Jerry Falwell and Pat Robertson interpreted the events of 9/11 precisely as the just deserts of 'sinful' American hedonism and materialism.

Differences

But there are substantial differences between the 'spectacle of the real', in this case, and the Hollywood equivalent; differences that clearly code one as 'reality' and the other as part of the realm of fictional-entertainment spectacle. Certain aspects of the images function as markers of *modality*, signalling their status as one or the other; the term, from linguistics, is used by Robert Hodge and David Tripp, in a different context, to suggest 'ways of situating messages in relation to an ostensible reality' (1986: 43). A number of modality markers made it clear that the real images on September 11 were not something from or 'just like' a movie. For a start, it would be abundantly clear to viewers with any media literacy that what they were watching on the day was of the nature of a 'breaking' live news event, an intrusion into normal programming or into normal news coverage. This is made apparent through numerous familiar conventions, including commentary by news anchors, reporters and 'experts' and through graphics presented on-screen. These are not absolute guarantors of authenticity, given that such devices are sometimes used in fictional works, precisely because of their power to evoke an impression of the real. Recent examples include some sequences in the BBC television production *Smallpox 2002: Silent Weapon* (2002), which employed real news anchors as part of its realization of an imagined smallpox outbreak, although in this case in a production that presented itself as a retrospective analysis. Any viewer unsure of the status of the coverage on 9/11 could have any doubts dispelled, however, as some reported at the time, by changing channels: the fact that the same material was being presented on all networks at the same time underlined its status not just as 'reality', but as reality considered to be of a high order of impact and importance.

Looking in closer detail at the images, many of the modality markers of real/actuality television in this case were to do with what was missing, what was absent, in comparison with the Hollywood-fictional equivalent. One of the markers of real, genuine authenticity in audio-visual media generally is a reduction often in the plenitude of images, as suggest by Amy West elsewhere in this volume. This applies to both 'real' reality coverage and the fabricated version found in some fictions. Absences or reduced quality of images – such as shaky camerawork, dodgy focus or awkward zooms – signify that events have not been staged for the convenience of the production of images. Coverage reacts to the events, rather than the events being created for, or through, the images themselves. In the case of September the 11th, there were numerous such signifiers of actuality.

There was initially no footage of the first impact at all, a key absence, a guarantor of authenticity (what spectacular disaster fiction would leave so crucial an event unseen, other than in the event of a severe lack of resources?) that was not filled until the following day. Our view of the second impact was obscured, rather than clear and complete. Depending on which channel viewers were tuned into, the impact happened either behind the first tower to have been hit, or behind the tower that was now being hit. In both cases, viewers could see – in multiple repetitions throughout the day – the plane approaching, momentarily disappearing from sight and then only the great billow of flame that emerged out from another side of the building. The moment of impact was teasingly out of view.

There was also an absence of close-ups or images of what was going on inside the tower: the kinds of scenes of panic, death, rescue or escape that would be expected in a movie. There was no human scale to which to relate what we were watching – very much the essential stuff of the Hollywood-fantasy version, in which we would expect melodramatic sequences, focused around central individual characters to whom we had been introduced in advance, depicting tragic and heroic encounters inside the twin towers. There was also a considerable and sometimes sustained confusion in while-it-was-happening coverage. The BBC, for example, reported at one point that another plane had hit, when what had happened was the collapse of the first tower. For all the real drama and its extraordinary nature, there was also a slower passage of events than would be found in a fictional version such as the rapid, intense, multiple impacts of the meteor shower on Manhattan in *Armageddon*.

Shifts to be more 'like a movie'
Some of these absences were gradually removed as coverage developed, and the gap

between reality and movie images was reduced in some respects. Footage from ground level, at the time of the impacts and of the collapse of the towers, was supplied quite soon, providing a more up-close-and-personal impression of the events, including eyewitness testimonials on September 11 and images of people running for and taking cover. It did not take long for a villain, Osama Bin Laden, to be suggested, in comment and analysis that sought to create some kind of narrative context for the events; again, something that would be expected in a movie version.

More images generally became available of the key moments, filling in some of the gaps left in the initial coverage. As more time passed, missing parts of the picture were supplied and, significantly, something closer to a cinematic assemblage of images was offered. One interesting example came in the BBC Six O'clock News on the 11th, the first example in the footage I have seen that creates a precise continuity match between two images of the impact of the second plane. The sequence starts with the by-then-familiar shot of the plane disappearing from sight, behind the smoke-belching tower that had already been hit. Just as the first part of the impact becomes visible on the other side of the tower, a cut is made to a new angle, in which a fuller view is given of the fireball coming through the far side of the tower. A match-on-action, a standard device from the conventions of cinematic and televisual continuity editing, is used to establish a seamless cut from one image to the other.

By the second day, footage was available of the first plane hitting the trade centre. A number of clearer views of the second impact were also broadcast, providing unobscured images of the moment of contact from several different cameras. These were put together in repeated sequences, although not edited in tight continuity style. Each image of the impact was usually seen in its entirety before cutting to the next. One example starts with Jules Naudet's footage of the first impact, from what subsequently became the CBS documentary *9/11* (2002). Naudet's camera, engaged in recording a routine call-out to a reported gas leak, as part of what was planned to be a film about the experiences of a new probationary firefighter, lurches sideways to catch the final approach of the plane and the first moment of impact in the background of the shot. A closer shot zooms clumsily in to capture an image of the billowing fireball, zooming back out, in and out again, its uncertainty registering the moment of shock, before settling on a more stable medium-long-shot. This is followed by the now-familiar shot of the second plane's approach, disappearance behind the tower and the blossom of flame on the other side. Next comes a striking low-angle shot from relatively close to the foot of the towers, not seen on the 11th. The camera, like many others, has been positioned after the first impact. The second plane suddenly enters the frame, knifing into the side of the tower closest to the camera. It disappears, *Matrix*-helicopter-like, for a second, before the fireball explosion erupts from the side of the building oriented most fully towards the camera, the shock registered in this case not by movement of the camera, which remains largely impassive (it moves slightly but in a composed manner, to reframe the explosion at the centre of the image), but by the abrupt withdrawal from the frame of the low-angle figure of a man standing in the lower left-hand corner of the screen. Next comes a long-range, slightly wobbling shot of the smoking first tower which pulls out and pans a fraction to the left, just in time to catch the second impact from the same side as the previous shot but rotated more towards the 'exit wound' side of the tower. What happens in this sequence is rather like the organization of images found in some fiction films created in the early years of cinema, in which action was played out from one perspective and then repeated in a overlapping manner from another, before the adoption of the conventions of temporal continuity with which we are familiar today. Allowing the impact to be seen in full from each view is privileged over any drive towards processing it into a more integrated assemblage.

The tendency to make the assemblage of images closer to that familiar from Hollywood fiction increased in later documentary coverage. A number of examples are found in the HBO production *In Memoriam: New York City* (2002), which offers a wide range of views of the action from different cameras put together into continuity sequences. There seems to be an impulse here to render the events of real spectacle in a form closer to that we would usually associate with fiction productions. One sequence starts with a long shot that tracks the movement of the second plane from a greater distance than usual from the trade centre. The camera pans with the plane until it enters the tower. The shot is held until the point at which the fireball begins to emerge from the near side, at which point a cut is made to a closer and lower-angle shot from the same side, during which the fireball emerges close to its full extent. The following images give a number of different perspectives on the development of the fireball: a shot that shifts the angle of view by about 90 degrees from the previous image; a very long-range shot from across the water that zooms rapidly in to frame the fireball; and a medium-range, long-lens shot that frames the towers from the facing side bearing the scar of the point of entry of the first plane, in which we see the latter part of the fireball and the thick muscle of smoke that follows.

This sequence is particular interesting, in comparison with the fictional explosive spectacles produced in Hollywood, because of the way it both obeys, and 'cheats' within, the strict conventions of continuity. A broad sense of continuity is established in the last few shots, which generally take the fireball from initial development to dissipation. There is a significant degree of overlap between each shot, however. This should not be understood as a 'failure' of continuity on the part of the editor/s, however. It closely resembles a regime often used in the editing of Hollywood fireball/explosions, in which the impact of the explosion is increased by the deliberate use of slight temporal overlap (for more detail on this see King 2000). Hollywood action films often cut into major special-effects explosions, to increase their impact. A quick series of cuts to different viewpoints emphasises the percussive effect. It is common to overlap these cuts slightly, effectively to get more 'bang for the buck'; a series of explosive impacts that build rapidly, one after another, from a number of angles. This is precisely the effect created in the sequence analyzed above. Each shot of the fireball starts just before the stage of its development reached in the previous shot; not a complete overlap, which would destroy any sense of continuity, but a significant moment of repetition, the overall effect of which is to heighten the impact of the fireball.

This very 'fictional' effect, a 'cinematic' construction of spectacular impact, is mixed, however, with many traces of the authentically real. These include unsteady camerawork and awkward zooms and the slightly different visual qualities of each of the images, taken from different cameras. The fact that this is a montage of separate components is made explicit by the use of captions that situate each of the shots, in terms of both the identity of the cameraman and the location of the camera: Park Foreman, Brooklyn Heights; Scott Myers, View from John Street; Michael Kovalenko, View from King Street; Ronald S. Pordy, View from Long Island City; Mike Toole, View from Desbrosses St. A similar combination of smooth continuity editing and visibility of separate components characterizes the cut from the Six O'clock News cited above. The first shot has no identifying marks but the second has different visual qualities and carries a large '5' logo, an overt reminder not only of the fact that a cut has been made but also of the ownership-rights surrounding such images and the fact that the BBC has had to 'borrow' the shot from elsewhere in order to create the continuity effect.

Sound plays an important role in this process of construction, also functioning both to increase the continuity effect and to establish the modality as that of the real/authentic. The sequence from *In Memoriam* starts with just ambient background noise and the sound of the plane's engine. Both the engine note (briefly) and the sound of the explosion from the first shot continue into the second, creating a sound-bridge, a classic continuity editing device in which continuity of sound helps to smooth the juncture between separate images. This process continues throughout the sequence. The background roar of the explosion and of ambient sound remains more or less consistent across all of the separate shots, including the very long shot from Long Island, in which case the sound could not possibly have been that accompanying the shot. A single sound perspective is maintained regardless of camera distance – another classical convention in the use of sound in continuity editing. Most shots come with their own 'reality' sound effects, however, in the form of the startled reactions of people close to the camera, comments mostly in the nature of 'oh my god' and 'holy shit'. The result of this combination of modalities suggests, if not a 'postmodern' collapsing of reality and fiction-spectacle, at least a penetration of certain ways of organizing fictional images into the realm of coverage of the real. A number of paradoxes result, indicating the relative nature of constructions we associate with the real and the fictional, spectacular or otherwise.

If a limited view and problems of access signify authenticity, something not set up for the cameras, such qualities also tend to draw our attention to the process of mediation. A dialectical relationship exists, as Jay David Bolter and Richard Grusin (1999) suggest, between the qualities of immediacy, the illusion of no mediation, and of hypermediacy, a state in which multiple markers exist of the process of mediation itself. We are likely to be aware of what is lacking and frustrated by such limitations (especially the urge on September 11 to see the first impact and an unobstructed view of the moment the second plane hits the building). Conversely, the fictional type of assemblage of images can become less noticeable in itself, precisely because of its familiarity. We are very familiar with the practice of cutting from one viewpoint to another to get a better overall perspective on the action. This version can give the impression of more objective and unmediated access to what is happening, despite the fact that it is more densely constructed and mediated, and that in this case many of the markers of the separate components remain visible. It offers a comfortable familiarity that moves smoothly and seemingly effortlessly from one shot to another. There is a widespread tendency in documentary, as Bill Nichols (1991) suggests, to use Hollywood-style continuity devices to efface the process of mediation in favour of a concentration on the material presented.

This is a paradox that, I would suggest, is symptomatic of the ways in which media constructions of the real-authentic and the fictional-image-spectacular generally exist in a dialectical relationship, in which each is mutually implicated in the other, and in which neither can entirely be separated out from the other. To argue this is not to surrender any distinction between notions of the real, including the spectacularly real, and the entirely fictional, but to recognise that a complex relationship exists between the two. The events of September 11 were, clearly, extremely 'real', in terms of their impact on those directly involved and on future American policy both at home and abroad. The domain of spectacular imagery is part of that reality, however, even aspects that might seem to have been experienced beforehand in the realm of out-and-out Hollywood fantasy. It is worth remembering that the enormous reality of September 11 probably would not have happened at all if it had not been for its potential to produce the spectacular imagery – because of the importance the imagery has for the project of those who carry out such attacks (it is notable, for example, that big strikes by the IRA in Northern Ireland and on the British mainland were known by the organization itself as 'spectaculars').

A shift towards a more cinematic-continuity assemblage of images might be understood as part of the process of implying some kind of mastery or control over the events, reducing to some extent their potential to shock. In two now-classic essays on television coverage of disasters, Mary Ann Doane (1990) and Patricia Mellencamp (1990) characterize television as a medium that both thrives on and provides relief from the potential anxieties generated by catastrophe, both natural and man-made. Catastrophe is characterized by both Doane and Mellencamp as discontinuous, a sudden and unexpected intrusion into the usual flow of television discourse. It is particularly noteworthy, in this context, that what comes to be imposed on images such as those of September 11 is precisely a form of *continuity*, a restoration of some kind of order. For Mellencamp, what is involved is 'a shift between the safe assurance of successive time and story and the break-in of the discontinuity of the real in which the future hangs in the balance [...]" (244). Assemblage of images according to the conventions of continuity editing implies a more secure viewing position, in which the depicted events are clearly located in the (recent) past, the immediate future less likely to be hanging unsettlingly in the balance.

Television coverage of catastrophe has a therapeutic effect, Mellencamp suggests; while producing anxiety, it also discharges it, especially through constant repetition of key images such as the Zapruder film of the John F. Kennedy assassination or the explosion of the space shuttle *Challenger* in 1986. The simple repetition of such images might also signal a process of shock, however, a stunned shock in which images including those of September 11 are repeated constantly in relatively unprocessed fragments. Throughout the immediate hours after the planes hitting the World Trade Center, broadcasters showed a constantly updated series of montage sequence: planes hitting, towers collapsing, dust-shrouded survivors, a fire engine doomed to keep passing the same street corner time after time. The therapeutic effect attributed to repetition by Mellencamp, in an account drawing heavily on Freud's theory of repetition-compulsion, might be achieved more strongly by the subsequent process in which such fragments were in some cases knitted more tightly into continuity sequences. Only up to a point, however. As Doane suggests, in a passage worth quoting in full:

> The televisual construction of catastrophe seeks both to preserve and to annihilate interdeterminacy, discontinuity. On the one hand, by surrounding catastrophe with commentary, with an explanatory apparatus, television works to contain its more disturbing and uncontainable aspects. On the other hand, catastrophe's discontinuity is embraced as the mirror of television's own functioning, and that discontinuity and indeterminacy ensure the activation of the lure of referentiality.

(234)

As well as seeking to contain it, Doane suggests, television's commitment to concepts such as liveness and actuality result in a striving 'to mimic the experience of the real, a real which in its turn is guaranteed by the contact with death' (234). There are limits to the extent to which television can 'contain' or reduce the impact of momentous events, especially something as shocking as those of September 11, even if it 'wanted' to – although terms such as these suggest a volition on the part of the medium that is not warranted. If the tendency of television coverage is partly to assuage and partly to thrive on the thrill of the impact that comes from the discontinuity of catastrophe, however, the formal qualities of the coverage of 9/11 could be said to contribute to both, although with the component that contributes to assurance and mastery increasing with the passage of time.

As for Hollywood itself, it might still be too early to draw any definitive conclusion about the fate of its images of spectacular destruction in the wake of 9/11. The immediate aftermath of the attacks was a time of nervousness, in which discomfort was felt about the use of any image of the twin towers – most notably the abandonment of planned sequences on the towers in *Spiderman* (2002) - despite the fact that the buildings were celebrated and memorialized in many other areas of popular culture, from the twin beams of light shone into the sky on the site to the myriad photographs and other memorabilia that immediately went on sale in the immediate vicinity. Some have suggested that Hollywood has since shied away from images of disastrous destruction, but it is far from easy to attribute this to any specific causal factors. The pre-millennial disaster and SF/disaster movie cycle of the second half of the 1990s had already run its course, while any shift in the centre of gravity towards more all-out fantasy, in the shape of blockbuster franchises such as the *Lord of the Rings* and *Harry Potter* series, was already in train well before the events of September 2001. Not that disaster in the contemporary American landscape has been entirely abandoned. The espionage thriller *The Sum of All Fears* (2002) features the explosion of a nuclear bomb in the city of Baltimore, although the destruction is shown obliquely – a blast wave hitting the locations of central characters, distant shots of the mushroom cloud, the local aftermath of burning buildings – rather than being given the full spectacular treatment that might have resulted pre-9/11.

References

Bolter, Jay David, and Richard Grusin (1999) *Remediation: Understanding New Media*. Cambridge, Mass. & London: MIT Press.

Doane, Mary Ann (1990) 'Information, Crisis, Catastrophe' in Patricia Mellencamp (ed.) *Logics of Television*. London & Indianapolis: BFI & Indiana University Press.

Hodge, Robert, and David Tripp (1986) *Children and Television: A Semiotic Approach*. Cambridge: Polity Press.

King, Geoff (2000) *Spectacular Narratives: Hollywood in the Age of the Blockbuster*. London: I.B. Tauris.

Mellencamp, Patricia (1990) 'TV Time and Catastrophe, or *Beyond the Pleasure Principal* of Television' in Mellencamp (ed.) *Logics of Television*. London & Indianapolis: BFI & Indiana University Press.

Nichols, Bill (1991) *Representing Reality: Issues and Concepts in Documentary*. Bloomington &
Indianapolis: Indiana University Press.

4. Reframing Fantasy:September 11 and the Global Audience

Kathy Smith

It was a hot afternoon. I was sitting on a bed in a small white room in North Africa, watching CNN when the storm broke. I switched on the television in time to see a plane hit a skyscraper. Another disaster movie. It took seconds to realize – from the shaking images, the silences broken by the clattering of the cameras and exclamations of bystanders, then the shocked and shocking commentary – that this was not a film. I called to my companion sitting outside on the terrace, who arrived just in time to see the second plane, in 'real time' impact on its target. The image then changed to the Pentagon, where smoke was billowing from within. For those few moments, America was under siege, and no one was quite sure what would happen next.

08.46 a.m. A hijacked passenger jet, American Airlines Flight 11 out of Boston, Massachusetts, crashes into the north tower of the World Trade Center, tearing a gaping hole and setting the building afire.

09.03 a.m. A second hijacked airliner, United Airlines Flight 175 from Boston, crashes into the south tower of the World Trade Center and explodes.

09.17 a.m. The Federal Aviation Administration shuts down all New York City area airports

09.21 a.m. The Port Authority of New York and New Jersey orders all bridges and tunnels in the New York area closed.

09.40 a.m. The FAA halts all flight operations at U.S. airports, the first time in U.S. history that air traffic nationwide has been halted.

09.43 a.m. American Airlines Flight 77 crashes into the Pentagon.

10.05 a.m. The south tower of the World Trade Center collapses, plummeting into the streets below. A massive cloud of dust and debris forms and slowly drifts away from the building.

10.10 a.m. A portion of the Pentagon collapses. United Airlines Flight 93, also hijacked, crashes in Somerset County, Pennsylvania, southeast of Pittsburgh.

10.24 a.m. The FAA reports all inbound transatlantic aircraft flying into the U.S. are being diverted to Canada.

10.28 a.m. The World Trade Center's north tower collapses from the top down as if it were being peeled apart.

(Prieto 2002: 5)

The events of September 11 2001 impacted significantly across the discursive formations of our culture, effecting what might be described as a seismic shift in terms of our construction and understanding of fantasy: on that day, the world of the possible expanded in directions which had previously only existed in imagination, delivered to a global audience through the medium of television. This was not fantasy. These were real events, happening to real people, affecting real lives. The scale of the devastation was, for some time, beyond the imagination, and beyond speech; and until it could be reconciled – in Lacanian terms – from the Real to the Symbolic, it was beyond words, existing in a visceral realm of shock and pain.

In the context of an aesthetics of reception with regard to theatre audiences, Susan Bennett explores the notion of a 'horizon of expectations', noting that '[a]vant-garde texts are [...] never completely "new" – if they were they would be incomprehensible – but merely contain instructions to the reader which demand revision of the horizon of expectations of earlier texts' (1997: 49). In the instance of the initial images of the events of September 11, however, the spectator's 'horizon of expectations' became irrelevant, as what was taking place was unprecedented; it was the spectator's horizon of *imagination* which was transgressed. The occurrence of these events *in reality* was beyond imagination. This was an audience that recognized, in those first and momentarily unmediated moments, that this was not a Hollywood blockbuster, but something quite different. The televisual frame was recognizable, but only served to further alienate that which was taking place within it; and this, in its difference, required and elicited a different intellectual and emotional response.

This was an event formerly confined to representations of fantasy, mainly within the genre of 'action' or 'disaster' movie, and the future experiencing of fictional representations of such a trauma, for the spectator, was fundamentally changed by this event. Such an event challenges accepted notions of pleasure in fantasy, and gives rise to questions concerning the allure of representations of disaster: why are fictional representations of disaster, 'disaster movies', pleasurable; do we respond differently to representations depending on whether we understand (and therefore frame) them as 'fantasy' or as 'reality'; and, for the spectator, how does the experience of watching 'fantasy' differ from that of watching 'reality'? Shoshana

Felman would argue that trauma can be accounted for only in a fragmented manner, that '[i]t is in the very nature of trauma to resist being accounted for in a completely coherent or easily comprehensible way' (Buse 2001:181). This paper attempts to engage with this moment of rupture in culture, considering the response of a global audience, an audience reading televisual rather than embodied images; and in doing so, to give account (albeit fragmented) of the economy – during those few moments of mesmerized paralysis – of the likely psychical relation of the audience to this event.

Stage and Screen

Considering first, then, the economy of the relation between spectator and representation in respect of the medium through which this event was witnessed, it is widely recognised that the experience of the televisual spectator necessarily differs from that of the cinematic or theatric spectator. Wendy Wheeler and Trevor Griffiths acknowledge the *immediacy* of theatre, observing that

> *In the theatre, and unlike film, the economy of seeing and hearing we are offered is just as immediate and as vital as the drama of the family from and through which we negotiate our precarious subjectivity. The danger of the theatre, the possibility of failing to maintain the illusion, of extraneous noises which should not be heard, of the collapse of the role and of the fiction of assumed identities, of fluffed or forgotten lines, of props which make noises which they shouldn't, all combine to reproduce precisely the erotic, libidinal danger of the Oedipal family.*

(1992: 188)

Christian Metz considers the relation to fiction of theatre and of film, as experienced by the spectator, observing that

> *In the cinema as in the theatre, the represented is by definition imaginary: that is what characterises fiction as such independently of the signifiers in charge of it. But the representation is fully real in the theatre, whereas in the cinema it too is imaginary, the material being already a reflection. Thus the theatrical fiction is experienced more – it is only a matter of a different 'dosage', of a difference of economy, rather, but that is precisely why it is important – as a set of real pieces of behaviour actively directed at the evocation of something unreal, whereas cinematic fiction is experienced rather as the quasi-real presence of the unreal itself.*

(1990: 66-7)

In terms of content, the representation in both cinema and theatre is – by definition – imaginary. In cinema, as Metz points out, the form also is imaginary: in his words, the projection is a 'quasi-real' presence.

The economy of the relationship between the televisual image and the spectator is, again, different. Televisual representations enter the private domestic spaces of the subject in a way in which theatric and cinematic representations cannot. The experience of the spectator in this instance (although shared with a global audience) is not communal, not estranged by the environment; and as the images enter his/her own home, s/he has a certain control over their reception, a control which is not present in the environment of a cinema or theatre. John Ellis observes that

> Broadcast TV proposes itself a very different spectator from that of cinema. The viewer for TV is very far from being in a position of producing a totalising vision of the truth from an initial stance of curiosity. For broadcast TV, the regime of viewing is rather one of complicity with TV's own look at the passing pageant of life. TV's regime is not one of enigma and solution of enigma, but rather one of continuous variety, a perpetual introduction of novelty on the basis of repetition which never reaches a final conclusion. Broadcast TV's viewer is therefore a bystander, but a bystander in very specific circumstances, those of home.

(1988: 160)

Theatric representation is characterised by physical embodiment, the *danger* of a re-presentation which is always a first performance, never a repetition or exact copy of the last. Cinematic images, on the other hand, offer a certain distance and a narrative certainty, in that they can be replayed; and televisual images domesticize, contextualizing and juxtaposing spectacular images within the familiarity of the domestic space. In the first few moments of the destruction of the Trade Center, however, the distinction between these three kinds of relation was momentarily blurred and compromised, and the libidinal danger of the theatric representation of real bodies overflowed into the quasi-spectacle of a Hollywood blockbuster viewed through the delimited lens of a television by a horrified and confused spectator who – momentarily disorientated – could not differentiate between the three. For those first few moments the schisms between content, medium, and spectator were difficult to reconcile into a coherent response.

Over the days which followed, the global audience seemed both fascinated and horrified by the developing narrative. Those first few moments, however, were moments of inadvertent spectatorship, where the spectator had to accommodate the realisation that what s/he was watching was not fantasy, but reality, and to reframe the experience accordingly. The medium (and the expectation of it) is likely to account to some extent for the disorientation of the spectator. The psychical economy of this moment of shift, the nature of the desire of the spectator immediately before and after, and the effect on the spectator's subsequent construction of fantasy might bring us a little closer to understanding the allure of the 'unpleasurable'.

In Pursuit of Pleasure

Why go to the theatre or the cinema at all? Why watch representations of things and events which are often of a distressing nature? What is the allure of the seemingly unpleasurable? Tim O'Sullivan *et al.* observe that

> *The relation between language and the unconscious has been shown to be one of the determinants of pleasure – even in such apparently desexualized activities as watching television or cinema (especially the latter) there is an element of voyeurism from which the pleasure may derive. But such pleasure is also textual, a product of the relation between the viewer and the text's specific representations.*

(1996: 229)

Metz observes that the visual and auditory drives have a special relationship with the absence of their object because, as opposed to other sexual drives, the 'perceiving drive' (combining the scopic and the invocatory drives) *'concretely represents the absence of its object* in the distance at which it maintains it and which is part of its very definition: distance of the look, distance of listening' (1990:59).

There are a number of models available, particularly if the discussion extends to an exploration of the theatric or cinematic gaze; the purpose of this project, however, is to move towards an account of the pleasure of the spectator within Freudian and Lacanian models. These offer some account of the pleasure to be found in representations in fantasy of events which, in reality, would be experienced as unpleasurable.

Pleasure in the Unpleasurable: The Allure of the 'Disaster Movie'

Returning, then, to a consideration of the allure of the 'disaster movie', and the role of the spectator in respect of the pleasure of the representation, Sigmund Freud (in his account of 'Psychopathic Characters on Stage') suggests that the spectator is

> *a person who experiences too little, who feels that he is a 'poor wretch to whom nothing of importance can happen', who has long been obliged to damp down, or rather displace, his ambition to stand in his own person at the hub of world affairs; he longs to feel and to act and to arrange things according to his desires – in short to be a hero. And the playwright and actor enable him to do this by allowing him to identify himself with a hero.*

(1988:121-122).

The spectator, as vicarious hero, runs no real risks in terms of danger to his personal security; and he (or she) is aware that it is only a game. The relevance of this particular idea to the spectator of the 'disaster movie' requires very little explanation.

Freud develops this account into a discussion of the construction of the 'neurotic spectator' and the 'non-neurotic spectator', noting that 'suffering of every kind is [...] the subject-matter of drama, and from this suffering it promises to give the audience pleasure'. He cites religious drama (man v. divinity), social drama (man v. society) and drama of character (man v. man). In each of these examples, two conscious impulses are in conflict. He moves on to differentiate psychological drama and psychopathological drama, defining the first as being where the struggle that causes the suffering is fought out in the hero's mind itself, a 'struggle between different impulses', and the second as 'when the source of the suffering in which we take part and from which we are meant to derive pleasure is no longer a conflict between two almost equally conscious impulses but between a conscious impulse and a repressed one' (1988: 125).

Within the notion of psychopathological drama, Freud offers two possible positions of spectatorship: the neurotic and the non-neurotic. For the neurotic spectator, the pleasure of the representation lies in the balancing of recognition and control of repressed impulses (as, presumably, an overwhelming return of the repressed would ultimately cause unpleasure, in a failure of resistance). For the non-neurotic spectator, whose control over the repressed is more robust, the experiencing of pleasure is slightly more complicated in that it involves the drama serving to avert attention from the impulse which is struggling into consciousness (and thereby averting a tendency to resistance) by ensuring that the spectator is in the grip of his emotions instead of 'taking stock of what is happening'. Elizabeth Wright comments that

> *The neurotic spectator will react to the lifting of repression with a mixture of enjoyment (on account of the energy saved in not having to hold down the repression) and resistance (on account of the anxiety that may be caused). The dramatist, says Freud, must proceed with care to attune the non-neurotic spectator, whose gain is not so obvious; he must draw him in 'with attention averted', lower his resistance, so that he does not know exactly where his emotions are leading him.*

> (1993: 34)

In terms of the disaster movie, for the neurotic spectator the pleasure might lie in the visual and auditory realisation of his fears, but from a safe distance: he can recognize that the situation represented is one which is to be feared, but that he himself does not have to face that fear, as it is firmly placed within the realm of fantasy. For the non-neurotic spectator, the sheer scale of the cinematic experience, in terms of colour, light and sound, might distract his attention away from the maintenance of the repression of that which he fears, so that – at moments of particular drama – he may be 'taken by surprise'.

A further Freudian model may also be relevant to the disaster movie, a model which addresses fantasies which are masochistic and sadistic in nature: the paper 'A Child is Being Beaten' (1987: 159-193) concerns the yield of pleasure, in terms of fantasy, in watching the imaginary suffering of another. In reality, Freud points out, these scenes are met with repugnance. It is within fantasy that there is a yield of pleasure; and this yield of pleasure in the observation of something unpleasurable, coupled with the repugnance at the reality, may contribute to an account of the lure of the disaster movie and the repulsion/compulsion response to 'reality'.

The compulsion to repeat, in an attempt to achieve mastery over the situation, is another mechanism identified by Freud. He opens his discussion of the repetition compulsion anecdotally by describing his observation of a boy of eighteen months playing a game with a cotton reel: a game of disappearance and return. The infant compensated himself for the absence of his mother by staging the disappearance and return of objects. This raised the question for Freud – a question also of relevance to that of the pleasure of the spectator – of how repetition of a distressing experience as a game reconciles itself with the pleasure principle. Freud suggested two possibilities: the first concerned the yield of pleasure in mastery – the child was able, through repetition of the game, to change a situation in which he felt passive into a situation where his role was active. Freud also suggested that it was an act of revenge on his mother for leaving, an act suppressed in real life. Both these ideas have obvious resonance in terms of the pleasure of the spectator of the disaster movie: watching the repetition of the movie gives the spectator a certain amount of mastery over it; furthermore, the spectator is to a certain extent (and particularly with regard to television) in control of the manner of its reception.

Alternatively, the fiction might be considered a fetish object masking the truth, which is where the pleasure and the need of the 'disaster movie' may be found. Drawing on Freudian and Lacanian thought, Metz considers absence an underpinning principle in cinematic fiction:

> *The Law is what permits desire: the cinematic equipment is the instance thanks to which the imaginary turns into the symbolic, thanks to which the lost object (the absence of what is filmed) becomes the law and the principle of a specific and insti-tuted signifier, which it is legitimate to desire.*

(1990:76)

and he observes that

> *Because it attempts to disavow the evidence of the senses, the fetish is evidence that this evidence has indeed been* recorded *(like a tape stored in the memory). The fetish is not inaugurated because the child still believes its mother has a penis (=order of the imaginary), for if it still believed it completely, as 'before', it would no longer need the fetish. It is inaugurated because the child now 'knows very well' that its mother has no penis. In other words, the fetish not only has disavowal value, but also* knowledge value.

(1990:76)

Following this line of thought, the 'truth' is the recognition of castration, which the fiction of the 'disaster movie' masks, in that it represents a trauma which 'turns out all right in the end'. The problem with real disasters is that they do not, and the outcome is unpredictable. The spectator observing minor disasters of a nature previously experienced might feel some discomfort (or perhaps not, if their repetition in similar form leads to a sense of mastery): the scale of the disaster in the case of the World Trade Center was, however, beyond most people's experience, and on a psychical level might be experienced in a similar manner to that of the original trauma: uncontrollable, leading to unimaginable loss.

All Too Real: When Fantasy Becomes Reality

In moving towards an account of the pleasure experienced by the spectator in the act of watching a 'disaster movie' or other fictional representations of a seemingly 'unpleasurable' nature, several models have been considered: identification with a 'hero'; the control of repression by the 'neurotic' or 'non-neurotic' spectator; masochistic and sadistic fantasy; mastery through repetition; or fetishization. These same models are likely to have extended into the spectator's initial experience of the events of September 11, with disorienting effects, as the ability to 'frame' became temporarily inadequate.

Returning first to Freud's notion of the psychopathic character on stage; if one considers this model of the spectator/representation relation and the psychical process involved in identification with the 'hero', an account of the psychical process of watching the first images of September 11 might concern the inability of the spectator to maintain the conventional and practiced role of the 'hero' because, firstly – and unlike most disaster movies – there is no 'hero'; secondly, 'good' does not necessarily triumph, effort does not necessarily produce results, and finally the outcome is totally unpredictable. The result, for the spectator of this disaster, is that there is no longer a tenable position from which to spectate. One can only stare in shock, in a kind of mesmerized paralysis.

For the 'neurotic spectator' of Freud's theory, the overwhelming effect of the initial images may well have temporarily unbalanced his/her tenuous grip on the boundaries of repression, the result being an upsurge of repressed material leading to a temporary lapse of control (resulting in panic, anxiety and grief). For the 'non-neurotic spectator', this particular event would have caught him/her 'off-guard': distracted by the scale of the event, the boundaries of repression would have been made vulnerable and breached, again resulting in an upsurge of repressed material.

Through *nachträglichkeit* – the making sense of earlier experience through later experience – the psychical economy of early sado-masochistic fantasy might have been re-invoked: the notion that these events are happening, but elsewhere (and again, this could be related to Freud's notion of identification with a 'hero', with whom one does not have to die in order to return the world to status quo), evoking contradictory, complex and disturbing responses of simultaneous relief (arising from the recognition that it is happening 'elsewhere') and revulsion (arising from the recognition that it is happening at all, and also from a recognition of the response of relief).

In terms of repetition compulsion, the connection between Freud's theory and the media representation of September 11 is clear. One of the lasting images of the events of September 11 is the image of the second plane impacting on the second tower, replayed again and again throughout the day and over the days which followed, in a global attempt to admit its possibility and to come to terms with the act.

Beyond the Horizon of Imagination

It has been observed that Freud's paper 'Beyond The Pleasure Principle', with its exploration of repetition compulsion, offers the foundations of a more recent theoretical model, that of Trauma Theory. Peter Buse cites Cathy Caruth's definition of trauma, observing the debt owed by 'trauma theory' to Freud:

> In its most general definition, trauma describes an overwhelming experience of sudden or catastrophic events in which the response to the event occurs in the often delayed, uncontrolled repetitive appearance of hallucinations and other intrusive phenomena. The experience of the soldier faced with sudden and massive death around him, for example, who suffers only in a numbed state, only to relive it later on in repeated nightmares, is a central and recurring image of trauma in our century.

> (Buse 2001: 174)

There are a number of psychical frameworks available to the spectator in terms of finding pleasure in the 'disaster movie'. Applying these frameworks to the unmediated 'breaking news' of September 11 is, however, problematic, for as Dori Laub observes, 'Massive trauma precludes its registration; the observing and recording mechanisms of the human mind are temporarily knocked out, malfunction' (Felman and Laub 1992:57).

On September 11, the images were arriving within the familiar frame of a television screen; but it quickly became obvious that the frame of 'disaster movie' was not appropriate, as these images, in spite of their appearance on a screen, were not fictional. These were moments when the representation was exceeding the frames of reference provided by our culture, and moving beyond our horizon of imagination, moments when – in Lacanian terms – the spectator was momentarily experiencing something outside of the symbolic, something in the Real. This 'something' in a moment of extreme experience, was an all too real physical reminder of a moment of psychical trauma and unimaginable loss, akin to the archaic psychical experience of the pre-subject and the original loss: a violent moment of *nachträglichkeit*, where a global recognition occurred of a first event, through a second. Although it could be argued that this kind of event has taken place before (perhaps resulting in the mass outpouring of grief and loss which followed the death of the Princess of Wales, or of John F. Kennedy), rarely has the quality of shock – in terms of the breaching of the limits of imagination – been so evident.

Witnessing this unimaginable event on a television screen resonates with the processes of Lacan's mirror phase: the global audience, mesmerized by these images, tried to make sense, to make coherent a fragmentary reality. In order to do this, the spectator has to revise the frame through which 'reality' can be read; and this revision was also evident in the rebuilding of a 'frame' around the event by the media, by first trying to 'contain' it (Who was responsible? What is happening and where? How is it being controlled?), and then through 'eye-witness' testimony, and later through documentary treatment and 'historicizing' of the event. This revised frame, or horizon of imagination, however, has now to include the possibility of the recurrence of an event of this scale, something previously unimaginable.

Angelica Rauch, in her study on trauma, explores the hermeneutics of a therapeutic encounter within which questions of language, culture, history and behaviour are situated. She cites Arnold Modell's observation that

> The analyst or therapist becomes an unwitting collaborator in the recreation of the past, while still retaining a proximity to the present time. The therapist becomes the person with whom one can experience trauma within a new context or experience for the first time what has been absent in the past. Affects belonging to the past that were never expressed then can now be recontextualized in current time. This is not just a

simple catharsis but an actual reorganization of memory. It is the process that pro-
vides a second chance.

(Rauch 1998:112)

Modell is speaking here about the analytic encounter; but this idea of a 'new context' might also describe the relation between the spectator and the traumatic event itself, to which s/he will later bear witness, but which is itself the 'second chance' to experience for the first time what has been absent in the past.

The events of September 11 might be regarded, in these terms, as an opportunity to experience communally: to negate the separation and loss, to temporarily 'heal' the gap. This global 'coming together' in grief and shock, to a temporary consensus (albeit not total), might be read as an attempt to close the gap opened by the original loss of (m)other. Through shared trauma, is there a possibility of acknowledging a shared sense of loss, and in this communal acknowledgement, (re)gaining a sense of wholeness with everything around? Rauch suggests that

By subjecting one's mental representations or memories to the configurations of unfa-
miliar signs, another experiential construction emerges as figure: hence an altered
horizon of imagination prepares the subject for a new historical experience, rather
than constantly reliving a fixated past in the present.

(1998:115).

Rauch is, of course, referring to analysis. Whilst not wishing to suggest that we repeat the events of September 11, it might be that the psychical engagement of the spectator with the 'unfamiliar signs' of this particular event would effect this altered horizon of imagination on the erstwhile spectator of the 'disaster movie', preparing the subject/spectator for a new historical experience.

The Return to Fantasy

I suspect that in the wake of September 11, disaster movies will no longer hold the same appeal: it is one thing to watch from the safety of the knowledge that 'this could never happen', and quite another to watch in the knowledge that it could and has, that the distance has been lost. The event has required the mobilising of different forms of spectatorship; it has altered our framing of such events, and significantly altered our horizon of imagination.

It may be fortuitous for Hollywood that by the time of September 11, a shift had occurred towards more fantastical productions such as the *Harry Potter* and *Lord of the Rings* series; and in the wake of the realisation of events previously confined to disaster movies, the global audience looked for a different kind of fantasy into which to escape, a 'guaranteed' fantasy, the reality of which was securely beyond imagination.

Magical narratives have – until now – been pleasurable, perhaps because they are securely sited in fantasy. Three-headed wolves, twelve-foot-high trolls and broomstick lessons have always been from the realms of fantasy, and scary only in an irrational, nightmarish kind of way. However, maybe the lesson of September 11 is that reality might not be too far behind, that the horizon of imagination is itself an illusory line, which – like any horizon – shifts as we approach. And maybe the allure of cinematic representations of fantasy (whether of disaster or of magic) would not be so compelling if we began to suspect that, just beyond that horizon, reality lurks, and that what might today be comfortably fantastic might, tomorrow, be painful reality.

References

Bennett, Susan (1997) *Theatre Audiences: A Theory of Production and Reception*. London: Routledge.

Buse, Peter (2001) *Drama + Theory: Critical Approaches to Modern British Drama*. Manchester: MUP.

Ellis, John (1988) *Visible Fictions: Cinema Television Video*. London: Routledge.

Felman, Shoshana and Dori Laub (1992) *Testimony: Crises of Witnessing in Literature, Psychoanalysis, and History*. London: Routledge.

Freud, Sigmund (1987) 'A Child is being Beaten', in Angela Richards and Albert Dickson (eds), *Vol.10 On Psychopathology*. Harmondsworth: Penguin Books, 159-93.

Freud, Sigmund (1988) 'Psychopathic Characters on the Stage', in Angela Richards and Albert Dickson (eds.), *Vol.14 Art and Literature*. Harmondswoth:Penguin Books, 119-127.

Metz, Christian (1990) *Psychoanalysis and Cinema: The Imaginary Signifier*. London: Macmillan.

O'Sullivan, T. et al. (1996) *Key Concepts in Communication and Cultural Studies*. London: Routledge.

Prieto, Robert (2002) *The 3Rs: Lessons learned from September 11th*. London: Royal Academy of Engineering.

Rauch, Angelika (1998) 'Post-Traumatic Hermeneutics: Melancholia in the Wake of Trauma' in *Diacritics* vol 28.4, winter 1998, 111-120.

Wheeler, W. J. and T. R. Griffiths (1992) 'Staging the "Other Scene": A Psychoanalytic Approach to Contemproary British Political Drama' in Adrian Page (ed.) *The Death of the Playwright*. Hampshire: MacMillan, 186-203.

Wright, Elizabeth (1993) *Psychoanalytic Criticism: Theory in Practice*. London: Routledge.

In Memory of Neil Powney

1961-2003

Courage Has Many Faces.

5. Teratology of the Spectacle

Dean Lockwood

Rational critique, for Walter Benjamin, belonged to a world of innocent vision, 'where perspectives and prospects counted and where it was still possible to take a standpoint' (1979, originally 1928: 89). This world no longer existed for Benjamin, and now, even more than in his time, the eye is constricted and clouded by proliferating representations. An Enlightenment critic such as Marx had recourse to the visual rhetoric of traditional metaphysics, opposing the 'natural vision of natural objects' to the technological spectacle of the *camera obscura* as metaphor for the ideological inversion and deformation of our circumstances (Cohen 1989: 103). Marx believed clear eyes could spy an escape route from this darkened chamber. Benjamin, however, perceived no clearly posted exit from the riotous, overlit showcase into which we are plunged in the thoroughly mediatized world. As Margaret Cohen has shown, in Benjamin's *Arcades Project*, ideology is phantasmagorical rather than reflective. His appropriation of visual rhetoric takes its lead not from the transparency of the mirror but from the opacity of the painted slide, as in the magic lantern show (1989: 93-4). Today, more than ever, we sense that representations do not reflect or invert reality in any simple or direct manner. Everywhere it is confirmed that behind images we will find only other images. Nevertheless, we might follow Benjamin in insisting that the phantasmagorical spectacle itself holds out hope. Against the corrosive abdication of critique in some postmodern theory, I wish to take literally this claim (although not in this instance exploring Benjamin's own methodology) that ideology as spectacle carries within itself an anticipation of its own demise and a seed of the future. As I wish to put it, it produces monsters. If rational critique is beyond us, we may seek to mobilize these monsters to our own 'ideologically disruptive ends' (Cohen 1989: 103).

The Spectrality Effect

The word 'teratology', meaning the study of monsters, usually now refers to the biological study of birth defects, but a teratology was, in the Middle Ages, a collection of tales about disturbing natural occurrences, often taken as signs of God's wrath or warnings of some impending cataclysm. An inkling of what I mean by the spectacle as teratological can be found in Maxim Gorky's perplexity on attending a showing of Lumière Brothers' films touring Russia in 1896. Of the experience, Gorky wrote: 'It seems as though it carries a warning, fraught with a vague but sinister meaning that makes your heart grow faint. You are forgetting where you are. Strange imaginings invade your mind and your consciousness begins to wane and grow dim' (cited in Gunning 2000: 317). For Gorky, the screening opened up a spectral realm, a strange borderland existence between real and imaginary that he takes as an 'intimation of life in the future' (316).

We can track this kind of experience back to those earlier visual technologies that preoccupied Benjamin. Take, for example, Étienne-Gaspard Robertson's device, the phantoscope, a late eighteenth-century variant of the magic lantern (my account is based on Castle 1988). For his shows, Robertson often took as subject matter the recent horrors of the French Revolution, artfully transforming the perpetrators into phantoms hovering in a pitch black exhibition space. Images, painted on glass slides, were projected onto a screen that itself could not be seen, so that they seemed to float above the audience, and could be increased or decreased in size by moving the apparatus on rollers. The phantasmagorical experience had an occult, ritualistic and séance-like character. In a bizarre act of sympathetic multimedia magic, blood, incense and written reports of the events of the revolution were burnt on a brazier; smoke, light and sound effects accompanied the projection. Although Robertson hawked the trick as a pedagogic exercise and believed that his device contributed to the debunking of the supernatural, the entertainment actually had an ambivalent relationship to post-Enlightenment rationalism. His machine was, despite its master's stated intentions, dedicated to the conjuration of horrors and the creation of an astonishing effect of spectrality. The spectre-shows paraded the supernatural as an artificially produced illusion but also traded on the uncanny effect of the objective, visible presence of the ghosts floating before the audience.

With the success and proliferation of similar entertainments across Europe, a host of developments and improvements were set in train which sought to render more vivid and convincing the presence of the spectral. Such visual phantasmagoria signalled the opening up of a new psychological space. The modern rationalist conception of the mind was founded upon a 'primal internalization of the spectral' (Castle 1988: 29). The modernization of consciousness depended upon evacuating the world of any supernatural content. The logic here was that the subject only becomes self-conscious and truly rational when it reflexively recognizes that the external appearance of ghosts is actually a matter of projection, of its own subjective production: 'The true "Phantasmagoric" apparatus is the human brain itself' (1988: 46). In the nineteenth-century mentalist discourse, as Castle points out, the subjective production of phantoms was not restricted to psychopathological states. Ordinary thought was also 'spectralized'; powers of imagination were equated with powers of conjuration. It was as if ordinary thoughts constituted a spectacle that could not be possessed or controlled by the thinker. The subject could not say with any confidence whether what played across the screen of his or her mind was being produced internally or externally. It was 'as if there were, at the very heart of subjectivity itself, something foreign and fantastic, a daemonic presence from elsewhere, a specter-show of unaccountable origin'

(1988: 59). The phantasmagorical experience, then, marks a point at which boundaries between real and imaginary, subjective and objective are breached. The rational is contaminated with its other. With the spectral technology of the phantoscope, as with the modernized imagination, 'ghosts now seemed *more real than ever before*' (1988: 58).

For Gunning, this demonstrates an occluded instability at the birth of cinematic representation, a simultaneous embrace and disavowal of the medium's spectral ontology. He refers to Bazin's discussion of the 'myth of total cinema' – the belief that the medium constituted a move towards 'a total and complete representation of reality [...] a perfect illusion of the outside world' (cited in Gunning: 236). This fantasy of visual totalization appears to have gone hand in hand with a growing anxiety about the virtualization of life, its transformation into ambiguous images. A battery of illusionist techniques, originating in pre-cinematic visual entertainments and developed in cinema, was dedicated to creating a perfect illusion, to fooling the senses, but the more effectively it achieved this goal the greater the disturbing sensation of unreality.

In his study of Marx, Derrida outlines the 'hauntological' status of all ideological construction. As is well known, Marx begins the *Manifesto of the Communist Party* by asserting that 'a spectre is haunting Europe – the spectre of Communism. All the Powers of old Europe have entered into a holy alliance to exorcize this spectre' (1968: 35). Communism is spectral, or monstrous, in that it threatens to manifest a radically altered 'future-to-come'. As Derrida tells it, in order to certify their legitimacy and their claim on the future, the European powers were compelled to abjure, or renounce, that which threatened them, to forestall the coming to actuality, the enfleshing of the dreaded spectre. However, to invest so much in the attempt to exorcize the virtual in the name of the actual itself keeps alive the threat. It is itself simultaneously a kind of invocation, or conjuration, undoing the line that has been so decisively drawn. The European hegemony struggled to expel the threat but continually spooked itself in doing so: 'Exorcism conjures away the evil in ways that are also irrational, using magical, mysterious, even mystifying practices' (Derrida, 1994: 48).

I would argue that, in like manner, Robertson's phantasmagorical experience both exorcizes and revivifies the horrors of the Revolution. The lantern spirits away the insurrectionary ferment but also testifies to it and glamorizes it. By extension, we might say that a spectre haunts total cinema, threatening to invade and unsettle the spectatorial subject, to dim the light of reason. The line between living and dead, real and unreal, virtual and actual is constantly undone. That which disturbs the fantasy of visual mastery is pronounced dead, but the death certificate revokes itself. The attempt to see clearly, without remainder, to cancel out the ghostly, must fail. Note that Marx was as guilty as the European powers of attempting to draw the line. Marx was driven by the quest to conjure the future – the promise of Communism – into being, into presence. However, for Derrida, manifesting revolution must always foreclose it. Revolution is always 'still-to-come'. The future must be conceived as a promise that 'dislodges any present out of contemporaneity with itself' (1994:73). Promise must not be allowed to degenerate into mere programme. Derrida embraces the monstrous for its emancipatory non-contemporaneity. In a similar spirit, I wish to argue that the teratological phenomena I am discussing here also possess a radical, deconstructive potential. I now go on to suggest ways in which this teratological effect of spectrality manifests in the contemporary media spectacle.

The 'Passion for the Real'

The seminal work on the spectacle is, of course, Guy Debord's *The Society of the Spectacle* (1999, originally 1967). Debord proposed that under late capital social reality is visually organized. More than this, the modern media spectacle dispossesses humans of the use of their powers of creative praxis and immerses them in a wraparound imagistic consumerist environment that alienates them from 'real life' – that is, their constructive relation to social reality.

Since Debord, some commentators have drawn attention to the unanticipated consequences of the spectacle. The homogenizing, totalizing spectacular society theorized by Debord seems to have inadvertently produced various new phenomena. Jean Baudrillard, in particular, has sought to develop the notion of the media spectacle and its implications. Baudrillard's analysis corroborates Debord's nightmare of the spectacle as a homogenizing machine. For Baudrillard, it is based on the principle of prophylaxis, laundering out and reducing all traces of contaminative otherness, all traces of contingency. However, if, for Debord, 'real life is elsewhere', for Baudrillard, 'we have abolished "elsewhere"' (Baudrillard 1993a: 145). In his estimation, there is no elsewhere which remains intact. The disappearance of reality spurs attempts everywhere to nostalgically resurrect and retrieve the real. In Baudrillard's words, 'There is an escalation of the true, of the lived experience [...] And there is a panic-stricken production of the real and the referential' (1983: 12-13). The proliferation of spectacles of the real attempts to conceal the fact of reality's disappearance but ironically services and accelerates the virtualizing work of the simulation industries. Looking at movies, we might say, for example, that recent reflexive critiques of simulation spawned by Hollywood such as *The Truman Show* (Peter Weir USA, 1998) or *The Matrix* (The Wachowski Brothers USA/Aus, 1999), built as they are upon clear distinctions between the fake and the real, are products of panic, attempts to reassure us of our awakening as clear-eyed free agents. In *The Truman Show*, Truman Burbank, unwitting star of his own reality TV show, comes to realize that his whole world is merely an elaborate stage set contained in an enormous dome, and the film ends when

Burbank literally punches a hole in this artificial world and breaks through to the other side. In *The Matrix*, the protagonist, Neo, is hailed by a group of subversives as the One destined to rescue the citizens of the world from their computer-imposed slumber. Both these films set up an unambiguous opposition between illusion and reality and are ultimately concerned with prophylactic boundary-maintenance.

Baudrillard's account is fairly familiar. Another account of the kind of phenomena engendered by spectacularization is provided by Slavoj Zizek, which I think may prove instructive here. There are points of overlap between Baudrillard and Zizek, but there are also major points of difference. Against Baudrillard, the notion of the Real foregrounded in Zizek's work is the substantial, irreducible 'hard kernel' theorized by Lacan. This hard kernel is extradiscursive and cannot be symbolically assimilated. This is the lack that drives the constitution of the subject. As Donahue explains, 'the subject is constituted through, yet simultaneously split by, the object-cause of desire such that the "it" is always already there before the "I" can be recognized' (2001: online, para. 21). Identity is both driven by and forged in the teeth of the Real's traumatic excess. Subjective identity and objective reality are ideological constructions organized against the trauma of this radical alterity: 'The function of ideology is not to offer us a point of escape from our reality but to offer us the social reality itself as an escape from some traumatic, real kernel' (Zizek 1989: 45). However, it is inescapable. In setting these limits we simultaneously produce otherness as a remainder. It ineluctably invades symbolization, erupting within our ideological constructions to frustrate and corrode these brief certainties. In Zizek's Lacanian formulation, the Real constitutes that which the Symbolic order refuses but which it is powerless to prevent returning.

In his recent work, Zizek has described the world as virtualized, apparently hollowed out of its substance, stripped of its 'hard kernel' (Zizek 2002). In such a world, it has become difficult to experience events as anything other than a movie. This is what the journalist Charles Shaar Murray has referred to as 'numbing down' (Murray 2001: 6). For Zizek, the numbed-down world recalls Nietzsche's account of 'passive nihilism', where 'whatever refreshes, heals, calms, numbs emerges into the foreground' (Nietzsche 1968, originally 1901: 18). In this world, we are happy to drug ourselves, to forego the tiresome business of setting ourselves goals. However, dialectically, the opposite tendency rears its head. A violent, destructive force appears – Nietzsche's 'active nihilism' – involving the overcoming of uncertainty in acts of affirmation for which we are willing to put everything at risk, even to sacrifice human lives (from extreme sports through to catastrophic terrorism). Here, _i_ek draws on Alain Badiou's notion of the 'passion for the Real' in which living authentically means willingness to destroy false appearances. He points out that the eruption of the Real into symbolization is a theme that defines much of twentieth-century culture, from Ernst Jünger's post-WWI explorations of the ecstatic states of consciousness achievable in the modern battlefield through to the contemporary delirium around the experience of the bodily Real (2002: 5-6). Recently, for example, we have witnessed the passion for the Real in the gruesome fascination exerted by Professor Von Hagen's 'plastinated' corpses in his *Body Worlds* exhibition. The exhibition opened in 2002 at the Atlantis Gallery in London after a successful tour of Europe and Japan during which it had attracted more than 81 / 2 million visitors. In November 2002 Von Hagen conducted an autopsy on a German businessman in front of 400 people. An interval was arranged for the audience to get a closer look which was eagerly taken up. This was the first public autopsy since 1830 and was also televised by Channel 4.

It is perhaps on television where the passion for the Real has mutated into some of its more innovative forms. For Mary Ann Doane, television is a 'catastrophe machine'. The reporting of a 'death event', a catastrophe such as a plane crash or terrorist attack, may disrupt the flow of information at any time. These 'moments when information bristles' fascinate because they link us briefly to the Real (Doane 1990: 228). This is television's thrilling promise, the bait of the referential, rendered possible by live transmission. However, Doane supplements this analysis with the observation that whilst television embraces catastrophe and legitimates itself by this referential lure, it must also work to defuse the anxiety this engenders in a retroactive movement of disavowal. Television 'seeks both to preserve and annihilate indeterminacy' (234). It quickly moves to ameliorate the shock, to restore our numbed-down passivity through the palliative ritual of couching events in a context of explanatory commentary or narrative.

In light of Zizek's account, we can understand the work of the catastrophe machine in terms of an entwinement of Spectacle and Real, a vicious dialectic. The attempt to penetrate reality's veils of illusion invariably 'ends up in the pure semblance of the spectacular effect of the Real' (Zizek 2002: 9-10). Many commentators have noted the way in which media coverage aestheticized and thereby numbed down the tragedy of 9/11, and the way those events could not but evoke the memory of Hollywood blockbusters. As King points out in his contribution to the present volume, these terror events were modelled by perpetrators who will have been fully conversant with the power of the images entailed. At the moment we cut through reality to the Real, the Real appears at its most staged, an entirely phantasmagorical experience. In effect, the intruding Real is always already plastinated. The passion for the Real is thus the ultimate avoidance strategy (Zizek 2002: 24). Baudrillard says something similar in his discussion of French reality TV. On the one hand, he hypothesizes, here we have a desire to 'achieve total nudity, find absolute reality, consume live and raw violence'. On the other hand, the reverse hypothesis also rings true – what we really want is verification of the fact that 'there is nothing to see' beyond the final veil, that there is no 'final clue' (2001: on-line).

Let me summarize the discussion thus far. I have suggested that there are historical traces of an ominous hauntology in experiences of early visual technologies. A fantasy of visual mastery was undermined by anxieties over the unreal and fantasmatic nature of these experiences. The result was that the security of the boundary between subject and object was disturbed. This resonates with anxieties today. Unintended consequences of the spectacle's displacement of the Real in the nostalgic fantasy of authentic brushes with the Real have resulted in a simultaneous laying claim to and disavowal of the Real. We are tormented with both the desire to see everything, to have the world on hand, 'live and raw', and the suspicion, ultimately reassuring, that there really is 'nothing to see'. The monster's radical, deconstructive potential seems to be immediately short-circuited wherever it appears. As Derrida writes, 'monsters cannot be announced. One cannot say: "here are our monsters", without immediately turning the monsters into pets' (1989: 80).

Viral Strategies

Baudrillard, for his part, suggests that the spectacle's prostitution of the Real compels what he calls 'evil' to re-emerge in new, terroristic forms. Attempting to write the other out of the world, we have forced it to take on a secret form, a form that we will be unable to tame and pat on the head: 'What springs up in order to combat the total homogenization of the world is the Alien – monstrous metaphor for the corpse-like, viral Other: the compound form of all the varieties of otherness done to death by our system' (1993a: 130). Baudrillard's alarming suggestion is that, rather than deploring the way things are, we ourselves must abet the viral strategies of the Alien. Citing Nietzsche, Baudrillard urges us 'to push that which wants to fall' (1993b: 209).

Zizek's discussion of the terror events of 9/11 intimates one shape such strategies might take, albeit not one that Baudrillard, presumably, would endorse (2002: 35-8). These events, he believes, constitute the last act of spectacular warfare, a terrorism still locked into the histrionics of the passion for the Real. Conflict in the twenty-first century is probably not going to be about blockbuster-style infernos. First signs – scares involving the discovery of anthrax and ricin, for example – indicate that the new terrorism will be waged invisibly, or, rather, it will frustrate the fantasy of total visuality (hence the desperation evident in the Pentagon's recently announced data-mining project, 'Total Information Awareness'). Terrorism tends to deconstruct the distinction between friend and foe. As Zizek comments, 'Every feature attributed to the Other is already present at the very heart of the USA' (43). The enemy, like the virus, infiltrates and reproduces itself within the host. It becomes inseparable from the host, neither properly part of the body nor entirely alien. In effect, it becomes invisible, undecidable. It cannot easily be destroyed without jeopardizing the host (see Lechte 2003: 216).

As a viral phenomenon, the media escapes subjective control and frustrates any attempts to subordinate it to social ideologies and agendas. It may have made sense two or three decades ago to level the charge at the media, as Noam Chomsky and others have done, that it constitutes a propaganda machine, functioning to serve the agendas of the wealthy and powerful. However, this analysis is no longer adequate. Douglas Rushkoff, like Debord and Baudrillard, argues that the media are no longer distinguishable from everyday life. They no longer simply observe and represent reality; they generate and present events as spectacles. In other words, 'the media' (singular noun) possesses a life of its own. It is a living thing, promulgating its own hidden agendas, which emerge spontaneously and spread quickly throughout the cultural body. The sticky shell of the media virus, itself composed of media – perhaps an event, a celebrity, a scandal or a particular image – clings to the healthy cultural 'cell' and its errant ideological code worms its way into the cell's centre, overwriting the host's code and sending out the instruction to replicate (Rushkoff 1996: 9-10).

Rushkoff outlines three varieties of media virus (1996: 10-16). Firstly, there are those viruses that the media spontaneously generates. Secondly, there are 'bandwagon' viruses, initially of the spontaneous variety but quickly seized upon by groups seeking to introduce their own agendas into the cultural body. Finally, and most importantly, there are entirely intentional viruses. These can be either manufactured and disseminated by parties with a commercial interest, attempting to diffuse brand names or images, or they can be designed with a more subversive intention in mind. Rushkoff delights in detailing how a media-literate generation – the children of Baudrillard and Sunny D, we might say – are packaging their own radical agendas within apparently innocuous entertainment forms. These 'information bombs' are set to fascinate and to simultaneously detonate all kinds of otherwise unacceptable ideas into the purview of public debate. For media viruses, like dreams, manifest repressed concerns, anxieties and desires: 'Viruses present us, in cartoonish simplicity and amplification, with the unspoken issues of our cultural present' (1996: 319).

Although Rushkoff refuses to decide whether this viral phenomenon is good or evil, he tends to paint an appealing picture of a process of media mutation which is beneficial overall. However, his analysis equally implies runaway, anarchic forms of the spectacle, predisposed to blow up in the face of those who wish to master media hype. This notion of viral strategies comes close to certain versions of the recent sociological thesis of reflexive modernization, which foreground the unintended consequences of the modern imperative towards the monitoring and control of objects by subjects. According to Scott Lash, the will to envision, clarify and pin down objects is inevitably frustrated. The subject's tenacity is rewarded only by greater exertions on the part of objects to wriggle free from its clutches and establish autonomy. This must ultimately compel the subject to reflexively question the very foundations of its envisioning project (Lash 2002: 50). Lash argues that the uncertainties inadvertently thrown up by modern practices suggest 'life is on the side of the pathological. Life, with David Cronenberg, is viral' (2002: 215). Classical social theory obsesses over the question of what makes society possible, and dwells on the reproduction of order and the ways in which societies strive to root out pathology. Lash suggests we should be attending to the ways in which flows of information through real-time telematic media are forcing a crisis of representation, undermining social reproduction, making society *impossible* (210).

Against this, Nick Couldry has recently argued, from a post-Durkheimian position, that such ideas drastically underestimate ideological processes that continue to naturalize notions of reproduction and order. Even if society is chaotic rather than ordered, we are still encouraged to believe that there is a functioning social whole because of powerful 'rhetorics of social integration' (2003: 10). Western media ritualistically naturalize the idea that the social world is cohesive and centred and that media provide the key point of access to this centre. This is how the media legitimates its concentrated symbolic power (2). Closely linked to this is the ideology of liveness permeating contemporary media. Again, this reinforces the idea that society revolves around a 'shared ritual centre' and guarantees access to this shared reality as it happens (98-9).

Couldry would reject the viral concept of media. Proponents of the idea of the impossibility and disorderly nature of society may well grasp the nettle of media power but they ultimately fail to penetrate the everyday rhetorical workings of media (18). I think this is true, and I accept that such abstract ruminations do need to be displaced by more concrete analyses of mediatized power. However, I think there is still some mileage to eke out here from thinking in an abstract mode. Let me conclude by stating that Western practices are predicated upon a 'depth grammar', a set of meta-rhetorics and metaphors that underpin the rhetorics of media outlined by Couldry. Central to this grammar is the schema of the spectacle, or the 'videological conception of the world' (Sandywell 1996: ix, 59, and see also Sandywell 1999). In the Western representationalist construction of the world, the subject gazes upon the other only to describe it as object. The subject, in supposing itself to gaze out upon a 'unitary, bounded, immobile totality', certifies itself as unified and centred (Sandywell 1996: 46). This is the origin of the fantasy of total visuality. The consequence of this ancient Western 'mirror game', informing the visual tropes of modern critique, is that truth is conceived only in terms of the 'visible presence of existing things'. As Sandywell notes, what is no longer present or yet to be present must be recovered from or extrapolated into a virtual realm. There is an implicit temporal mode of being here – that of presence – licensing a static schema of past, present and future that precludes any attempt to think time as emergent, to think life as heterogeneous rather than reproductive

(56). Life, however, *is* emergent. It is a matter of creation and alteration; it is never fully present to itself, never unsoiled by absence and alterity. Yet anything that does not surrender to the gaze, anything that is not visible or representable, makes itself felt as monstrous and must be disavowed. On this view, the traumatic, viral indeterminacies I have discussed in this chapter can be understood as the inadvertent result of the spectacle practically dismantling naturalized boundaries between subject and object, self and other, precipitating its own deconstruction and intimating, to recall Gorky, 'life in the future'. The spectrality effect indicates the break point in the spectacle, a constant prompt to seek to interrogate and shake the schema of the spectacle. With Derrida, what is monstrous is precisely the promise of the future.

References

Baudrillard, Jean (1983) *Simulations*. New York: Semiotext(e).

Baudrillard, Jean (1993a) *The Transparency of Evil: Essays on Extreme Phenomena*. London: Verso.

Baudrillard, Jean (1993b) *Baudrillard Live: Selected Interviews*, ed. Mike Gane. London: Routledge.

Baudrillard, Jean (2001) 'Dust Breeding' Ctheory. Accessed online at http://www.ctheory.net/text_file?pick=293

Benjamin, Walter (1979) *One-Way Street and Other Writings* [1928]. London: Verso.

Castle, Terry (1988) 'Phantasmagoria: Spectral Technology and the Metaphorics of Modern Reverie' *Critical Inquiry* Vol.15, No.1 (autumn), 26-61.

Cohen, Margaret (1989) 'Walter Benjamin's Phantasmagoria' *New German Critique* No.48 (fall), 87-107.

Couldry, Nick (2003) *Media Rituals: A critical approach*. London: Routledge.

Debord, Guy (1994) *The Society of the Spectacle* [1967]. New York: Zone Books.

Derrida, Jacques (1989) 'Some Statements and Truisms about Neologisms, Newisms, Postisms, Parasitisms, and other small Seismisms', in David Carroll (ed.), *The States of Theory*. New York: Columbia University Press, 63-94.

Derrida, Jacques (1994) *Specters of Marx*. London: Routledge.

Doane, Mary Anne (1990) 'Information, Crisis, Catastrophe', in Patricia Mellencamp (ed.), *Logics of Television: essays in cultural criticism*. London: BFI, 222-39.

Donahue, Brian (2001) 'Marxism, Postmodernism, _i_ek' *Postmodern Culture*. Vol.12, No.2 (May). Accessed online at http://muse.ju.edu/journals/pmc/v012/12.2donahue.html

Gunning, Tom (2000) '"Animated pictures": tales of cinema's forgotten future, after 100 years of films', in Christine Gledhill and Linda Williams (eds), *Reinventing Film Studies*. Oxford: Oxford University Press, 316-31.

Lash, Scott (2002) *Critique of Information*. London: Sage.

Lechte, John (2003) *Key Contemporary Concepts*. London: Sage.

Marx, Karl and Frederick Engels (1968) 'Manifesto of the Communist Party' [1848] in *Selected Works in one volume*. London: Lawrence and Wishart, 31-63.

Murray, Charles Shaar (2001) Numb and Number, *The Guardian*, 15th June, 6.

Nietzsche, Friedrich (1968) *The Will to Power* [1901], ed. Walter Kaufmann, tr. Walter Kaufmann and R.J. Hollingdale, New York: Vintage.

Rushkoff, Douglas (1996) *Media Virus!: Hidden Agendas in Popular Culture*. New York: Ballantine.

Sandywell, Barry (1996) *Reflexivity and the Crisis of Western Reason: Logological Investigations Volume 1*. London: Routledge.

Sandywell, Barry (1999) 'Specular Grammar: the visual rhetoric of modernity', in Ian Heywood and Barry Sandywell (eds.), *Interpreting Visual Culture: Explorations in the Hermeneutics of the Visual*. London: Routledge, 30-56.

Zizek, Slavoj (1989) *The Sublime Object of Ideology*. London: Verso.

Zizek, Slavoj (2002) *Welcome to the Desert of the Real*. London: Verso.

Part II: Reality/TV

6. Caught on Tape: A Legacy of Low-tech Reality

Amy West

Caught-on-tape must be one of the more evocative entries in television's phrase book. The object of capture is a moment of crisis: a natural disaster, a criminal act, a private perversion, a hilarious physical blunder. Because the incident is unforeseeable, the circumstances of capture can be characterised as inadvertent, meaning that the recorded moment arises out of a critical co-incidence of rolling camera and spontaneous or aberrant incident. Notions of entrapment and containment offered up by the term 'caught' are delusory. In fact this model of audiovisual capture is one in which both pro-filmic event and the mechanisms of its capture are spontaneous, aberrant, random or inadvertent. The curious circumstances of its production, however, are not the only aspect of this televisual form flagged by the caught-on-tape label; the specific technology of that production is also indicated. The candid honesty of 'tape' acknowledges the sub-broadcast quality of all material aired under this label. It also nods at a multitude of anonymous authors wielding home handycams, storefront CCTV sets and police chase helicopter-cams. Portable, cheap and impermanent, video tape has a kind of innate applicability to the subject material of these accidental recordings. The label caught-on-tape thereby gestures towards a medium, a subject and a particular process of production; all of which are fleeting, mutable and often literally on the run.

Thus caught-on-tape announces its own processes of production and makes a virtue of them. By advertising its own processes caught-on-tape footage defies the seamlessness of television production and by specifying the kind of technology used (non-professional, sub-broadcast quality) it aligns itself with a domain of image production outside the parameters of the television industry. The circumstances of production – both the incident of capture and the mechanisms of tape recording – are actively promoted in this way to a particular end. They are made to serve as certification of the product's authenticity, promising as they do the intersection of an unprecedented (thus unstaged) dramatic crisis and an amateur (thus innocent) recording medium.

Out of this formulation arises a specialised aesthetic of television realism; one which not only announces its preferred medium (video tape) but freights this process of production with connotations of the amateur, the ordinary and the inadvertent. This article concentrates on the audio and visual signatures of this particular brand of realism, arguing that these caught-on-tape formats – now largely superseded by the professionally produced and narrative-led reality programmes of the turn of the century – have embedded a particular construct of low tech reality in televisual culture.

Part 1: The aesthetics of amateurism

The caught-on-tape video-clip show proliferated, as legend has it, in the late eighties as a burgeoning number of cable stations, hungry for supply, came up against a screenwriters' strike in Hollywood. An abundant, United States-wide resource of pre-recorded images from personal handycams, store security cameras and police video archives proved the antidote, and much to the chagrin of the writer's union, 'unscripted TV' was born. Short extracts from these video tapes were quickly formatted into television series; presented as non-narrative collections according to certain themes, including domestic comedy, law and order or natural disaster. All of the extracts violated conventions of audiovisual broadcast standards. Whether footage derived from the home handycam or the closed circuit surveillance camera, images and audio were consistently poor quality. Low-grade video stock and amateur handling generated images which were poorly composed, lacking in tonal contrast or textural detail, unfocused, over or under exposed and accompanied by a muffled and distorted audio track. The basic unintelligibility of much of this material necessitated a format structure which leant heavily on post-production framing devices such as studio links, voice-over and captioning to give this decontextualized footage an easily accessible meaning. Material was sorted into over-simplified genre classifications – horror, humour, tragedy, shock – and made to stick there. Thus the televisual form of caught-on-tape became relegated by critics to the ranks of tabloid TV and its status as amateur disparaged as unsophisticated.

For the fan of caught-on-tape television, however, the intersection of amateur and accident made a special promise of authenticity. As suggested, the status of caught-on-tape moments – however diverse their subject-matter – is that of crisis; a dog attacks its owner, a stunt plane explodes over a crowd of spectators, a bride trips in the aisle. Accidents and aberrations such as these stake their claim in the domain of the real by asserting their status as unpremeditated. The sudden and unexpected nature of these events is always emphasised by the rhetoric of caught-on-tape formats because it serves as a guarantee of truth. Events such as these cannot be predicted, pre-planned or staged – thus they cannot be faked. But this assertion of the unfakability of content is not enough. Without a correlative promise of a truthful medium, this putative reality is as suspect as that of any other re-presented event. This is why the flag of amateurism is waved so high in the field of caught-on-tape television. The self-evident non-professionalism of footage screened under the caught-on-tape banner certifies that the represented event is not staged, because both the technology utilised and the operator controlling it lack the sophistication to fake. Thus amateur image production is coded as transparent. Compromises in audio and visual pleasure which this mode of production may entail are traded off against a heightened feeling of the real – a trade audiences are more than willing to make. The poor quality of caught-on-tape footage thus becomes a marker of realness because it signals certain circumstances of production. The co-incidence of unpredictable content and unprocessed medium adds up to a powerful and pervasive sense of the real.

The sources of the video extracts presented by these caught-on-tape shows – and thus the impulse behind their production – are varied. A single show may include footage derived from security tapes recorded on CCTV, vehicle or helicopter mounted police video, or the handycam wielded variously by the tourist, the passer-by, the accident investigator, the 'mom'. Each is freighted slightly differently according to the context of production. Too easily lumped together (all the better to dismiss), caught-on-tape footage generates many fine distinctions according to the technology used in the recording, the subject's relationship with the camera, the impulse behind the recording (professional, archival, memorial, personal) and not least the controlling force behind the camera (be it human or mechanical).

The latter distinction is a productive one, generating two distinct categories: hand-held camera and fixed camera. The hand-held handycam is the embodiment of human point-of-view image capture, resonating as it so often does with the physiological responses of the operator. In contrast, the unblinking, mechanical eye of the wall-mounted surveillance camera betrays no investment in the recorded scene. The construction of reality necessarily occurs differently within these contrasting modes of image production. The first 'feels real' because it fulfils a 'powerful urge for a sense of contact with the real', as it 'inscribes' this physiological contact on the recorded text (Fetveit 2002: 130). This is a kind of real which is heightened by evidence of human error – the swoops and slips of a running, dancing, laughing, crying camera – which testifies to the amateur authenticity of production. On the other hand, the second model 'feels real' because its inflexible recording position signifies its infallible and impartial omniscience, recording whatever occurs within its range 24/7 without preference or participation.

Selected at random from a promisingly entitled Fox special *The World's Most Shocking Moments: Caught on Tape* (a regular smorgasbord of am-cam captured crises occasioned variously by natural disaster, mechanical failure and human error or malice) two different extracts illuminate the formal characteristics of both handycam and surveillance caught-on-tape footage. The sequence entitled 'Deadly Mudslide' exemplifies the strategies and affects of hand-held, handycam footage.

According to the format principles of this particular show, the video recording of a mudslide in a hilly suburban neighbourhood of Portland, Oregon is heavily framed by narrative devices – voice-over, digital titles, canned music and witness interviews – which code the event as fraught with a dangerous unpredictability. They also work to establish the credentials of the footage as inadvertently 'caught'. The circumstances of production are announced by the presenter's voice-over as the sequence begins; two contractors 'are driving to a job site to inspect potential damage' in the rain-sodden neighbourhood. They bear with them a personal camcorder to document the site. The handycam is contextualised here as a tool of the trade, its usage is routine and professional. When the muddy bank upon which the camera is trained begins to slip ('What was about to happen would turn the next two minutes into a heart-pounding experience') the contractor's reaction to it (to keep recording) forces a formal shift into the domain of caught-on-tape. This shift is determined by the nature of the pro-filmic event as much as by the operator's cognitive process. At the very beginning of the extract, when the muddy bank is yet to slide, its status is mundane and the impulse behind the recording camera is that of routine engagement with the everyday. When the mud starts to slip, it becomes something special and the impulse to continue recording is predicated on a palpable desire to capture something rare, powerful and fleeting.

Once the circumstances of production have been marked in this way, the key footage of the mudslide is screened in its unedited entirety. At approximately 1.5 minutes in duration, the mudslide is a long-held shot for television but one which easily sustains viewer attention. A single hand-held tracking shot, this footage performs a perfect narrative trajectory from the mudslide's initial discovery, through its hair-raising pursuit of the camera operator downhill to its subsidence at the base of the sloping street. The footage bears all the hallmarks of handycam caught-on-tape material. Low-resolution tape stock means that colours are washed-out and textural detail limited. The camera is hand-held throughout the sequence and its swoops and jumps replicate the physiological journey of its operator. Initially calm in its survey of the muddy bank, the camera jerks with interest as a voice calls out 'The hill's going – have you got it?', an exclamation which is at once a warning to bystanders of oncoming danger and an urgent appeal to the gods of am-cam spectacle to ensure the safe capture of event (even at the potential cost of human safety). The camera and operator then jump from the street into the back of a truck and the recorded view wheels crazily, showing glimpses of a rain-lashed sky, running feet, battered umbrellas and the contents of the contractor's truck.

The footage generated by the operator's ascent into the truck is typical of the kind of 'proof of production' material included in caught-on-tape shows. Although it forces attention away from the mudslide itself, it rewards viewers with a heightened affect of immediacy and authenticity. For one thing, it shows that the camera was never turned off and that the sequence is being broadcast just as it was recorded; a production/reception trajectory which promotes a belief in an unmediated real. For another, this wheeling camera effectively expresses the physical and emotional state of its operator; the jump into the vehicle tray and the steadying of the camera(man)'s body against the back of the cab is imbued with urgency, excitement and fear. Moreover, the movement from the street to the truck is ambiguous; does this moving vehicle provide its occupant with a means of escape or a more effective shooting angle?

Am-cam footage such as this mudslide sequence thus entails a double strand of fear and suspense; the fear of damage to the body as opposed to the fear of the loss of spectacle, as the aberrant external force – in this case several tonnes of speeding mud – threaten to overwhelm both. The particular reality effect of the handycam aesthetic derives from this interconnection of human body and recording device. In 'Deadly Mudslide' the verbal and physical responses of the camera's operator – expressing awe, excitement, fear and delight – are traced over the representation of recorded events. As the contractor turned cameraman urges on the truck driver, shouting 'faster' and 'go, go, go, go' (his voice rising in pitch with every word), it becomes evident that this footage is telling more than the story of the pro-filmic event. Rather, the 'Deadly Mudslide' recording reanimates the extreme physiological journey of a man running for his life and as such produces a specific aesthetic of a visceral, subjective real.

Another, much briefer clip from the same programme entitled 'Out of Control', shows surveillance camera footage of a prison riot. The contrast with 'Deadly Mudslide' is complete. Welded to a corner of the ceiling, this unblinking eye betrays no sensitivity to the scene of violence it holds within its gaze. True to its form, the camera misses nothing. A high-angle position and a wide-angle lens encompass every inch of the concrete room. And yet the result is characteristically low-visibility. The convex lens distorts perspective, the low-resolution stock eliminates detail, the high-angle shot makes it difficult to distinguish between guards and inmates. To add to this level of unintelligibility, every other face is digitally blurred to protect the subject's identity – a strategy typical of crime-based caught-on-tape material. The overall effect is an unindividuated blur of flailing limbs and batons, without narrative or resolution. In contrast to the handycam, which tells such vivid stories in its replication of the experiences of its human operator, CCTV material has no narrative of its own making. This means that broadcast footage of the prison brawl pushes the limits of television tedium at just under thirty seconds, a third of the time given over to an unedited extract of the 'Deadly Mudslide'. Even though the surveillance camera (which runs endlessly) would have caught the outbreak and subsequent containment of the violence, the programme producers have been obliged to edit this footage down to its dramatic core. The screened extract therefore begins and ends *in medias res*, a narrative lack which exacerbates the unintelligibility of the extract. Nevertheless, the 'reality effect' of this footage, if it can be quantified, is high. The sheer unintelligibility of the images presented to view testifies to a lack of design, either in terms of subject or representation. The singularity and simplicity of the recording impulse behind the prison surveillance camera – just to see everything and go on seeing everything endlessly – defies the precepts of television entertainment. Narrative, style and visual pleasure are sacrificed to the insistent demands of omniscience. Thus the all-seeing and never-ending medium of the surveillance camera produces an experiential real predicated on transparency of intent.

This 'transparency of intent' is the keystone of am-cam realism. The intriguing formal differences between hand-held handycam and wall-mounted CCTV do not detract from the common ground of all caught-on-tape footage. Located as 'other' to professional broadcast-standard television production, this material asks audiences to invest in an innocent camera, one which always tells the truth because it lacks the art to dissemble. In the case of the surveillance camera this artlessness is that of an automaton – pre-programmed, indifferent, ongoing. In the case of the personal camcorder the recording impulse is not so different. As the dangerous mudbank begins to slip, the human instinct ('the hill's going – have you got it?') is to stay and watch rather than run and hide. Like a possum in the headlights, the cameraman is transfixed by the glory of the spectacle and unable to prioritise his escape from it. Thus, in moments of spectacular crisis, the human-held camera is as unable to turn away, or turn off, as the CCTV set. The resulting footage, in either case, seems to tell the truth of the event depicted because its sole intention is just to see and go on seeing until the end.

Part 2: The legacy of low-tech reality

At first glance, much reality programming of the early twenty-first century bears little resemblance to the non-narrative, crash-edited, episodic madness of *When Good Pets Go Bad* and other classic titles. The elaborate studio-based contrivance of the *Big Brother* household, the cheerful transformation arc of property makeover shows, the self-reflexive selection processes of *Popstars* and other talent quest formats or the convoluted set-dressing of historic formats such as *1900 House* is now typical of the reality genre. Termed 'second generation' reality programming, all these shows present character-driven narratives which sustain interpersonal relationships over an entire season in a way antithetical to the short, sharp shock antics of video clip collections. In terms of aesthetics, broadcast standards are the norm; a multi-camera set-up allows for a seamless edit and a conventional 'hero's journey' narrative arc. Post-production layering adds titles, voice-over and presenter links to this representation of real experiences. However, the legacy of low-tech realism lives on. Never likely to settle for a single strategy when several will fit, contemporary reality television formulations allow for the discreet deployment of caught-on-tape style representation. The mechanisms of the am-cam ethos are reworked to suit the purposes of this character-driven realism and to serve the sophisticated palette of a new generation of reality television viewers. Retained by some of these new formats is the selective use of the techniques and/or audiovisual markers of amateur video-cording and the deployment of associated discourses (of the ordinary, the amateur, the unexpected). The self-reflexive acknowledgement (and often self-conscious display of) the process of production (even when these processes are not those of the amateur handycam) within second generation reality productions is also indebted to the strategies of the caught-on-tape brand of reality.

Magazine or makeover shows frequently incorporate amateur video footage into a professionally shot and edited programme. The UK's *What Not to Wear* – a fashion makeover format – makes a feature of hand-held handycam footage, which is both generated prior to and during each episode as the unwitting subject is caught committing her style crimes. Similarly the garden makeover show *Ground Force* cuts to a hidden camera carried by a family friend in a 'meanwhile' narrative construction to heighten suspense and emphasise the element of surprise. In both cases, part of the reality affect is the camera-innocence of the subjects – a potent indicator of authenticity embedded in the caught-on-tape catch-cry. These inserts are clearly delineated from the rest of the professional footage by the visual signatures of am cam – shaky framing, low resolution stock, washed-out colours and poor audio. They are further distinguished by superimposed screen titles (such as 'am cam') and framing devices (such as the flat screen television in the WNTW fashion stylists' workroom). Carefully labelled and framed by the programme in this way, these images bear the weight of Walter Benjamin's paradox of technology-permeated realism. For the am-cam footage 'offers, precisely because of the thoroughgoing permeation of reality with mechanical equipment, an aspect of reality which is free of all equipment' (1988: 233). At once more real-seeming and more manufactured-seeming than the professionally shot and edited material which sandwiches these video inserts, the connotative freight of amateur image production ensures that the am-cam clips on *What Not to Wear* are more real because they are more manufactured, or in other words, because they bear the aesthetic stamps of their particular circumstances of manufacture.

Likewise, personal journey or diary format reality television shows such as *Castaway, Faking It, 1900 House* or *Perfect Match* use confession cam or diary cam sequences to heighten the desired affect of intimacy and authenticity. Structured around the conventions of a 'heroes journey' narrative these programmes differ from the magazine-style makeover shows because they sustain a relationship with one set of participants over the entire programme season. This provides for the extended exposure of audiences to selected individuals and fosters promises of intimate knowing. As a special means of production and reception, the diary cam is thus emblematic of the diary format's affective intentions. The particular intimacy generated by diary cam sequences is predicated upon the operator being alone with a camera. This circumstance indicates that the camera is a non-professional one, and that it is being operated by the subject. This relationship is usually signalled to the programme's audience by the inclusion of footage which shows the video diarist leaning forward, momentarily fading out of focus and leaning out of frame, to switch the camera off. This brief instance, technically poor and so easily edited out, is included in the sequence for good reason. It stands as a marker of authenticity, confirming the amateur status of the image-maker and the all-alone status of the confessor. Both these affirmations serve the programme's promise of immediate and intimate contact with the represented participant. For a media-savvy audience the transparent acknowledgement of the means of moving image production serve an appetite for authentic shared experience better than the conventions of 'suturing'. As with the 'am cam' on *Ground Force*, these diary cam sequences are usually delineated from the rest of the programme by titles, focus lines or digital time codes which mimic the screen displays of genuine handycam footage. In this way the signatures of amateur video footage – shaky hand-held movement, poor focus or composition, digital graphics – are re-deployed by professional television formats in ways which authenticate a format which otherwise risks a diminished reality effect through its heightened professionalism.

Different in kind, but comparable in intent, is the international phenomenon of *Big Brother*. Where diary formats foster notions of personal agency (as participants record their own images and audience members are invited into an all-access domain of amateur production), *Big Brother* is all about delimiting the agency of individual participants. Nevertheless, as one of the most self-reflexive reality television formats of the age, *Big Brother* freely and knowingly performs its own processes of production. As with many reality formats, images of recording equipment are incorporated into the opening and closing title sequences and are signature elements of associated publicity material. Although specifics of production design vary from country to country and season to season, the emergence of each evicted 'housemate' into the studio world exterior to the closed set of the *Big Brother* house provides an opportunity for production transparency. The executive producer of the first *Big Brother* series in the United Kingdom, Ruth Wigley, has described the production of the weekly live 'Eviction Specials' in these terms:

> I wanted it to look live and exciting, I wanted viewers – and the contestants who were evicted – to see the control room, to get an idea of all the behind-the-scenes work. After all, this was not meant to be a piece of polished drama. We were filming it for real, and it was a virtue of the programme that viewers understood that.

(quoted in Ritchie 2000: 10,11)

In this formulation both participants and viewers are given the opportunity to bear witness to the technologies of their mediated relationship. The confession of representational processes thus exhibited heightens both the temporal thrill of liveness and the pull of the real. Wigley's statement also indicates the extent to which the self-conscious display of process is specific to the reality genre (as opposed to 'polished drama') suggesting that part of the 'reality' of the reality television label is its truth-telling about processes of image production. In the same interview, Wigley suggests that the pleasures of 'seamless' editing are lost on a new generation of viewers; 'The audience we attracted understand television, they've grown up with it, they know its grammar' (quoted in Ritchie 2000: 10, 11). Here, *Big Brother* rehearses the lessons of caught-on-tape formats, as it announces its own processes and makes a virtue of them.

Coda: Inadvertent television

As one of the slickest reality television formats in production, *Survivor* exemplifies the second generation shift away from an aesthetics of amateurism. Unlike some of the programme examples discussed here, *Survivor* resists self-reflexive references to television production and fashions itself on the 'polished drama' which Wigley's production design eschewed. In fact, the show's producer Mark Burnett strenuously resists association with the reality television label, coining the terms 'unscripted drama' and 'dramality' for his work. As a consequence this reality format suffers from a perceived loss of realism. Professional digital formats, high-tech sound and image reproduction, post-production visual effects, audio layering and a finely honed edit are all part of the 'dramality' signature. However, despite its allegiance to seamless production techniques and narrative shaping, the 'reality' precepts of the *Survivor* format (i.e. the 'unscriptedness' of the drama) make it vulnerable to the vagaries of human activity. Thus unanticipated and aberrant incidents – such as Michael Skupin's campfire accident in the 'Australian Outback' series – crack the well-polished veneer of the show's dramatic form. Curiously, this incident proved to be an aesthetic disruption as much as a narrative one. As Michael's accident was unanticipated, the camera crew was unprepared to cover the event. As a consequence the footage of this incident is much closer in tone to that of an amateur with a handy-cam than the professionalism of the usual multi-camera set-up. Shot from an awkward distance and including jerky movements as the cameraman runs to follow Michael into the river, the footage of this dramatic incident has no edits and no close-ups. Michael's screams are unintelligible and it is difficult to make out the extent of the burn damage to his face and hands. Suddenly we are in the domain of *The World's Worst Moments: Caught on Tape* as horrific injury and rolling camera collide. Brief though this momentary genre-devolution may have been, its impact on audiences was considerable. Cynical commentators noted that the producers would have liked to stage the event if they could, as it boosted ratings and generated bonus publicity. However it was the accidental clumsiness of this footage which accounted for its appeal. Fans, critics and watchdogs disagreed over questions of morality, safety and privacy raised by the episode, but nobody suggested it was faked.

The eruption of am-cam aesthetics at a point of real emergency indicates that the production of televised reality is ineluctably intertwined with certain processes of image-making. For caught-on-tape is *the* medium for the representation of unanticipated crisis. In this way, Michael's injury forced a formal shift in production for the *Survivor* crew, a shift which traded the visual pleasure of high-class cinematography for the pleasures attendant on viewing an accredited reality. As the entertainment tabloid *Who Weekly* reported, the *Survivor* team was not squeamish about the opportunity presented by the campfire incident. The programme's host Jeff Probst is quoted as saying: 'On one hand, it's horrifying to watch the skin peel off a human being. On the other, when things calm down, there's certainly a part of you saying, "Now that's gonna make for dramatic television". We have a responsibility to keep the cameras rolling.' More succinctly, Mark Burnett told a press conference that he would have sacked the cameraman filming Michael Skupin's accident if he had stopped shooting to assist the wretched man (Halfpenny 2001: 31). Both Probst and Burnett speak of the imperative of spectacle-capture, not only as a ratings puller but as some kind of grisly social mandate ('we have a responsibility...'). The compulsion to continue recording until the very end (think here of the final scene of *The Blair Witch Project*), as manifested by examples of caught-on-tape footage, becomes a marker of realness because it testifies to the mesmerising appeal of spectacle. It seems that the *Survivor* cameraman was never in any danger of losing his job because, as for the contractor from Portland or the female director in *Blair Witch*, instincts of self-preservation or human succour proved to be weaker than the instinct to keep shooting.

As I have suggested, second generation reality television programming is arguably at its most 'real' when it reverts to type in this way. Whether (real or faked) am-cam footage is inserted into the programme format, or the narrative supports the disclosure of technological process, or unanticipated crises prompt unprofessional recording practices, the legacy of low-tech realism lives on.

References

Benjamin, Walter (1988) *Illuminations*. Harry Zohn (trans.) New York: Schocken Books.

Fetveit, Arild (2002) 'Reality TV in the Digital Era: A Paradox in Visual Culture?' in James Freidman (ed.), *Reality Squared: Televisual Discourse on the Real*. New Brunswick, NJ and London: Rutgers University Press, 119-137.

Halfpenny, Kate (2001) 'Reality Bites' *Who Weekly* magazine, March 26, Milsons Point, NSW: Time Inc., 28-31.

Ritchie, Jean (2000) *Big Brother: The Official Unseen Story*. London: Channel 4 Books.

7. Love 'n the Real; or, How I Learned to Love Reality TV

Misha Kavka

Television by definition is a medium that invites questions about how real its version of reality is. Love by definition is oddly similar, always open to doubts about whether one is 'really' in love. As the Oracle tells Neo in *The Matrix* (1999), 'no one can tell you you're in love – you just know it, through and through, balls to bones.' Itself invisible, always begging to be proved or performed, love also has the putative power to skew one's view of reality. In the U.S. the reality TV series *The Bachelor* (ABC, 2002) and *Joe Millionaire* (Fox, 2003), like *Perfect Match* (Channel 4) in the UK, drew an enthusiastic viewership for the spectacle of winnowing down a field of suitors to a single one who 'wins' the affections of the bachelor/ette. The success of such shows has produced a tide of similar-but-different formats, announcing the era of Real Love TV.[1] It may seem perverse that the conditions for 'real' love are being relegated to television, whose cameras can only bastardize properly private emotion. Yet I will argue that this shift on our screens from telling love stories in fiction programmes to performing love-making through reality TV is curiously appropriate, for the confirmation of both – the reality of the televisual world and the reality of being in love – comes down to a matter of feeling.

The format draws in part on the ill-fated experiments in wedding-TV by the Fox channel (*Who Wants to Marry a Multimillionaire?* and *Who Wants to Marry a Prince?*) but also has links to other, more exotic examples of the real-love genre, namely *Temptation Island* and *Love Cruise* (both Fox, 2001 and 2002), which draw on the *Big Brother* format of isolating a group of people, introducing the stress of expulsion, and filming their interactions. What makes such programs interesting is their double structure: diegetically, the ideology of requited love prevails (even if, or precisely because, they consist of testing such an ideology), but in their form these programs urge us to love without return, since as viewers we expend a great deal of emotion on people who cannot see us back. In this chapter, I will focus on this sudden surge of real-love TV, arguing that the coupling-based derivatives of the *Big Brother* docu-soap teach us a lesson not about social interaction, or even about the woeful dissolution of the private sphere, but about media intimacy.

I. Reality – with Feeling

For detractors of reality TV and/or sentimentalists, the difficulty with real-love shows is the same: love displayed for the camera cannot be real. Such a concern, however, is first and foremost rooted in a suspicion of the medium itself. Unlike film or cyberspace, television promises actuality but functions as a medium, a means of transmitting a view of a particular scene across distance (hence the etymology of its name). Even documentary or live transmission is thus open to questions about technological and narrative intrusions into the reality presented. Ideologically, television has been thought of as both a 'window onto the world'-that is, as a medium of information and/or communication-and as a phantasmatic screen whose pleasure lies in its imaginary appeal-that is, as a medium of spectacle, or entertainment. In terms of emotive function, 'feeling' has no place in information programming, which strives toward objectivity, while fiction programming thrives on the production and consumption of feeling. These two definitions of television's role suggest radically different relations to the real, but they have been kept comfortably separated by genre expectations: the tradition of news/public service programming fulfils a different social function than the tradition of fiction programming. With the onset of the much bemoaned trend toward tabloidization, however, these two functions have begun to collapse into one another, so that information is increasingly harnessed for purposes of spectacle, and entertainment is more spectacular when based in actuality (see Langer 1998).

No genre has been more in the firing line than reality TV, which commits a double crime of conflation: on the one hand, it blurs television's promise of information with its penchant for entertainment; on the other hand, it highlights the paradox central to television itself that actuality may seem most real when mediated. Offering a kind of 'best of the worst' showcase of television as apparatus, reality TV programmes produce a sense of reality as an effect of seemingly *direct* transmission. They are thus sites of 'constructed unmediation', where the technology involved in both production and post-production shapes a final product that comes across as unmediated, or real.

This has important implications in the age of media globalization, where the demand for an 'ethics of actuality', or a guarantee of strict overlap between reality and its representation, is being overwhelmed and reconfigured by reality in the service of entertainment (see Nichols 1994: 43-62). The criticism that reality TV is not in fact 'real' because the shows are heavily manipulated (read: nobody actually lives like that!) assumes a dumbed-down viewership that conflates what plays out on one side of the screen – framed as spectacle – with what happens on the other – grounded in the experiential world. Rather than assuming such a stark division and chastising the populace for failing to see it, the more serious jumping-off point would be to credit viewers with having watched enough TV to know perfectly well that the reality of RTV is mediated, even manipulated (the programmes tend to highlight rather than hide this). To accept both – that viewers know that it is a set-up and yet the level of actuality in these shows is important – would be to understand that the appeal of reality TV lies precisely in its performance of reality in a way that *matters*.

There is no question that global media culture is having a profound effect on what we take to matter. The term 'reality' need not be limited to palpable or documentable experience, but must increasingly be thought in terms of techniques of documentation which produce a sense of immediacy (see Bonner and West in this volume). This is not to say that we no longer recognize the external world as real – I do not wish to argue for the full-scale paranoization of media society – but it is to say that what we can touch often matters less to our lives than what we see on the screen. The reality effects of the mediated real, what I am calling 'constructed unmediation', often have a greater urgency and a paradoxically greater immediacy than the world around us (a good example here is the bemused refrain heard after the death of Princess Diana: 'I didn't feel like this even when my grandmother died'). This immediacy serves as the grounds for what we take to be real, and is itself known or measured through our affective response. The relationship between viewer affect and the constructed unmediation of reality programming is thus a reciprocal one; our affective response 'proves' that this reality matters (i.e., it must be real if we care so much), while the fact that the actions and faces on screen belong to 'real' people serves to justify our having an affective response (i.e., real people give us a reason to care). The feeling guarantees the reality, and the reality justifies the feeling.

Reality TV is both compelling and threatening because these programmes bridge the once-firm division between spectacle and experience, between the staged event and actuality, through mediated intimacy. For the participants on such shows, intimacy is mediated by performance (they must first do as though they feel), while for the viewers intimacy is mediated by the television screen itself. Mediation in this case, however, does not necessarily mean a lessening or blocking of feeling, or the affect of intimacy. It turns out to be possible for the participants to love, hate or feel strongly about someone they have just met despite the presence of cameras (this has become something of a refrain during *Big Brother* post-eviction interviews). On the other side of the screen, it turns out to be possible to love, hate or feel strongly about someone you've never talked to, never touched – someone who does not even know you exist because they cannot see you watching.

I am talking in terms of affect, or feeling, in an attempt to give some grounding to the term 'intimacy' which has begun to appear in media and television studies but without much theoretical specificity. I use affect in order to distinguish it from emotions; affect is both more and less than emotion, since affect covers the entire range of feelings but before they have been assessed or identified in relation to a particular object. Affect is the zone of potential emotions – emotions which have not yet been perceived as such and thus constitute a 'primordial soup' of feeling. To this I want to add another dimension, for affect can also be said to serve as a cusp between the individual and the collective psyche, that shared pool of feeling whose production and recognition glues individuals into a particular social body. In other words, feelings may be individually owned but must be socially resonant; any feeling that is *too* individual will mark the subject as pathological (i.e., the hysteric, the rage case, even the serial killer). This cusp between the individual and the collective obviously takes any number of forms, but in our media age one material version of this cusp lies in the TV screen itself, that conjoining divider which connects real people on one side of the apparatus with the real people, in a different sense, on the other.

Christina von Braun, in an article on *Big Brother* written in response to the first series in Germany, has referred to this intimate connection as 'an act of union between the people in front of the camera and those in front of the television' (2000: 57; my translation). She goes so far as to name this union an openly sexual one, claiming that as viewers we engage not necessarily in group sex, but in sex with the group. The function of *Big Brother* for the social unconscious, according to von Braun, is to establish an erotic relationship between the collective and the individual psyche. I agree with this formulation, but would wish to lay stress on the affective rather than on the strictly erotic experience of being 'intimate with' the Big Brother participants. On the one hand, the notion of the erotic is too specifically object-oriented, too dependent on particular visual images. We cannot, after all, discount the banality built into a show like *Big Brother*, which makes even sex on camera look and feel not unlike watching someone you know make the bed (think of the various acts of huddled humping caught on a night camera). Though the U.S. real-love shows increasingly find ways of incorporating shots of women in bikinis, especially in contact with someone's pecs in a hot tub, there is a certain mundanity, through over-familiarity, in such soft-porn representations. In these shows, rather than being voyeurs of hot-tub scenes, we are voyeurs of emotion – but equally participants in it, drawn in by what I call the affect of intimacy. What is pertinent to reality TV is not the issue of erotic representation or even voyeurism (which would require one to stand outside of the intimacy on show), but rather the capacity of the television screen to act as both a transparent lens *and* a conduit of social affect. The paradox of constructed unmediation comes back into play here: the screen is 'not there' because it appears to be transparent, and yet its mediating presence works to intensify the feeling of becoming intimate with someone, of knowing them well enough to love them. Thus a show like *The Bachelor* encourages viewers to be caught up in the reality-testing of the feeling of love ('no one can tell you if you're in love . . .'), both from the perspective of the love-seeker and the suitors longing to be claimed.

Admittedly, one could say that the setting of reality TV simulates as well as stimulates intense intimacy. There is no question that the setting is artificial, whether participants are placed in a house with neither media nor physical access to the outside world, as on *Big Brother*, or billeted together in a chateau in France and sent on romantic excursions in different pairings, as on *Joe Millionaire*. In each case, the setting, whether found or purpose-built, is there to simulate the scene of intimacy: flatting together in a house on *BB* or falling in love in the land of romance on *JM*. What is questionable, however, is to conflate the simulated setting with a necessarily simulated intimacy. I would argue, rather, that the simulated setting *stimulates* feeling, in part because the removal of the participants from their normal surroundings strips them to nothing but the space and affect of social interaction. The intimacy that arises out of this amplified situation is real – both for the participants and for the viewers. The participants, given the structure of the shows and the living spaces, cannot but perform intimacy, and in the process they come to have intimate knowledge of each other. In *Joe Millionaire*, as in *The Bachelor*, the women and the 'regular Joe'/bachelor behave from the start as though they were already potentially in love, not least because the 'romantic' setting dictates that they should. This is less a matter of acting in the sense of simulation than of *acting out*, a performance of the self which creates feeling; hence, the most common refrain spoken by the women participants in the direct-to-camera cutaways on *Joe Millionaire* is 'I think I'm falling in love'. To those who are sceptical about how 'real' this statement is, I would only recall my opening analogy: love, like television, must be performed to be real. The performance of love will generate the effects of love, just as the performance of reality will generate reality effects.

Similarly, as viewers engaged in, if not sex, then love with the group, we too feel caught up by the performance of love, and we respond affectively. This is a point not understood by the broadcasters in various countries which have attempted to ride the RTV wave by stringing *Big Brother* series back to back (such as in Germany on RTL II), only to be surprised by a radical drop in ratings with each new series. The reason is simple: viewers cannot fall out of love with one group quickly enough to accept intimacy with another one just like that. We need time to mourn the end of one group affair before we can turn our mended hearts to another (Channel 4 in the UK, I might add, has been more attuned to this need, staggering *BB* series once a year, though I would say that CBS is beginning to push its luck with the rush to produce more *Survivor* series).

II. Matching Up *The Bachelor*

Characterized by the formatting trope of group isolation, the programming trend initiated by *Big Brother* (1999 and after) can be usefully termed the 'intimate strangers' genre. These programmes all bring together a group of people with no previous connections and place them in a setting geared to intensify intimacy; according to Paddy Scannell these shows involve 'not so much the merely as the purely sociable' (2002: 277). In my formulation, I would say that the 'intimate strangers' genre is so successful precisely because of the way it produces the 'real' in a reciprocal relation of mattering to viewer affect. It is in the RTV-inflected dating show, however, that the function of intimacy becomes most visible, for in this subgenre intimacy is directly thematized as both the content and the motor of the programme. Countless numbers of dating shows are being produced across the world, versions of a fairly low-budget, multiple-vignette format (e.g., from *Blind Date* to *Dismissed*) which has a history as old as *The Dating Game* from the 1970s. Those now having the most impact on the ratings, however, certainly in the U.S., are competition-based relationship shows that commit to one person's search for love for the duration of a six- or eight-week series. Derived from the innovative but crass experiment in wedding-TV, *Who Wants to Marry a Multimillionaire?* (Fox, 2000), a show whose place in the annals of television history has been secured both by an on-screen wedding and by the later revelation that the 'millionaire' in question had a police record for violence against women, ABC's *The Bachelor* attempts to replace the Fox freak show element with Hollywood elegance.

Aired initially in 2002, *The Bachelor* uses the simple premise of allowing one man to choose his potential bride from a group of 25 women, with each episode culminating in a cull of the available women until there are only four, then three, then two, and then – the engagement. The initial series, with Bachelor Alex, proved so popular that ABC soon after ran a second series with Bachelor Aaron. In both cases, the bachelor chosen to be the centre of the programme was required to be youthful, attractive, educated, financially solvent and, crucially, articulate (all but the last being, not uncoincidentally, the standard description run in a personal ad). After two series, the mould was already being updated: in early 2003 Fox pitted *Joe Millionaire* against ABC's *The Bachelorette*. In *Joe Millionaire*, the bachelor is chosen for youth, attractiveness and articulacy, but crucially *not* for money – the women are told he has recently inherited $50 million when in fact he is a lowly construction worker. In *The Bachelorette*, the 'gimmick' is sex-reversal, though with the added attraction of bringing back the sexy runner-up of the first *Bachelor* series – who herself had thought, along with the majority of viewers, that she was a shoo-in for Alex's full and final affections – to be the girl in the middle. As a boon, this third series brought another layer of intimacy to the first episode, for the suitors who arrived to meet the bachelorette Trista seemed already to 'know' her – from having been viewers, just like us, of the first programme.

The trappings of mediated intimacy are all here: the oscillation between group surveillance and the individual interview, the omnipresent yet invisible cameramen, the personal microphones miraculously attached to skimpy clothing, the ritualized setting and rhetoric of the send-off, the close-ups of faces contorted by emotion or dissolving into tears. Rather than simply serving as a reflective surface, or pedagogical model, for group intimacy, as with *Big Brother*, these real-love shows take it one step further: they spur mediated intimacy by thematizing intimacy itself in its most basic, sexual definition. In *The Bachelor/ette*, Christina von Braun would be heartened to know, the (wo)man at the centre of the format really does engage in group (if serial) sex. The format, followed loosely by *Joe Millionaire*, starts with group dates, then moves in later rounds to individual dates, visits 'home', and finally an overnight trip-for-two, before culminating in a scene set for a proposal. The *Bachelor* producers' discreet offer of the use of a 'fantasy suite' on the overnight trip makes it more than clear that pre-marital sex is now considered an acceptable (and even necessary) step in the search for love.[2] But even the glimpses of pre-coital intimacy in these episodes, however often replayed in the programme trailers, are ultimately there as a support and instigation for what really matters on these shows – feeling. This is not strictly the emotion of love, which is so hard to prove, but the more visible and visualizable emotions that surround the search for love: the agony of deciding who to reject, the anger and pain of being (publicly) rejected, the jealousy evoked by the polygamous setting, and the joy of a happy choice (however temporary).

One reason why such an unlikely format can work, at least for the viewers, is because of the implicit analogy made between the *structure* of the 'intimate strangers' show and the *practice* of selecting a mate for marriage. Do we Westerners not allow ourselves to make intimate connections with a select few, people chosen as appropriate by familial and social institutions, and then on the basis of further, regular contact do we not decide to break off relations with all but one, sending each rejectee home to his/her invisible daily life, and ending up with one ultimate 'winner' who reaps the full benefit of our monogamous affections? Is it not, in fact, as though each time *Big Brother* or *American/Pop Idol* produces another winner, the viewing community has made precisely such a commitment, after an extended, ritualized period of ever more focused intimacy, a commitment to the 'one' whom they will love forever – at least for a few months, before s/he gets shunted to a late-night presenter's spot? When the presenter of *The Bachelor* intones in the beginning of the first episode that 'this is no ordinary relationship show; the stakes are considerably higher,' he is suggesting that this is a reality TV show which will touch a nerve because of the analogy *already* in place between mediated intimacy and 'real love'. These shows make sense because it turns out that constructed intimacy is a lot like the way real love works, at least in the ideological terms of Western romance.

This development of the RTV genre is not a dating game so much as a televisual arranged marriage. The U.S., like other countries in the West, is a society which, in the course of 100 years, has moved from a notion that marriages should be socially and economically 'appropriate' to taking on the full ideology of romantic *choice*. The real-love programmes, on the one hand, celebrate choice, which is an important and oft-repeated word throughout this subgenre (as can be seen on *Temptation Island*, where presenter Mark Walberg repeatedly intones, 'this is all about the choices you make'). Indeed, *The Bachelor/ette* fetishizes choice in the format itself, balancing the rhythm of dates with regular expulsion ceremonies that rely on the bachelor/ette publicly announcing her/his choice and bestowing a rose on the favoured suitors. On the other hand, though, these programmes seem to offer a response to the confusion of having *too much* choice, of being burdened by romantic choice. The suitor's 'normal' field of choice is both expanded by people s/he would not otherwise have met and radically contracted to a pre-selected twenty-five suitors. Real-love TV thus has a double, even contradictory, effect: it offers to show us how romantic 'choice' works, by breaking it down into its components (first meeting, first date, first kiss, etc.), while it also marks a return to the socially approved arranged marriage. Now, rather than choices being made by and within the family, the television offers the medium of arrangement; the potential mates are vetted in pre-production or on air – by producers, family and friends, and viewers themselves. The format of *Perfect Match* itself revolves around the social arrangement of romantic coupling, with the final choice of viable suitors placed in the capable hands of a 'panel' consisting of the love-seeker's family or friends (as well as the ubiquitous relationship expert). [3] What these shows assure us is that romantic choice is not in fact a lonely or even an individual process, but is something performed within and for the social group. Television has taken over the role of the village matchmaker.

Intimacy, whether in face-to-face scenarios or across the screen, must always involve an element of selection, and hence of judgement, for only the 'arrangement' of emotion allows it to be focused on a particular recipient. If real-love shows are about romantic choice, performed through mediated intimacy, then viewers join in at both the level of feeling and of judgement. In *The Bachelor*, the judgements that participants and viewers of RTV shows are regularly called to make will count 'for real': the bachelor in search of a bride will truly narrow his field of potential commitment (and potential romantic gain) every time he 'votes' a woman off. In fact, once he is down to the last four women – and having to fly across the country in order to meet all their families as the boy they bring home – he seems quite daunted by how 'for real' his intimate judgement calls will now be. Admittedly, there is a difference between the Bachelor and RTV viewers who engage in making judgements on the basis of mediated intimacy. Whether the format allows viewers to voice their judgement by poll or not, the 'intimate strangers' genre always draws viewers into making a choice in the eviction round; the construction of the format around the Bachelor/ette's 'choice' means that we too have a favourite or favourites, groaning or cheering if the Bachelor/ette has discarded our favourite or allowed her/him to stay. And yet we remain anonymous, never running the danger of being personified on screen. Such programmes thus allow us to make highly invested personal judgements about others without having the effects of judging revert back on us as individuals. We are, in other words, making judgements based in affective investment but on the part of the group; we even make these judgements *for* the group, to be heard and incorporated into the impassioned discussions with other viewers and in the media that follow. In this sense, Bachelor Alex is woefully on his own, individuated and highly visible, having to take the brunt of responsibility for his judgements just because, on his side of the screen, they are 'for real'.

And yet, Alex is protected by the analogy between reality TV and real-love as well. Following the ritualized format of *Big Brother* and *Survivor*, where the person who has been evicted must leave within a very short time frame, *The Bachelor* also gives the rejected women a 'few moments to say your good-byes' and then marches them out of the room. What the Bachelor is spared, in other words, is the emotional fallout of having rejected someone, particularly in the mass culling of the first few episodes. Like the viewers who make a choice but are freed of personal responsibility for the effects, Alex's job is just to make the decision, not to clean up afterwards (that seems to be the lamentable role of the producers behind the camera who conduct the final interviews with the rejected women). The analogy between reality TV and real-love, then, has effects in both directions: televised love rituals reveal something about the basic structures of intimacy and judgement underlying the appeal of reality TV, while reality TV offers to cleanse cultural love rituals, both of the nasty aftershocks of making a judgement and of the overabundance of choice. Both effects, of course, operate in the realm of collective fantasy, but are no less real for that.

III. Ethics of Emotion

There is no discounting the fact that by peddling the ideology of requited love, these shows foreground a certain moral imperative about how, and whom, one should love. And inevitably, a moral imperative attached to practices of love will have gender implications. Indeed, there is something quite uncomfortable about a programme which screens close-ups of women crying while the man at the centre of it all poses thoughtfully elsewhere and muses calmly about the seriousness of what he is doing. There is also something uncomfortable about a show which knowingly sets up monogamy as the goal but polygamy as the process, encouraging a rhetoric of 'honesty' and 'trust' but a practice of 'cheating', since it happily sends the Bachelor on three overnight dates with three different women. Nor is the power differential, which is so obvious when twenty-five women are asked to fawn over one man, exactly corrected by reversing the gender positions and running *The Bachelorette* in the third series. As much as the producers may have tried for equality through gender-reversal, the voice-over in the first series' credits, 'when one man is involved with more than one woman, there's bound to be trouble . . .', does not and cannot reappear when the gender positions are simply reversed. In *The Bachelorette* series, the presenter draws attention to the social oddity of a woman 'calling the shots' rather than taking for granted any 'trouble' to come amongst men vying for the same woman (and, in fact, scenes from the men's house suggest that they got along fine). This programme, like *Temptation Island* before it, begs an ethics of emotion. By stressing the idea that this series of choices is 'for real', that the man and woman at the end will form a monogamous, till-death-do-us-part couple, the show attempts to make its use of emotions (particularly the women's) serve an ultimately ethical end. *Temptation Island* does the same thing, by setting itself up as a self-help programme for devoted but commitment-phobic couples, while the deceit of the women participants on *Joe Millionaire* is exonerated by the outspoken justification that only such a practice will weed out gold-diggers in favour of 'true love'. It is not too difficult to see how precarious such a balance between the exploitation of emotion and the ideology of monogamous romance is, hence the uncomfortable aspect of these programmes.

What is harder to see here, I think, is that these shows draw on the very same emotional structures, and romantic ideologies, that drive our desiring lives. They are not so much discomfiting because they are artificial and exploitative; rather, these shows perturb because, in confronting the conditions of love in a simulated setting, they bring to light aspects of love practices that are indeed conflictual and contradictory. It is here, rather than in the more simple moral imperative of finding 'Mr. Right', that an ethics of emotion truly comes into play. The conflictual polygamy of these shows is underwritten by the medium of television itself. Narratively, the ideology of requited love prevails, but in their form these programs urge us to love (or, just as possibly, to hate) without return, since we expend a great deal of emotion on people who cannot see us back. Our affective response, in other words, is excessive, and thereby in excess of the moral imperative or normatizing ideology built into the format (which suggests that the 'truth' and 'honesty' of our feelings will, if such, be requited). As inchoate, floating or excess emotion, not fully recuperated by format, our affective response constitutes a kind of burgeoning ethical sphere, for it becomes an object of interrogation and articulation in a variety of places, forms and conversations – not least those in our own living rooms.

Real-love programmes teach us a lesson about media intimacy: it is in fact possible, and pleasurable, to become intimate with someone by performing the rituals of love, just as it is possible to become intimate with someone across the mediating screen by joining in the rituals of the televisually arranged marriage. Such intimacy does not abrogate the 'proper' sphere of privacy, nor undercut the realness of love, but rather indicates the expansion, through mediatization, of the field of the intimate itself.

References

Langer, John (1998) *Tabloid Television*. London and New York: Routledge.

Nichols, Bill (1994) *Blurred Boundaries*. Bloomington: Indiana University Press.

Scannell, Paddy (2002). '*Big Brother* as Television Event', *Television and New Media*. Vol. 3, Issue 3 (August), 271-282.

von Braun, Christina (2000) '"Big Brother" oder Der frei zirkulierende Eros', *Tages-Anzeiger* (Switzerland), 5 December, 57.

Notes

1   Fox, for instance, followed up *Joe Millionaire* with *Married by America* (2003) and *Mr. Personality* (2003). Recently, Bravo has launched the first gay real-love show, *Boy Meets Boy* (July 2003).

2   Interestingly, Trista was quite staunchly unapologetic, on the show and in media interviews, about her intention to 'do what it takes' to find the right man, that is, reserving the right to sleep with the men remaining at the overnight stage of the programme. She was well aware, presumably, of the double standard still prevalent that judges men who 'sleep around' differently from women.

3   *Perfect Match* seems fully aware of the implications of the arranged marriage having come to television; in one 2003 episode, the love-seeker is a British Asian woman whose parents are trying to carry the traditional arranged marriage into the modern age by sitting on the panel. Together, however, they count as only one member, so that the modern form of social arrangement can be represented by a friend and the relationship expert (for an interesting fan review of this episode, see www.dooyoo.co.uk/tv/tv_channels/bbc_1_in_general/_review/386440/ (accessed July 2003).

8. Looking Inside:Showing Medical Operations on Ordinary Television

Frances Bonner

Much has been written from a cinematic and cultural studies perspective about medical imaging and films of operations, but the principal focus has been on the medical interpretation of such imaging and the use of documentary film by the medical profession, rather than what will be the concern here – the televised screening of such material to a lay audience. Both Lisa Cartwright (1995) and José van Dijck (2002), notable scholars in the field, have published historical studies of early medical documentary films which detail how any 'spilling over' of such material into popular exhibition was considered a scandal or at the least a misuse. More generally, writing on medical and health issues on television (apart from that concerned with drama) tends to look at traditional documentaries and focus on the utility of the information conveyed and the degree of support exhibited for medical personnel (see for example Hodgetts and Chamberlain 1999, Belling 1998). The touchstone is overwhelmingly the medical informational part of the proceedings, with Catherine Belling, for example, approving televised operations despite her warnings about their constructedness, because of their role in demystifying patients' understandings of the insides of their own bodies (1998: 19). An exception to this perspective is provided by studies of surgery to separate conjoined twins, which despite the rarity of such surgery, comprise a significant proportion of writing in cultural studies concerned with non-fictional medical operations. David L. Clark and Catherine Myser, for example, are largely concerned with matters of embodiment and the way in which surgical considerations are shown as unquestionably primary in issues relating to decisions about separation, compared even to psychiatric ones (1996: 346-8).

I want to consider both the televisual site and the content involved when comparatively unexceptional medical sequences become part of ordinary non-fiction infotainment television, not to consider how well medical data is conveyed, but how it is framed for popular consumption. How is it that serious and arguably gruesome operations performed on ordinary people have become part of the regular content of domestic infotainment television? In such programmes, medical matters are the focus and the assumption is that viewers come to know more about the issues at hand, but the pill is sugared by various entertaining devices which may well be far more to the (televisual) point than data about the human body. What does it mean that we can sit in our living rooms and observe catheters being inserted into a stranger's heart through a vein in the thigh and regard this as just part of an evening's viewing?

I will be arguing that one of the ways in which entertainment is produced is by the generation of spectacle, but that the informational component means that programmes showing 'real' medical operations on ordinary television produce a distinctive spectacle and need also to contain the extent of the eruption of spectacle. In this, I am running counter to the customary way in which the term spectacle is used in television studies. The normal use is to cover programmes which are anything but ordinary television; rather they are special events, news or media events, to use Dayan and Katz's terms (1992). Spectacles of these kinds – both pre-planned and (hastily) scheduled media ones such as Royal funerals or unanticipated news spectacles that suddenly disrupt the schedule, such as September 11th – are extended, given space to signify their importance, which the very act of disrupting regular programming indicates. Even when the news event itself takes only a matter of moments, its coverage is open-ended and the salient moments are repeated into excess. The long durée is precisely the point of the coverage. An alternative possibility for television studies would be to use 'spectacle' to talk of special effects within television dramas, especially now that science fiction has returned as a popular televisual dramatic form. This does not appear yet to be a common usage but might be more viable when a higher proportion of the population have very large widescreen sets with digital capability and commensurate sound.

It is my belief that non-fiction televisual spectacle is currently of a different order, one more in keeping with the comparatively small scale of the image and its domestic location. It is possible that televisual spectacle compensates for its inability to overwhelm the viewer on a cinematic visual and aural scale by seeking an intensity focussed around the reality or actuality of what is being displayed, whether the rare destruction of skyscrapers or the more frequent medical incursions into the bodies of ordinary people. What I am suggesting in the medical televisual instance is that viewers might be paying a mundane, perhaps only desultory, amount of attention to a non-fiction program (this is certainly a common mode of viewing television programmes generally; see Ellis 162), the people being followed more or less engaging, when suddenly the modal quality of the programme shifts. Bloody flesh or normally concealed body cavities fill the screen and the viewing engagement becomes of a different order as we enter what Clark and Myser call the 'theatre of surgery' (1996: 339). In this theatre, although the spectacle is mediated, the actuality of the event is stressed; we are assured, often repeatedly, that this is not a fiction, that what we are shown really happened to a real person. But because it is just an uneventful part of the regular schedule, ordinariness must be maintained and the spectacular reasonably quickly circumscribed.

This is part of my continuing work on British and Australian 'ordinary television' – popular non-fiction programming covering a somewhat larger field than that designated either by the rather old term 'light entertainment' or the newer 'infotainment'. This televisual growth area looks at mundane matters, uses ordinary people on-screen and is characteristically of the long-run form – rather than being either one-off or short prestige series of the kind that, in the realm of medicine, are presented by Robert Winston (Bonner 2003). At the time of writing, there were few dedicated medical examples on British television that focused on people, although the popularity of programmes about vets meant that animal health and animal operations were commonly to be found. A late night Channel 4 series entitled *Under the Knife with Miss Evans* did show operations in the manner discussed here, but atypically produced its entertainment frame through a disjunction between the type of operations and the manner of the surgeon. As a urinary-genital surgeon, Miss Evans conducted penis enlargement and sex-reassignment surgery as well as operations to deal with prostate cancer, but the sensationalism inherent in televising her specialism was undercut (or perhaps estranged) by her gruff, down-to-earth approach and her Home Counties delivery.

At the same time, Australian television had far more instances of ordinary medical programming during prime time, including *Good Medicine*, the Tuesday edition of the ABC (public broadcasting) magazine, *New Dimensions*, and the one I will focus on here, *RPA*. This latter was modelled on *Jimmy's*, a highly popular British series which had a long run on ITV during the 1980s and 90s (and could readily be revived), following the surgical experiences of patients at the St James Infirmary in Leeds. *RPA* is a similarly high-rating Australian networked commercial series based in the Royal Prince Alfred hospital in Sydney which usually follows, over several episodes, the experience of three or four patients from diagnosis to discharge. The core of the coverage is the operation or the principal investigative procedure, but the significant time spent with the patients and their families before and after the procedure ensures that viewers are not watching anonymous bodies being observed and treated but seeing the organs and flesh of people with known histories and personalities. Whether or not dedicated shows are present, in both the UK and Australia, medical segments are common on programmes such as morning and talk shows and the operations which are my main concern can easily be found across many of the types of ordinary television.

That not all viewers want to see operations, or that perhaps there is something particularly shocking about viewing the 'opened' body, is usually made quite apparent. Operations have long been televised to much larger audiences than can be assumed to have immediate or even long-term need of the information they convey, and for an equally long time, viewers have been warned about them. Belling begins her study of the US series *The Operation* by quoting as an epigraph the televised warning that the program was not for everyone since it showed a real medical operation (1998: 1). Such warnings happened even before the standardised contemporary system which simply announces that the programme about to follow contains 'medical operations' in the same terms that it would warn that it contains strong language or nudity. This reflects the change in censorship practice from one based in the dominance of a singular expression of morality to one that accepts the existence of a range of audience positions. 'Offence' can be triggered by a wider range of material, some of which may not have a particular moral component. Operations, despite being designed to cure or to heal, might be regarded as offensive to watch, because of their ability to shock – that is to produce an excess of affect.

Despite the possibility of its showing of medical procedures causing offence, the popularity of ordinary television, and of its presenters, makes them ready conduits of medical information. While not all ordinary television programmes can incorporate medical matters directly, promotional work in newspapers and magazines, across a range of other programmes on the same network, ensures that health issues have the opportunity to be discussed somewhere suitable. John Burgess, an Australian game show host, allowed footage of his face-lift operation and a discussion of his reasons for having it, to form a component of the health magazine programme *Good Medicine's* 1998 special on cosmetic surgery. The network's publicists' judgement was that this would attract more viewers to his own programme than would be offended either by the spectacle of the operation itself or the revelation of male vanity.

The popularity of ordinary television makes it especially attractive to public health campaigners wanting to inform the general public about particular medical issues. A good example of this is the case of American daytime presenter Katie Couric, who was credited with prompting a 20 per cent increase in the number of Americans having colonoscopies when, following the death of her husband from colon cancer, she agreed to have a live on-air colonoscopy. This was the 'cornerstone' of a five-day public health campaign, so could be argued to be purely informational, but it was the entertainment component of Couric's persona that was held to have made the difference (Dobson). Roger Dobson's article on the subject focuses on the medical consequences (unsurprisingly since it was published in the *British Medical Journal*). The story is of the increase in real-world procedures, not of the way the colonoscopy was presented or why people were watching it. Dobson pays no attention to the spectacle of the public display of some of the most private parts of a major American celebrity, yet this surely was instrumental in many people's decision to watch.

To investigate further the way infotainment television presents medical operations, I want to consider in detail two procedures screened on a single episode of *RPA* broadcast during 2002. One is of invasive orthopaedic surgery on the leg and the other a non-invasive investigation of a case of bleeding in the upper bowel. As was indicated earlier, in both cases the programme follows its usual practice of introducing the patient during his (both patients are male, as are their surgeons) initial consultations, allowing viewers thereby to become familiar with them and the problem with which they have presented.

The orthopaedic surgery patient had been injured many years earlier during service in the Vietnam War (the passage of time has meant that the socially divisive aspects of Australia's involvement in the war in Vietnam no longer inhibits the representation of soldiers from this conflict as war veterans equal to those from battlefields less marked by domestic debate). He had a severe limp caused by a fusion of hip and thighbone and had presented hoping for a hip replacement to return a degree of mobility to his right leg. Investigation revealed that this would not be possible, but some improvement in his gait was promised by an operation to remove a wedge of bone and realign the thigh.

The camera spends more time during the operation looking away from the operating table, filming the surgical team and giving long shots of the anaesthetised patient on the operating table, than in close-up on the area being manipulated, but it is this blood, bone and marrow that dominates the screen. The apparently primitive procedure, starting with the incision then following with a cutting away of the flesh to reveal first the fused hip and then the part of the upper thigh from which the wedge will be removed, looks more like a butcher boning a dead carcass than any instance of surgical precision. It fills the screen and tests the viewer's capacity to deal with bloody images insistently marked as 'real' by their location and the surgeon's words, even if the 'reality' of the person to which they are attached seems, for this segment, absent. A V-shaped section of bone is removed, the surgeon leans on the patient's leg to force the gap created to close (there is an audible crack) and then a plate is attached to hold the bone in its new position. The final scene of the operation involves the screws on this plate being tightened with a tool looking and sounding remarkably like a handyman's electrical screwdriver, producing a particularly uncanny conjunction of the medical and the mundane. The comments about the violation of the body that pervade cultural studies of medicine appear especially apt, yet the programme cuts rapidly to the patient recovering in his hospital bed, his wife by his side, and then to his first (painful but already less lurching) steps. Clark and Myser comment on the documentary coverage of the separated conjoined twins that 'this is the accelerated hyperreality of television, in which medical crises are by convention resolved within a miraculously compressed temporality' (1996: 349). Certainly the narrative of the man's arrival with a medical problem and its partial alleviation has proceeded quite swiftly and its logic pulls the viewer on, but the visceral affective power of the operation scenes lingers, perhaps especially because there has been no complete cure and so closure is not quite complete.

Intercut with this is the second case, which concentrates on diagnosis. The patient had a suspected disorder of the upper bowel – apparently beyond the investigative reach of a colonoscopy – which is examined by a swallowed miniaturised camera whose broadcasts are picked up and screened on a computer monitor. This leads to a very different representation. The patient remains much more present during the procedure since he is conscious throughout. The actual staging is initially very similar to the previous sequences, introducing the patient and his problems. Instead of being marked by bloody flesh, the procedure part of the case is marked by the display of technology; the patient swallows the miniaturised camera and his marvelling at the technology (echoed by the doctor) is designed to parallel that of the viewer. Although it is for a much shorter time than for the orthopaedic patient, he too disappears for the 'money shot', when we look inside his body and are guided by the doctor in what we are seeing. This is much less a test or challenge for the viewer since the body is observed from the inside, rather than cut open with the inside exposed and then reconfigured. Here we actually have to be told which part of the image is blood. The violation is so much less dramatic and the patient so consciously present, that it may be difficult to argue that violation has occurred, though it has. The sense of wonder that is generated here is an intellectualized one, focussed on the capabilities of the technology.

In both instances I want to argue that we are being presented with spectacles, but that unlike the case with cinematic special effects spectacles, here televisual requirements act to ensure that any suspension of the narrative to marvel at the representation is minimal. Most importantly, the commentary holds us close to the continuing stories, especially through emphasising the reality of what we are watching. Television is predominantly an aural medium and the words we hear ensure that we are reminded that this primitive butchery is actually happening to a real person, and that this sequence of shots is actually of the insides of a real man's intestine as he is standing in a doctor's rooms, and that it has been taken by a piece of technology smaller than the man's fingernail. The commentary itself is part of this reality; presented not in voice-over, but by the doctor speaking to the man about his condition and the surgeon speaking to his operating team (ostensibly; he seems to be giving information designed for a lay audience, although directed at his fellows). The distracted viewing that typically characterises our engagement with television, in comparison with the greater attention given the cinematic image, is part of this – made possible by the aural information being so rich and also meaning that sequences when the visual comes to the fore are rendered comparatively more compelling. In addition to these consequences of televisual location, programmes such as these are rarely longer than a commercial half-hour (i.e. 22-23 minutes) so the total time available is quite short. For the most part, and certainly for *RPA*, more than one story is being told in the individual episodes and these are more often intercut, as here, than placed sequentially. The intercutting keeps the viewer from falling too far into the spectacle, since we are only briefly present at each site.

Yet despite the brevity of the sequences showing the procedures and their spectacular character, the mechanisms of engagement that they offer are very different. The operation is comparatively unmediated; the television camera shows us the body opened, violated and displayed and challenges us to watch or look away. The diagnosis is much less challenging, especially since much of our attention is focussed on the wonders of the technology.

To consider this further, I want to go back to the matter of the early medical films scandalously screened to the general public. Van Dijck discusses the case of the 1902 French film of a separation of conjoined twins. The intention of the surgeon, Eugène-Louis Doyen, in having the operation filmed was that it would be used to instruct other doctors and that it would never be screened without a surgeon providing a commentary, but his assistant circulated copies more widely. Doyen sued the assistant and the distributor Pathé to reclaim the copies and prevent them being shown to the general public as entertainment (2002: 543-4). Van Dijck's argument is about the continuity of the screening of the operation with the freak show, a general feature of writing on conjoined twins (see Clark and Myser) that can be applied to varying extents to representation of other medical or medicalised conditions. The context, however, is that in which Tom Gunning's analysis of early film as a 'cinema of attractions' can be applied. Both the film as an example of the marvels of the cinematograph and the content showing the marvels of nature and of science would have been fascinating to the audience of a hundred years ago. It is also worth recalling Gunning's comment that people went to see demonstrations of the cinematograph machines 'as they did for other technological wonders such as the widely exhibited X-rays' (1994: 42); medicine, or at least anatomy, was thoroughly imbricated with entertainment, then as now.

In my examples, these two aspects are more separate, though the intercutting ensures we shuttle between them rapidly. For the operation, the visual technology seems irrelevant, as viewers confront and are confronted by the 'reality' of the violated, revealed body (though as I have suggested above the almost domestic nature of the medical technology involved may draw the attention). For the diagnosis, the visioning technology takes precedence and viewers are invited to marvel at it and what it can do. The fascinations which can be hypothesised are more visceral and, despite the commentary, more visual in the first instance and more intellectual and aural in the second. Discussing the fascination of the Visible Human Project, Catherine Waldby calls on Stephen Heath's term 'machine interest', which he used before Gunning to describe the initial appeal of the technology of the cinematographic apparatus. Walby argues the term's usefulness to describe 'instances where technologies become [...] objects of cultural attention over and above their specific products' (1997: 4). While I acknowledge that one could trace the whole panoply of the medical institution whose operations *RPA* and other programmes display as just such a technology, I do not want to do this since it obscures the distinction between the two examples.

The 'machine interest' so evident in the diagnosis is unavailable in the operation, though this is not always the case; far from it. I chose to examine an orthopaedic example precisely to separate out components that much televised heart surgery, for instance, would collapse. Of recent operations with advanced (visualizing) medical technology, van Dijck has noted how the 'convergence of media and medical technology results in an enhanced sense of the real, the suggestion of increased transparency, when it comes to capturing the activities and anxiety involved in medical operations' (2002: 548). I believe the juxtaposition of the two chosen instances enables this to be taken a little further. Not only does the increased transparency enhance our sense of the real in the case of the swallowed diagnostic camera, but a similar enhanced sense of the real is produced from mediated medicine without much in the way of medical technology, when it presents the blood work of low-tech surgery. The real can be enhanced in more than one way. Only the convergence of technologies provides this through increased transparency, however; it is the primitive arresting power of blood that testifies in the other case.

There remains the matter of the way the two terms 'spectacle' and 'real' interact with televisual infotainment, in both its informational and entertainment aspects. It would be wrong to suggest that the 'real' speaks to the informational while spectacle provides the entertainment, since it has already been shown how central the revelation of the 'real' is to the production of spectacle, both through the indexical exhibition of blood and bone and through the technological marvels of visualising technologies that allow viewers to see the actual functioning of hidden parts of the body without invasion to bring them physically to the surface.

Even though both may be thought to interrupt narrative, both spectacle and information are embedded in narratives which provide much of the entertainment. Standard health narratives have no difficulty in following the classical narrative pattern, as is evident in the outline in which an equilibrium disrupted by the discovery of symptoms is explored before treatment brings closure with a return to equilibrium. Thus while the orthopaedic patient does not receive the desired hip replacement, his condition is still sufficiently improved for the story to end happily. Very few programmes involving operations are broadcast live; there is time for producers to be selective so viewers can be assured that the overwhelming majority of outcomes of televised medical procedures screened will be positive. Every now and then a programme will return to a person who had been pronounced cured or left with alleviated symptoms, to reveal a worsening of the condition. Instances like this tend to shift the programme more fully into the melodramatic mode, where emotions such as sorrow and pity are more readily encompassed; it is rare for these to feature spectacle.

Even stronger is the convention that patients whose operations are displayed continue to live. *Jimmy's* did once include an instance of a patient who died, but whose relatives were persuaded to grant permission for the case to be broadcast for its instructive value to potential patients and their families. The emphasis on the instructive (on information) was in keeping with the genesis of *Jimmy's* in a programme designed to show children facing hospitalisation what the experience would be like. The popularity of this initial short series led to its expansion to deal with adults as well. However common it may be in hospital dramas, death is not at all common in non-fiction medical television.

Despite these exceptions, both dedicated and occasional medical television are dominated by the trajectory from ill-health to cure, with the operation providing the key punctuation. It is worth examining this through the structure of the most pervasive of recent ordinary televisual genres: the makeover. This highly popular ordinary television type follows the case of a person with a problem who, thanks to skilled intervention, becomes a person with the solution. Obviously medical stories differ from 'secret' makeovers, such as those conducted in the gardening programme *Ground Force*, but in many regards the formula is the same. The major difference is located in what those producing makeover shows call 'the reveal', when the transformed situation is shown to the person concerned and viewers observe their reaction. This provides the climax and the affective high point of the programme (Bonner 2003: 130-6). While televised operation stories frequently conclude with the patient revealed as restored to health, providing the pleasure of happy closure, this is not the affective, nor often the dramatic high point; that is here the intervention, the operation, with all its blood, gore and technology. The cured person is the person returned to equilibrium, which is much less exciting, and calls for less viewer affect, than the testing under the knife.

The operation serves as testimony to both the authenticity and seriousness of the experience. There are some actual medical makeovers, where cosmetic surgery produces a transformed individual. Once this would have involved the simple presentation of 'before' and 'after' shots, but this is now less common than items that include intermediary footage of the body under the knife. A British example of this from 2002 occurred in the light documentary *Vain Men*, which inserted graphic footage of the insertion of pectoral and other implants to separate a man's earlier statements of dissatisfaction with his body from his later happier state. The operation shots functioned both to give an element of spectacle and to reduce the extent to which the man could be seen as just a figure of fun. Operations conventionally serve as indexes of pain and the body under duress, so the inclusion of procedures in which the body is exposed, bleeding and violated indicates that viewers are to take the man's dissatisfaction more seriously than might otherwise be the case. The frequency with which cosmetic surgery is shown being performed using the same televisual devices as surgery to treat diseases or rectify the consequences of injury, acts to place it in the same register, making it harder to dismiss as the indulgence of the vain. The televised operations can in these cases be seen as acting in part to promote more widespread adoption.

In conclusion, then, I want to argue that ordinary television provides instances that create a (small scale) spectacle of the real and that arguably the most dramatic of these happen during the operations which are at the core of non-fiction medical television, whether these are invasive or not. Both kinds of televised operation encourage viewers to remind themselves that the events by which they are transfixed actually happened. The invasive examples do this by providing sufficient gore and exposed flesh to produce a spectacular, if gruelling, viewing experience. Those procedures that enter the body without cutting into it rely on visioning technologies that are themselves part of the spectacle at the same time that they provide a view of the actual functioning of normally invisible bodily processes. However the camera gets its pictures, they carry the stamp of authenticity that comes from looking where ordinarily we are forbidden – inside the skin of a living fellow human being.

References

Belling, Catherine (1998) 'Reading *The Operation*: Television, Realism and the Possession of Medical Knowledge'. *Literature and Medicine* 17.1. 1-23.

Bonner, Frances (2003) *Ordinary Television: Analyzing Popular* TV. London: Sage.

Cartwright, Lisa (1995) *Screening the Body: Tracing Medicine's Visual Culture*. Minneapolis: University of Minnesota Press.

Clark, David L. & Catherine Myser (1996) 'Being Humaned: Medical Documentary and the Hyperrealization of Conjoined Twins' in Rosemarie Garland Thomson (ed.) *Freakery: Cultural Spectacles of the Extraordinary Body*. New York: New York University Press, 338-355.

Dayan, Daniel & Elihu Katz (1992) *Media Events: The Live Broadcasting of History*. Cambridge, Mass.: Harvard University Press.

Dijck, José van (2002) 'Medical Documentary: conjoined twins as a mediated spectacle'. *Media Culture and Society* 24.4. 537-556.

Dobson, Roger (2002) 'Broadcast of Star's Colonoscopy Boosts Screening'. *British Medical Journal* May 11, 324.7346. 1118.

Ellis, John (1982) *Visible Fictions: Cinema: Television: Video*. London: Routledge & Kegan Paul.

Gunning, Tom (1994) *D. W. Griffiths and the Origins of American Narrative Film: The Early Years at Biograph*. Urbana & Illinois: University of Illinois Press.

Heath, Stephen (1980) 'The Cinematic Apparatus: Technology as Historical and Cultural Form' in Teresa de Lauretis and Stephen Heath eds *The Cinematic Apparatus*. London: Macmillan.14-22.

Hodgetts, Darrin & Kerry Chamberlain (1999) 'Medicalization and the Depiction of Lay People in Television Health Documentary'. *Health* 3.3, 317-33.

Walby, Catherine (1997) 'Revenants: The Visible Human Project and the Digital Uncanny'. *Body and Society* 3.1. 1-7.

9. Hell in a Cell and Other Stories: Violence, Endangerment and Authenticity in Professional Wrestling

Leon Hunt

Wrestling is the only sport which gives such an externalised image of torture.

(Roland Barthes 1957/1973: 20)

Wrestling has become so good at creating the illusion of disaster that when disaster does hit, it's very difficult to tell the difference.

(Mick Foley 1999/2000: 485)

'That's not real! That's not real!'

(Chant sometimes heard at wrestling matches)

February 2000: The WWF/WWE Pay-Per-View *No Way Out* climaxes in a Hell in a Cell match.[1] Mick Foley (a.k.a. 'Cactus Jack'), beloved by fans for his risk-taking manoeuvres, challenges top 'heel' Triple H for the Heavyweight title as the culmination of a well-established feud.[2] A stipulation adds that if Foley loses, he must retire; an orchestrated pretext for Foley to genuinely retire his battered, damaged body. A Hell in a Cell match, a more violent variation on a cage match, places the wrestlers inside a steel mesh cage.[3] This 'demonic cell' ostensibly promises a brutal environment with 'No Way Out', but it is virtually mandatory that matters come to a head *on top of* the sixteen-foot cage; after all, if you don't climb to the top, how can you be thrown off? At the 1998 *WWF King of the Ring* PPV, Foley (in another persona, the Lecter-masked Mankind) had the most celebrated of all Hell in a Cell matches against The Undertaker, a bout that actually *began* on top of the cage. By the end, Foley had been thrown both *off* and *through* the top of the cage, not to mention being choke-slammed into a mound of drawing pins. At *No Way Out*, Foley and Triple H have a tough act to follow and so they, too, must make their way to the top. Triple H's face wears the proverbial 'crimson mask', soaked in blood. Foley stalks him with a length of wood wrapped in barbed wire, supposedly the instrument of Triple H being (as 'colour commentators' are fond of putting it) 'busted wide open!' The blood is certainly real, even if Triple H has, as in most wrestling matches that shed blood for dramatic effect, most likely inflicted the cut on himself with a concealed blade (the practice of 'blading' or 'juicing').

'What could be worse than a 2-by-4 wrapped in barbed wire?', screams commentator Jerry 'The King' Lawler. He does not have to wait long for the answer – Foley immediately produces a lighter and sets fire to the weapon. He holds it in the air to roars of approval from the crowd, but when he attempts to piledrive Triple H onto the flames, Foley is instead backdropped onto the cage. His body crashes through the roof and onto the ring below which also gives way beneath him. The crowd are audibly impressed; 'Holy shit! Holy shit!' they chant, one of the ultimate accolades.

Blood (and plenty of it!), barbed wire, cages, assorted weaponry ('foreign objects'), fire, falls from high places; these are the stock-in-trade of the so-called 'hard-core' wrestling match, one of the ways in which professional wrestling offers a Spectacle of the Real within an industry known by most of its fans to be staged, that is 'fake'. This chapter is concerned specifically with wrestling's intensification of risk, damage, and self-endangerment as a means of authentication. In exploring this corporeal dimension, I shall consider a pornographic (and documentary) dimension to wrestling's probing of imperiled flesh and bone. Finally, I shall look in more detail at a specific match, Foley/Mankind versus The Rock at the 1999 *WWF Royal Rumble* PPV. I have chosen this particular match because of its documentation across a range of texts; the original PPV (and subsequent video release), Barry Blaustein's feature-length documentary *Beyond the Mat* (US 1999) and Mick Foley's two autobiographies, *Mankind - Have a Nice Day!* (1999/2000) and *Foley is Good and the Real World is Faker than Wrestling* (2001). This extensive documentation, I want to argue, is a search for the 'real' within the fake.

'Not as Fake as You Think': The Real and the *Raw*

Sharon Mazer characterises pro-wrestling as 'a sport that is not, in the literal sense of the word, sporting; a theatrical entertainment that is not theatre' (1998: 3). Even more paradoxically, it is 'the one sport in which participants lose legitimacy when they move from 'amateur' to 'professional'' (4). Amateur wrestling is an authentic (if not especially popular) sport, while the WWE has coined the phrase 'Sports Entertainment' for its staged grappling. Some pro-wrestlers are authenticated by amateur backgrounds, like Brock Lesnar and Olympic gold medal winner Kurt Angle. But Angle – a 'heel' who never shuts up about his medals and whose entrance music facilitates chants of 'You Suck!' – would not be so popular if he did not know how to 'work' a (staged) match. He has good microphone skills, can 'put over' his opponents (make them look good), and even lose convincingly to wrestlers who would not last very long in a 'real' match against him. In other words, he is both (extra-textually) legitimate and the consummate 'pro'. Wrestling is most 'fake' as competitive sport and as a televisual form that 'mimics the structures and visual style of nonfiction television' (Jenkins 1997: 65). WWE's flagship shows *Raw* and *Smackdown!* include supposedly unrehearsed interviews, pseudo-fly-on-the-wall backstage antics, commentators 'surprised' by events; all of these, alongside decisions about wins and losses, 'face'/'heel' turns, long-running feuds and storylines, are the work of the scriptwriters. What professional wrestling takes from legitimate sport, Henry Jenkins suggests, is its implicit narrative and thematic structures (53) – titles changing hands, dramatic reversals of fortune, heroic battles against adversity, career-threatening injuries. Take away the uncertainty (and potential tedium) of actual competition, heighten the drama to 'Soap Opera' levels, push the athletic spectacle to a level of hyperbolic excess – That's (Sports) Entertainment!

One fan guide describes wrestling as 'like a live action movie, with the wrestlers playing dual roles as leads and stuntmen' (Mahoney 2000: 8). Stunts suggest a notion of the 'real' guaranteed by self-endangerment; thus a wrestler can be seen as authentic in the same way that Jackie Chan often is. While no one is meant to believe that Chan's onscreen fights are real, he authenticates himself by documenting pro-filmic risk and injury in the out-takes of stunts gone wrong that accompany the end titles of his films. Elsewhere, I have examined notions of authenticity in relation to Chinese Martial Arts films (Hunt 2003). One of the forms of authenticity I identified there has particular relevance to wrestling. 'Corporeal' authenticity locates the real in evidence of physical danger, in what the star is prepared to subject his or her body to. Mick Foley, like Jackie Chan, has a star persona characterised by self-endangerment, injury and a willingness to endure pain (both theatrical and genuine). The damage to Chan's body is well documented – one stunt almost killed him and left him with a hole in his skull. A famous image of Foley, first appearing on a T-shirt and then the back cover of *Have a Nice Day*, offers a diagram of his injuries; most dramatically, two thirds of an ear is missing after a match in Germany. There is one important difference, however. Chan's version of authenticity disavows the mediation of cinematic technology, offering a version of the 'real' that seeks to transcend editing and special effects; this is also bound up with a small film industry (Hong Kong) challenging and differentiating itself from a big one (Hollywood). Wrestling does not so much disavow as *compensate* for its illegitimacy as sport; it may be less 'real' than, say, boxing, but it can be more dangerous. When Foley reveals that he was briefly unconscious during his famous *King of the Ring* match, he seems to imply that wrestling can be *more* 'real' than sport; 'in a real sport, the action would surely stop if a player was knocked out. But no, we are not a real sport, and no, the action doesn't stop' (1999/2000: 658). Of course, wrestling is heavily mediated, too, by the apparatuses of television, but it also has the status of a live event.[4] When stunts go wrong or their impact is especially *visible* and *tactile*, they will not be recycled as out-takes, they will be inscribed into the main event; they may even make the match a 'classic'. Thus danger and risk take on a heightened presence, and promise a dimension that cannot be fully controlled by the participants. While the camera can just as easily be in the 'wrong' place, making a pulled punch look more fake, reminding us that 'That's not real!', certain images of televised wrestling seem to take us to the heart of the 'real'. During Foley's *King of the Ring* bout with The Undertaker, a famous close-up found one of his teeth stuck to his nose. Foley appeared to be smiling, a signifier of Mankind's deranged persona, but later claimed that he was trying to show his tongue protruding through a hole in his lip (1999/2000: 659). More recently, The Undertaker returned to the Cell against Brock Lesnar at *WWE No Mercy* 2002. When 'Taker was 'busted open', he bled copiously for the remainder of the match, at one point bleeding *into* the camera.[5]

Blood, and the use of folding metal chairs as weapons ('chair shots'), have long been a standard part of US wrestling. In *Exquisite Mayhem* (Cameron and Kelley 2001), a collection of Theo Ehret's black-and-white wrestling photos from the 1960s and 1970s, blood-soaked wrestlers land head first in rows of hard plastic seats, 'Classy' Fred Blassie bites the forehead of an opponent, The Sheik wreaks gory havoc with a variety of 'foreign objects', Abdullah the Butcher prepares to live up to his name. When Vince McMahon, the owner of the WWF, gave wrestling a new TV presence and arena-filling glitz in the 1980s, little of this 'Exquisite Mayhem' made it onto the small screen but was confined to regional, and largely declining, promotions. The generic notion of 'Hardcore' seems to have taken hold particularly in the 1990s, with the Japanese Frontier Martial Arts Wrestling (FMW) and the North American ECW changing its name from Eastern Championship Wrestling to *Extreme* Championship Wrestling. 'Hardcore' went beyond blood and chairs, to embrace fire, barbed wire (wrapped around the ropes, in place of ropes, electrified), broken glass, C4 explosions. FMW staged the first no-rope Barbed Wire Explosion match in 1990, and gave their matches names like 'Explosive Barbed Wire Land Mine Double Hell Time Bomb Death Match'. ECW, under the creative leadership of promoter Paul Heyman, took 'arena-wide brawling, table and ring destruction and stunt wrestling to a new plateau' (Martin 2001: 17). ECW remains synonymous with 'Hardcore' even after its demise and WWE's absorption of its former stars like Rob Van Dam and Tommy Dreamer, the 'Innovator of Violence' – wild stunts are often greeted with chants of 'E-C-dub!' Initially associated with the 'Indie' scene, 'Hardcore' also carried the aura of subcultural authenticity, where, in the words of *Power Slam* magazine, 'scarification became the bizarre badge of honour of the truly hard-core (or truly stupid)' (Hurley 2002: 35). What it lacked in terms of WWE's production values and Olympian stars, it made up for with corporeal audacity and violence; ECW's table-endangering Sabu was billed as 'homicidal, suicidal and genocidal!'

This subcultural (and wilfully 'stupid') dimension is taken further in Backyard Wrestling, the current folk devil of parent's groups, in which teenagers with camcorders slam each other through burning tables.[6] Backyard wrestling tapes make a virtue of their 'amateur' status through a lo-fi aesthetic (camcorder on-screen counters, fuzz and dropout, single camera set-ups) and homemade violence; the 'reality effect' guaranteed by 'ordinariness' that Amy West discusses elsewhere in this volume. Impromptu rings are set up in back gardens, stunts usually staged in well-upholstered rings take place on grass and even gravel; there is even a sub-genre of 'Extreme Trampoline Wrestling'. In other words, the 'everyday' provides fresh, and more 'real', sources of violence and danger. The quintessential Backyard 'spot' is the leap off a roof, usually onto a prone body lying on an eminently breakable table. This subcultural dimension flirts with the illegal; one match in *The Best of Backyard Wrestling* (2000) ends with the wrestlers being arrested. Early Backyard tapes carried an aura not dissimilar to snuff or violent porn; suburban teenagers mutilating each other for an underground 'grey' market. But as it sought semi-pro legitimacy, Backyard needed to disavow its more extreme associations. *Best of Backyard Wrestling* mocks the 'lard bucket pantomime dames of professional wrestling', but in its 'Don't Try This at Home' intro, challenges the 'misconception' that 'all backyard wrestlers are untrained'. Rather, they 'have spent countless hours practising and choreographing shows with safety in mind'. Professionally produced Backyard tapes and discs promise authentic danger and violence in 'everyday' settings, but temper it with a sense of the absurd ('Oh, he throws the cactus at him!'). Thus, they move closer to the good-natured 'stupidity' of reality stunt/prank shows like *Jackass* and *Crazy Monkey*.

'Hardcore' violence was co-opted by the WWF in the late 1990s as part of a calculated image change from the family values of Hulk Hogan and his 'Little Hulkamaniacs' to the edgier 'Attitude' era of Stone Cold Steve Austin and silicon-enhanced 'Divas' engaging in Bra-and-Panties matches. As WWF became more adult-oriented (albeit 'adult' in the most adolescent sense of the word), 'Hardcore' gave wrestling's mainstream a bit more authenticity. *Power Slam* observes that at *King of the Ring*'s Foley/Undertaker clash, the 'big boys had muscled in on ECW's territory' (Martin 2001: 19). But the WWF's notion of 'Hardcore' was more contained than the blood-soaked promotions it imitated; its more 'extreme' matches were confined to special matches and selected performers. Its now-defunct Hardcore division and title alluded vaguely to an anything-goes dimension more often than not manifested in poorly staged matches involving dustbins, shopping trolleys and kendo sticks.

At the start of *Beyond the Mat*, Barry Blaustein sets out his own position of belief. 'I know wrestling is a show', he acknowledges, 'but it's not as fake as you think – the result of the violence is *very* real'. But even the blood blurs the line between the 'fake' and the 'real'. On the one hand, blood is, as Mazer suggests, 'the most vivid sign' that 'the game has passed from simulation to actuality' (1998: 64). But the fact that it is largely self-inflicted pushes it towards the 'fake' again; albeit, a self-mutilating fakeness which may constitute another kind of 'real'. That blood is often referred to as 'juice' (a particularly bloody match is sometimes called a 'juice job') makes it sound like the 'Money Shot' of pro-wrestling. But as porn theorists such as Linda Williams (1990) argue, the Money Shot – the image of (external) male ejaculation in explicit sex films – is as much a substitute for the real as the (unrepresentable) thing itself. The phrase 'busted wide open' seems to testify to wrestling's pornographic (and documentary) 'desire to see and know more of the human body' (36).

From Money Shot to Chair Shot: Wrestling's 'Hardcore' Aesthetics

The word 'Hardcore' already suggests a pornographic dimension, in Williams' sense of a 'frenzy of the visible'. Pornography, as Tanya Krzywinska suggests, displays an investment in 'the encoding of "authenticity" and verisimilitude' (1998: 159), the 'generic promise to show everything and hide nothing' (165). In wrestling, the Hardcore gaze is embodied in fans' desire to see corporeal evidence of the real within a fictional spectacle. The 'sight of bodily pain' is one example Williams gives of a frenzy of the visible (203); the marks on naked flesh in S/M porn find their correlative in the red hand marks left by huge slaps in wrestling. Punches invariably look fake when pulled, but while slaps seem strangely 'unmanly' for such macho icons, they do leave physical evidence of the real. Roland Barthes' famous essay, 'The World of Wrestling', touches on this sado-erotic dimension – wrestling is an 'exhibition of suffering' (1957/1973: 20), with the wrestler frequently 'crucified in broad daylight and in the sight of all' (22). But like other forms of body-knowledge, the spectacle of suffering has to be taken partly on trust. Even the visible can, as Williams argues, only 'seem' to guarantee the reality of its referent. Extra-textual information plays a role here. Williams cites Marilyn Chambers' profession of the 'reality' of her on-screen pleasure and Linda Lovelace's claims of violent coercion; 'attentive viewers who have read Lovelace-Marchiano's story can look for the bruises on her body' (203). Similarly, Mick Foley's autobiographies promise to reveal body-secrets, those 'bumps' that really hurt and the injuries sustained. But this corporeal authentication is dependent, in some respects, on its mediation. Foley claims not to remember the *King of the Ring* match clearly, a result of the fall through the cage knocking him out, but 'video and time have helped me to not only see but remember almost everything' (1999/2000: 656). *Beyond the Mat* further supports this version of events by including an 'incoherent and rambling' message left on Barry Blaustein's answerphone after *King of the Ring* in which a euphoric-sounding, but slurred, Foley says 'they tell me it was good; I don't remember too much about it'.

Two pieces of wrestling terminology, seemingly polarised but in fact closely linked, are suggestive here; the 'work' and the 'shoot'. A 'work' is another word for a match, pointing to the performed, constructed, narrative qualities of wrestling; grapplers often talk of good matches 'telling a story'. To 'work' is to draw the audience into this performance, to 'sell' one's opponent's moves or 'put them over', to make fans suspend their disbelief. Contrary to a real competitive bout, some wrestlers are heavily criticised by fans for not putting others 'over', making their offense look weak; such selfishness both transgresses the collaborative nature of wrestling and makes a match less exciting to watch. But this, too, points to another 'hidden' dimension sought out by the fans' gaze; the locker-room politics that determine storylines and match outcomes. A 'shoot', on the other hand, is an unplanned or illegitimate excursion into the real; 'the plan is forsaken, an accident occurs, or a genuine conflict erupts with the violence spilling over from display to actuality' (Mazer 1998: 22).[7]

The dividing line between a 'work' and a 'shoot' is less a matter of the degree of violence than consent; Foley talks about the necessity of 'respect for your opponent's body' (1999/2000: 115). At the risk of wearing out the analogy with S/M, what seems important is the idea of a contract between wrestlers, an agreement over how much pain/damage is acceptable. For wrestling fans, the 'shoot' carries a frisson of authenticity, but how can they know it when they see it? Gullible wrestling fans are known as 'marks', yet Mazer suggests that even the more knowledgeable fans look to experience the real just as they 'revel in their own deception', celebrating 'the moments when they "marked-out"' (167). In this respect, 'Holy shit!' seems to translate into something like 'You made me believe'. This 'phantom of the real', as she calls it, 'is at the heart of professional wrestling's appeal' (167). But if phantoms are incorporeal – the 'ghostly' presence of media images – wrestling's real is ultimately sought in documentary evidence of the endangered body.

Beyond the 'Crimson Mask': Documenting the Body

Several times a year, I look at something and I say, 'This is going to be dangerous and it could turn out real bad, but it's got to be done for the sake of history'.

(Mick Foley, *Beyond the Mat*)

Beyond the Mat focuses on three wrestlers, former WWF star Jake 'The Snake' Roberts, and two 'Hardcore Legends', battle-scarred veteran Terry Funk and the younger, but scarcely less damaged, Foley. The film does not want for drama; Roberts' awkward reunion with his estranged daughter, Funk's emotional 'final match' (there would be many more, in spite of the severe degenerative arthritis in his knee). But the film's most powerful scenes follow Foley and his family – wife Colette, son Dewey and daughter Noelle – to the 1999 *Royal Rumble*. At the top of the card, Mankind defends the Heavyweight title against The Rock, still in his 'heel' phase ('The Corporate Champion'). It is to be an 'I Quit!' match; the loser will utter those words into a microphone after enduring an unimaginable beating.[8]

The Rock seems to be at a disadvantage; Mankind has never given up and seems to positively embrace pain. But what this really promises is that 'The Most Electrifying Man in Sports Entertainment' will dig deep into the well of unconscionable violence and take Foley to the brink. This is the 'work', then, but Foley's accounts of the match, written after its emotional appearance in *Beyond the Mat*, represent it as one which got out of hand, went beyond the contract and veered dangerously close to a 'shoot'.

The video sleeve of *The Royal Rumble* describes it as 'the most brutal match in federation history'. According to Foley, it was always planned for his wife to be there and, originally, for her presence to be incorporated into the 'work' (2001: 14); her distress would help to 'sell' The Rock as Barthes' 'perfect bastard' (1957/1973: 24). This was later changed and no reference is made to her by the commentators. The WWF broadcast avoids shots of Foley hugging Colette on his way to the ring that are seen in *Beyond the Mat*. She is only visible in the background during some of the out-of-ring action.

Beyond the Mat emphasises not only Colette's presence, but that of their two small children; we see them chatting with The Rock about a Disneyland visit, Foley reassuring them that the man who will shortly batter him senseless with a chair is daddy's friend. As The Rock rehearses and then delivers a characteristically slick promo, Blaustein's camera finds a nervous, pacing Foley; ominous non-diegetic music intensifies the feeling of impending doom. Blaustein keeps a camera on Colette, Dewey and Noelle throughout the match; there are a few winces early on (at least, the way the scene is edited), but they are on their feet as Mankind pursues The Rock onto a balcony. As Foley is pushed off onto a monitor, diegetic sound drops from the soundtrack, replaced by the song 'Stand By Me'. Isolated shots of each family member watching are intercut with 'flashbacks' of Foley playing with his kids or with Colette. As diegetic sound returns, we are into the chair shots; Foley handcuffed and helpless, The Rock pounding his skull. The Foley family are visibly and audibly distressed. Colette screams at each chair shot, tries to shield the children's eyes. Dewey and Noelle, both in tears, look terrified, and are led from the arena by their mother.[9] Backstage, a bitter Foley hopes that the audience got 'their money's worth', although later proudly claims that 'we touched a lot of people' as the huge gash in his head is stitched. This is emotive footage in any form, albeit undeniably manipulative. Notwithstanding Blaustein's profession of his status as fan, these are the sort of scenes one might expect in an effects-based critique of wrestling. When Foley watches Blaustein's footage, he observes sadly that 'I don't feel like such a good dad anymore'.

However, within the discourses of wrestling, *Beyond the Mat* further authenticates the match, and Foley's autobiographical accounts address Blaustein's film as much as the bout itself. Foley does not exactly represent the match as a 'Shoot', yet implies that The Rock exceeded the bounds of the contract; five (agreed) chair shots became eleven, microphone work allowing Foley to recover largely disappeared (2001: 22, 29). He also reveals that he underestimated how the handcuffs would diminish his ability to absorb the chair shots (28). According to Foley:

> *professional wrestling is at its best when the performers lose their own sense of disbelief and begin to actually 'feel it'. In a sense, the match becomes real, or at least real in that they actually 'become' their character, and actually 'feel' what the storyline is attempting to make the audience feel. As I took the beating up the aisle, I lost that sense of disbelief and began to actually 'feel' that I was the wounded Mankind, so beat-up that I could hardly stand.*

(24)

But an excess of the 'real' shocks him into something *too* real: 'my defiance was gone, as was my sense of disbelief. I knew exactly what was going on. I was in a match that had gotten carried away – I was suffering a great deal – and I wanted it to end' (32). Foley becomes legitimately angry – 'I looked The Rock in the eye and dared him to knock me down' (29) – and his opponent fails to pick up on nonverbal cues to deliver one last 'knockout' blow (is this wrestling's equivalent of the 'safety word'?)

But in pro-wrestling's Hardcore discourse, 'too real' can be just real enough; Foley even tells us of his ideas for incorporating his resentment towards the Rock into a storyline (1999/2000: 724-8). I am not, for one minute, suggesting that Foley's family's distress was anything but genuine (albeit uncannily close to the 'work' as originally conceived), but it has become part of the complex mythology of the match. The original PPV plays differently in the light of its documentary and autobiographical representations; we know that his family are just out of camera shot, we know when his jaw dislocated and The Rock went too far. Or do we? If *Beyond the Mat* appears to intensify (guarantee?) the reality of the 'I Quit' match, it also becomes part of a particularly labyrinthine 'work'. In any case Blaustein creates his own 'work' – the use of 'Stand By Me', the constructive editing, the commentary ('the sight of Mick being beaten up in front of his family haunted me'). In other words, in wrestling's violent spectacle, the 'real' and the 'fake', the 'work' and the 'shoot' are profoundly embedded in one another.

References

Aaron, Michele (ed.) (1999) *The Body's Perilous Pleasures: Dangerous Desires and Contemporary Culture*. Edinburgh: Edinburgh University Press.

Barthes, Roland (1957/1973) *Mythologies*. London: Paladin.

Cameron, Jamie and Kelley, Mike (eds.) (2001) *Exquisite Mayhem: The Spectacular and Erotic World of Wrestling by Theo Ehret*. Koln: Taschen.

Chatra, Mohamed (2001) 'So You Wanna Be a Wrestler?', *Power Slam* 83, 32-5.

Evans, Anthony (2001) 'Hard Men', *Power Slam* 82, 22-5.

Evans, Anthony (2001) 'Hard Men 2: Cashing In', *Power Slam* 88, 30-3.

Foley, Mick (1999/2000) *Mankind - Have a Nice Day!* London: Collins Willow.

Foley, Mick (2001) *Foley is Good and the Real World is Faker than Wrestling*. London: Collins Willow.

Hunt, Leon (2003) *Kung Fu Cult Masters: From Bruce Lee to Crouching Tiger*. London and New York: Wallflower Press.

Hurley, Oliver (2002) 'Wild Things', *Power Slam* 93, 34-5.

Jenkins, Henry (1997) ' "Never Trust a Snake": WWF Wrestling as Masculine Melodrama', in Aaron Baker and Todd Boyd (eds.) *Out of Bounds: Sports, Media and the Politics of Identity*. Bloomington, Indianapolis: Indiana University Press, 48-78.

Krzywinska, Tanya (1998) 'Dissidence and Authenticity in Dyke Porn and Actuality TV', in Mike Wayne (ed.), *Dissident Voices: The Politics of Television and Cultural Change*. London: Pluto, 159-75.

Mahoney, Jeff (ed.) (2000) *Checkerbee Fan Guide: Wrestling*. Middletown: Checkerbee Publishing.

Martin, Fin (2001) 'The Rise and Fall of ECW', in *Power Slam* 82, 16-19.

Mazer, Sharon (1998) *Professional Wrestling: Sport and Spectacle*. Jackson: University of Mississippi Press.

Twitchell, James B. (1992) *Carnival Culture: The Trashing of Taste in America*, New York: Columbia University Press.

Williams, Linda (1990) *Hardcore: Power, Pleasure and the "Frenzy of the Visible"*. London, Sydney and Wellington: Pandora.

Notes

1 In 2002, the World Wrestling Federation was forced to change its name after losing a long-running dispute with the World Wildlife organisation over the use of the initials 'WWF'. Recovering face with a suitably aggressive 'Get the F out!' campaign, the one-time 'Federation' changed its name to World Wrestling Entertainment. My use of the initials 'WWF' and 'WWE' in this paper is based on when cited matches and events took place.

2 Professional Wrestling hinges on a Manichean distinction between 'heels' (villains) and 'babyfaces' (heroes). 'Babyface', however, has increasingly become something of a misnomer for the more anti-heroic wrestlers of contemporary wrestling. The most popular 'face' of recent years is Stone Cold Steve Austin, the hard-drinking, middle-finger-giving 'bionic redneck' with an ongoing grudge against his (both real and fictionalised) boss, Vince McMahon.

3 A cage match has no roof on the cage – the most frequent route to victory is by *escaping* the cage. When combatants 'escape' from Hell in a Cell, fans know that things are just beginning.

4 This is certainly true of WWE PPVs and 'Monday Night' *Raw*, both of them broadcast live. *Smackdown!*, on the other hand, has been known to do re-takes of fluffed or dramatically unclear moments in matches, especially if they have particular narrative significance.

5 'Juicing' usually seems to produce just enough blood to cover the wrestler's face. The Undertaker, by accident or (attention-getting) design, seemed to cut himself deeper than usual; sections of the ring were stained crimson.

6 Little wonder Mick Foley is known as the 'Hardcore Legend'. As a teenager, he shot early versions of Backyard Wrestling and wrestled for FMW and ECW before bringing his particular brand of mayhem to the WWF.

7 The word 'shoot' is also sometimes applied to competitive combat sports such as the mixed martial arts/boxing/grappling Ultimate Fighting Championship.

8 The twist, not revealed until a subsequent *Raw*, is that Mankind only *appears* to quit. The Rock and the evil McMahons have made creative use of a tape recording of Mankind warning the Champion what *he* will say at the *Rumble*.

9 Comparing the soundtrack of the WWF tape to *Beyond the Mat*, they seem to have endured the entire match, but Blaustein's editing makes it look like they left before the end.

10. Docobricolage in the Age of Simulation[1]

Bernadette Flynn

Simulated factuality

Arguments by documentary theorist John Corner that we might be moving into a post-documentary period echo concerns raised earlier by Brian Winston that the documentary is facing some type of crisis (Corner 2000b; Winston 1995, 1999). These concerns are often placed in relation to the impact of new media technologies such as Web TV, Internet spycams, and interactive voting games. Richard Kilborn is one commentator who has argued that their use in contemporary forms of television such as reality TV and the docusoap have reconfigured notions of the 'real' away from the authentic towards the voyeuristic or fabricated (1994).

At the heart of these hybrid documentary forms is a playfulness that Corner casts as entertainment, diversion and a lightness of topic or treatment (2000b). Such a response reinforces a general belief that playfulness and the game-like challenge the purity of the serious documentary form and perhaps reveals an underlying Griersonian suspicion of pleasure.[2] This paper argues that, rather than signalling an unravelling or a dumbing down of documentary's purpose, emerging forms of factuality point towards more localised and participatory forms of communication that have been effaced in 'discourses of sobriety', with their distrust of the popular (Nichols 1991). Such 'gamedocs', rather than being an entirely new phenomenon, belong to the lineage of nineteenth-century *fin de siècle* experiments with their mix of the exotic, the factual and the illusionistic, as illustrated by the films of Méliès, early motion simulators and pre-cinematic games. Along with the panoramas, dioramas and mutoscopes, these phenomena contained elements of popular education and gaming that are now re-emerging in new forms of popular factual entertainment through computer visualization and simulation models.

My aim here is to frame these more interactive and playful types of factuality as a shift towards a new logic of simulation associated with the aesthetics of primarily symbolic or simulated actuality generated by computer systems and game engines. Such an aesthetics is most apparent in documentary's borrowing of game scenarios and play elements and the adoption in computer games of a type of factuality through AI (artificial intelligence) and the rules of emergence.[3] In applying the intervention of creative strategies, the simulated image moves beyond evidence and witness in a manner that evokes Grierson's notion of 'a creative treatment of actuality' (Nichols 1991). Rather than being inferior representations of actuality, simulation models instead provide sophisticated ways of modelling social behaviour and articulating real world conditions.

My focus is on the reality television program *Big Brother* (Australian *Big Brother 3*, 2003) and the computer simulation game *The Sims* (2000) as examples of convergence across interactive gameplay and documentary that express a similar self-conscious, playful, sometimes critical exploration of the authentic-seeming. In *Big Brother*, the housemates' playful mimicry and mastery of the rules of the house and audience involvement through telephone voting and SMS messaging function to extend the show from television event into gaming session. In *The Sims*, there is an extensive borrowing of the visualisation codes and observational documentary techniques used in *Big Brother*. These techniques are married with the rules of AI emergence in order for the player to observe and play with human-like behaviours.

Such an assemblage of appropriated documentary material and game techniques can be seen as a type of docobricolage or media poaching (from the French term bricolage for tinkering). The bricoleur (producer and to some extent audience/player) crafts and tinkers with materials lying around in the media landscape. Patched-up strategies from observational documentary, bits and pieces from network gaming, and re-worked models from medical and military simulations are incorporated into the hybrid projects of *Big Brother* and *The Sims*. In such examples of simulated factuality, documentary's cultural cache as the site of the real is combined with the instability and turbulence of emergent systems. These experiences move beyond simple notions of authenticity or representations of factuality to explore normalized models of sociality and in this sense model a more complex and responsive analogy of lived experience.

Cinéma vérité and the authentic-seeming

Commentators have noted how reality TV and *The Sims* take up aspects of the observational documentary (see, for example, Dovey 2000; Roscoe 2001; Winston 1999). From the late 1950s, practitioners of the US Direct Cinema movement asserted that shooting in sequence, the long take, the jumpcut and avoiding voice-over narration or the interview would permit a more accurate representation of reality. Contact between subject and camera operator/director was reduced to the absolute minimum to create the 'fly-on-the-wall' effect. Albert Maysles argued: 'To be really governed by reality you have to stick a camera in a wall, just like a fly on the wall, let it operate on its own' (Plante,2002: para 8). At the same time, in France, the *cinéma vérité* movement had similar aspirations towards veracity, but with a greater acknowledgment of the constructed nature of documentary production. As further evidence of reality, they included the image of the filmmaker on screen and applied extensive selection and editing. These strategies, with their sense of detached observation (direct cinema) and co-authorship (*cinéma vérité*) are evident in both *The Sims* and *Big Brother* as ways to suggest authentic relations within the dynamics of the domestic suburban environment.

The Sims emerged in 2000 from a simulation series developed by Will Wright in the tradition of arcade and training-based simulation. In *The Sims*, the player creates simulated humans in suburban homes and attempts to balance their needs for eating, sleeping, financial gain and social interaction against a tendency towards entropy and anarchy. *The Sims* uses AI and emergent properties to display lifelike behaviours and mimic social relations. Through these lifelike behaviours and *believable enough* social interactions, the Sim avatars become akin to a type of documentary subject within a nostalgic representation of US suburbia, complete with picket fences, regular newspaper delivery and neighbours who call by with cakes.

In an attempt to create a place of authenticity or emotional purchase through the vehicle of the simulated 'real' experience, *The Sims* adopts the observational documentary techniques of direct cinema and *cinéma vérité*. For game designers, the success of the simulation game rests on the same notions of believability that are central to the observational documentary. As Sherry Turkle comments, simulations enable us to think through questions about the construction of the real: 'What we are willing to count as real? What do our models allow us to see as real? To what degree are we willing to take simulations for reality?' (Turkle 1995: 73).

In *Big Brother*, the modes and conventions of observational cinema are imitated and exaggerated, to play with the boundaries between fact and fiction. On the one hand, the show deliberately draws attention to, and exposes the construction of, the television apparatus and the on-screen subjects; on the other hand, it constructs the householders as personal and intimate documentary subjects. Under the scrutiny of multiple cameras, the householders are legitimated as both authentic documentary subjects and simulacra in a virtual environment. *Big Brother* quite deliberately exploits the space between aspects of dramatic realism (the personal, subjective) and those of the artificial and performative. It is in this marginal space between the real and the simulated – in the 'flickers of authenticity' (Roscoe 2001c) – that one of the fascinations of the *Big Brother* project resides. In its visual coverage from wide aerial shots to eye-level close scrutiny, *Big Brother* vacillates between the direct address of participant film-making and a distinctly surveillance-camera point of view. In so doing, it reinforces and valorises both the voyeuristic and the intimate aspects of its programming. This splices notions of social control and visual neutrality associated with surveillance together with the notions of intimacy and subjectivity associated with the domestic camcorder (albeit simulating them through the extensive professional recording and editing apparatus) (Dovey 2000). The 35 hidden cameras and 40 hidden microphones (in

Big Brother 3 Australia) suggest that nothing will escape our gaze, that we are witnesses to all the intimate interactions in the household. In the diary room of the *Big Brother* house, the dynamic between the housemate and 'Big Brother' significantly extends the logic of the provocateur role of *cinéma vérité*. As Dovey points out, these approaches link to forms of the confessional associated with the lineage of soap operas and video diaries (2000).

In *The Sims*, the 'camera' viewing angles are created by player-controlled simulated cameras created digitally in real time. These 'cameras' adopt the aesthetic regimes of observational documentary techniques, and manipulating them becomes central to controlling the characters' actions and movement. The player, behind the virtual lens, is able to manipulate the speed of household events to play with the Sim avatar, build onto the house, shop for household goods or capture screen images for the html photo album. In *The Sims* the high angle – similar to the perspective of many games – is both a surveillance aesthetic and a 'God's eye view' that mimics and parodies the 'fly-on-the-wall' detached view of direct cinema. From this elevated isometric viewing position, the player can both direct the movement of the 'camera' and observe how the Sim avatar responds to the environment and other Sims.

The use of multiple perspectives is common in other computer games, including cameras at each point of the compass that can be switched at will; the chase-cam; the cockpit-cam and the famous shoulder-cam over Lara Croft's shoulder in *Tomb Raider*. In both game and reality TV households, players/audiences get to explore, practice and evaluate positions of constructed authenticity. For *The Sims* this play comes closer to the traditional concerns of documentary in attempting to represent the real.

In *Big Brother*, the mix of soap opera, *cinéma vérité* and game show tropes moves from the idea of the real towards that of the game event. From this position, any residue of the serious documentary shifts into a collision of simulated gestures, gameplay and increased audience engagement. Dovey usefully positions this shift towards simulation in relation to changing cultural circumstances as the world moves from nation state models towards global frames and markets (2003). As other commentators have also argued (Corner 2000b, Bondebjerg 2003) the nation state (and its association with public responsibility, civic life and social community) has become increasingly less relevant as a model for understanding contemporary life. In this context, the traditional documentary functions of exposition, observation and testimony (to use Corner's categories) are often inadequate to the task of assessing and interpreting current cultural changes and experiences. As Dovey suggests, increasingly complex models, such as simulation systems, are perhaps more useful ways of producing knowledge and interpreting real world phenomena. Such models not only take into account the uncertainties of everyday life and a re-evaluation of identity and ethics, but also enable a participatory 'embodied, direct and material' engagement with the underlying conditions of sociality (Dovey 2003). In such engagement, ethical values or underlying historical forces – once seen as central to documentary concerns – are absorbed into a responsive system of dynamic and variable outcomes.

Spatial Domesticity

Spatial construction and navigation of the house and garden is central to playing *The Sims*. In play mode, even without player-driven mouse action, the Sim avatars continue to move through space and engage in on-screen activity. The representational code of these navigable spaces is adapted from architectural modeling and the cinema to visualize the way humans and architectural spaces interact. As director, camera operator and production designer, the player has an active role within the visualization and is able to enjoy mastery of the environment through consumption of household goods, architectural construction and navigation. This sense of agency combines the fly-on-the-wall view with a vicarious sense of presence. While the player can direct a Sim to an activity in the environment, the environment itself is also responsive. Using terrain mapping, objects such as the fridge, toilet, chairs and bathtub are programmed to act as attractors. For example, when a Sim passes the fridge, it will send out a message: get food. Wright was initially more interested in architectural systems than people systems. In an original brief, the game was a simulation of a doll's house and enabled the avatars to walk around and comment on the environment built by the players (see Wright 2001). Elements of this approach remain in *The Sims*. If unhappy with the player's choice of interior design such as décor, furnishings or entertainment systems, an avatar will turn and directly express annoyance or displeasure through angry gestures and symbols that appear in comic-book speak bubbles above their head. For many players, the building and exploration of simulated domesticity is as significant and pleasurable as developing avatar-based social relations.

In creating believable worlds, reality TV also relies on the construction of exploratory spaces and the subject's navigation through screen space. The housemates/players spatial navigation – whether of an island, airport or the interior of a house – constitutes one of the main objectives and audience viewing pleasures of the reality TV formats. In *Big Brother 3*, housemates are set challenges day and night to position them into suitable camera viewing zones across the limited spatial dimensions of the house/houses. Reggie receives a challenge from Big Brother to add salt to the milk. Her action not only triggers debates about trust within the household but also ensures that housemates move between fridge, sink, cupboard and sugar bowl to try to resolve the problem. The construction of fabricated problems operating within simulated environments with simulated risks evokes the popular late 19th-century simulations. One simulation from 1892 represented the sinking of the French ship *Le Venger* during the revolutionary war against the British in 1792. As described by Vanessa Schwartz, spectators mounted the deck of *Le Hussard*, which pitched back and forth to the sound of gunfire, cannons, a chorus singing the Marseillaise and two actors reciting a lyric poem about the accomplishment of the sinking ship (Schwartz 1995). Early simulations, such as the sinking of *Le Venger*, established particular ideas about virtual mobility and spatialisation which can be traced through the filmic simulations of travel, such as Hale's Tours of 1905-1912, and which are reinvigorated in the spatial navigation in computer gameplay and in the more domesticated simulations of *Big Brother* and *The Sims*. [4] In *Big Brother* and *The Sims*, the action, exploration and colonization of the space become the central apparatus for the way stories emerge, as the characters apply the rules of the game to navigate and locate themselves through the house or terrain. Narrative and representation become subservient to navigable geography, mastery of the simulation environment and the pleasures of gameplay. This represents a shift to the agency of navigation based on emergent story and spatial exploration, away from documentary arguments, constructed debate or drama-based pre-determined causality.

In both *The Sims* and *Big Brother*, the minutia and triviality of domestic life – such as visiting the bathroom, washing dishes, emptying rubbish bins and watering plants – form the repetitious goal-orientated gaming activities. Players of *The Sims* and housemates in *Big Brother* must engage with these mundane activities of domestic order and maintenance in order to succeed in the game. For housemates in *Big Brother*, the house becomes the play environment and stage for modeling or performing domesticity to win audience approval. In *The Sims*, reduction in cleanliness or too radical a departure from the normal routines of domestic life will result in the Sim avatar becoming sick, refusing to eat and go out to work or, in a worst-case scenario, collapsing and dying. These activities create an electronic present that is strangely more compelling than undertaking the same activities in physical domestic space.

Jon Dovey draws on Ib Bondebjerg's work in arguing that the fuel for new reality genres (which I would extend to *The Sims*) is a new awareness of the self in public and private life (Dovey 2003). Dovey suggests that the intensification of our innate social curiosity, as reflected in the popularity of reality TV, is part of a broader cultural shift from observational to more reflexive ways of understanding the world. To use Dovey's terms, programs such as *Big Brother* actively produce the conflicts and practices of everyday life to explore issues of gender, power relations and sexual politics. However, unlike the tradition of *cinéma vérité*, with its emphasis on observable politics, these issues are treated as a form of popular entertainment. Evidence collected from surveys indicates that audiences respond to *Big Brother* primarily as a form of sociable team sport (see Jones, 2000; Johnson-Wood, 2002).

Corner describes this pleasure as 'a snoopy sociability' in which the viewer is 'an amused bystander to the mixture of mess and routine in other people's working lives' (Corner, 2000b). These popular forms of factual entertainment associated with the home and the feminine subsume documentary from Nichol's focus on arguments about the historical world into a concern with the minutiae of domesticity (Nichols 1991). Thus, local forms of communication marginalized in Nichol's 'discourses of sobriety' as trivia, chat and gossip are able to re-emerge. In this re-emergence, entertainment and life politics, the game and the documentary come together to create a simulated exploration of everyday domestic life based on playfulness.

Cybernetics for modeling behavior

As systems for simulating realism, *Big Brother* and *The Sims* deploy different but associated cybernetic models or game rules for exploring and understanding human sociability and thus engaging audiences/players. 'A typical simulation consists of a number of agents that are given an environment to live in and some rules to follow' (Ryan 2001:63). By changing variables the user can experiment with the model and experience different simulation outcomes. These simulation environments then conform to what Dovey describes as network logics, in which all events and behaviors may have multiple determinants and variable outcomes (2003). This is not to suggest that the player is engaged in detached observation of system dynamics. Instead, my argument is that the player is dynamically engaged with these systems in a gaming form of social learning that models suburban life. Gaming has been broadly described as ludic after the Latin term *ludus* for games. However using Roger Caillois' definitions more precisely, ludus is an institutional form of play at the opposite end of the spectrum to *paidea*, uncontrolled anarchic play (see Frasca 1999; Darley 2000). From these definitions, I would argue that *Big Brother* and *The Sims* operate more as paidic than ludic play spaces. Rather than any simple winning and loosing rule-based scenario, human relations are played out through the introduction of emergent disorder and turbulence in the space of the home.

One element that is foreground by this renewed focus on simulation as a method for constructing an impression of factuality is the redundancy of any residual belief in the neutrality of the camera lens. Since the development of photography, the image produced by the camera lens has been considered to have a close indexical relationship to a real-world referent. Underlying its status as the primary tool for observation and recording of the physical world is a belief in the objectivity or neutrality of the lens in capturing actuality. At the same time as cultural studies and documentary film theory have contested the ability of the camera lens to reproduce the real, the camera continues to retain its position as the privileged interface between the real world and its representation. In contrast, computer simulation models have been considered somehow suspect. As Nichols, remarks: 'The simulation displaces any antecedent reality, any aura, any referent to history. Frames collapse. What has been fixed comes unhinged. New identities, ambivalently adopted, prevail' (Nichols, 1996: 127).

Games like *The Sims* highlight the fact that digital simulations are complex and dynamic systems that create increasingly convincing representations of human behavior and sociability. *The Sims* is one of the most popular desktop computer games and has significant proliferation through photo albums that are posted on the Web (Sims version of 'my home page'), 'skins' (character or environment texture maps that players can design and import into the game) and the development of theme-based communities in *The Sims Online*. [5] Many players develop Sim households that explore their own family and relationship situations and develop significant bonds with their simulated creatures. The gameplay then occupies a similar position to the observational documentary in constructing the appearance of a lived situation. Indeed Mark J.P. Wolf puts forward the argument that a simulation might be special mode of documentary – a subjunctive documentary in the way that it employs simulation models to offer what might happen rather than to shape or construct a fixed subjectivity (Wolf 1993). In addition to the player's attempt to manipulate the Sims' identity and daily experiences, the avatar and the environment itself respond in unpredictable ways to reflect credible and often unexpected dynamic social interaction. The simulation relies on the believability of both the cybernetic self-regulating feedback loops and the emergence of behaviors that are not predicted by players, or even at times, the game designers. For example, what happens when a burglar steals an avatar's possessions? What happens if an avatar has not urinated? What happens when an avatar has a baby? Wright takes the position that human life on personal and social levels can be simulated, claiming that: '*The Sims* is really just a game about life' (Fehlauer, 2000). The underlying logic of *The Sims* is the maintenance of the status quo through the purchase of commodities. In order to increase happiness and develop social contacts, the avatars must move towards greater economic and social efficiency through buying products and technologies. The priority in the game is on keeping your Sims alive and happy (or subverting the rules of the game by making them unhappy and trying to kill them). In attending to the well-being and life (or destruction and misery) of these creatures, the player learns about their responses and engages in a dynamic feedback mechanism. This results in strong emotional attachments such as those associated with *Tamagotchi* or other virtual pets. As Stephen Poole describes it, *The Sims* is 'an open-ended process toy that attempts to simulate complex social relations' (2000: 250). This toy operates on potential events and probabilities – the 'what if' – opening up other possibilities and types of 'realism', away from the tyranny of the monocular camera lens.

Documentary codes and practices and techniques of simulation may seem like strange partners in the construction of factuality, as evinced by crisis narratives referenced at the beginning of the paper. The examples from *Big Brother* and *The Sims* mark a convergence across simulation worlds, interactive gameplay and documentary that are not altogether new, but relate to older and often ignored histories of representing the real. What is significant about these projects is the self-conscious, playful, sometimes critical exploration of factuality they incorporate. Their re-emergence in contemporary digital media opens up the traditional models of documentary to a different logic of media communication. This is one in which forms of sociability such as conflict, reflection and insight arise from within simulation environments, and through participatory engagement, rather than from an externally imposed narrative-based causality or a pre-formed argument. *The Sims* and *Big Brother*, as examples of hybrid factuality, construct a type of *docobricolage* which, rather than seeking to usher in a period of post-documentary (Corner, 2000), play with documentary forms and simulation techniques and their relationship to the real. In the resulting engagement with the more popular and interactive form of the game event, they constitute an exploration of how truth and identity are constructed. As such they belong to a broader context of cultural experiences that adopt a self-conscious, sometimes critical relationship to the authentic-seeming.

References

Bondeberg Ib (2003) 'The social and the Subjective Look: Documentaries and reflexive modernity'. Australian International Documentary Conference, Byron bay, February 2003.

Corner, John (2000a) 'What Can We Say About Documentary?' *Media, Culture and Society*, vol. 22, no. 5, pp. 681-88.

— (2000b) 'Documentary in a Post-Documentary Culture'. European Science Foundation, Changing Media – Changing Europe Program, Team One (Citizenship and Consumerism), Working Paper No. 1.

Darley, Andrew (2000) *Visual Digital Culture, Surface Play and Spectacle in New Media Genres*. London and New York: Routledge.

Dovey, Jon (2000) *Freakshow: First Person Media and Factual Television*. London: Pluto Press.

— (2003) 'Reality television game shows and the order of simulation'. 'Staging Reality' conference, Stirling, January 2003.

Fehlauer, Mike (2000) *Lord of The Sims*, Master game designer Will Wright discusses *The Sims*, Accessed online at www.playcenter.com/PC_Games/interviews/will_wright_the_sims.htm

Flynn, B (2002) 'Factual hybridity: Games, Documentary and Simulated Spaces', *New Factual Forms*, Media International Australia, no 104, August, 2002.

Frasca, Gonzalo (1999) Ludology meets narratology: Similitude and differences between (video) games and narrative, Accessed online at http://www.jacaranda.org/frasca/ludology.htm

Jones, Janet (2000) 'Big Brother – Whose Life are we Living Anyway. Consoleing[HP1] Passions conference, Bristol.

Johnson-Woods, Toni (2002) *Big Bother*. Brisbane: University of Queensland Press.

Kilborn, Richard (1994) 'How Real Can You Get? Recent Developments in 'Reality Television'', *European Journal of Communication* vol. 9, no. 4, pp. 421-39.

Nichols, Bill (1991) *Representing Reality*, Bloomington: Indiana University Press.

— (1996) 'The Art of Culture in the Age of Cybernetic Systems', in T. Druckrey (ed.), *Electronic Culture, Technology and Visual Representation*. New York: Aperture.

Plante, Mike (2002), *Albert Maysles,* Cinemad, no. 6. Accessed online at www. Cinemadmag.com/print_issue_six_albert _maysles.htm

Poole, Steven (2000) *Trigger Happy*: *The secret life of Videogames*, London: Fourth Estate.

Roscoe, Jane (2001a) 'Real Entertainment: New Factual Hybrid Television in New Television Formats', *Media International Australia incorporating Culture and Policy*, no. 100, pp. 9-20.

— (2001b) '*Big Brother* Australia: Performing the 'Real' Twenty-four-seven', *International Journal of Cultural Studies*, p. 4.

— (2001c) 'Flickers of Authenticity: Performing the Real', Visible Evidence IX, Brisbane, 17-20 December.

Ryan Marie-Laure (2001) *Narrative as virtual reality: Immersion and Interactivity in Literature and Electronic Media*. Baltimore: Johns Hopkins University Press.

Schwartz, Vanessa R. (1995) 'Cinematic Spectatorship before the Apparatus: the Public taste for reality in Fin-de-Siécle Paris', Williams, Linda (ed.) *Viewing positions - ways of seeing film*. Rutgers University Press.

Turkle, Sherry (1995) *Life on the Screen: Identity in the Age of the Internet*. New York: Simon and Schuster.

Winston, Brian (1995) *Claiming the Real*. London: British Film Institute.

— (1999) 'The Primrose Path: Faking UK Television Documentary, "Docuglitz" and Docusoap', *Screening the past*, no. 8. Accessed online at www.latrobe.edu.au/screeningthepast/firstrelease/fr1199/bwfr8b.htm

Wolf, J. P. Mark (1993) 'Subjunctive Documentary: Computer imaging and simulation', Gaines, Jane and Michael Renov (eds) *Collecting Visible Evidence*. Minneapolis: University of Minnesota Press, pp 274-291.

Wright, Will (2001) 'Design Plunder', keynote address at Game Developers Conference, accessed online at www.gamasutra.com/features/20010323/bytd_01.htm

Notes

1   This paper draws on and extends arguments from my previously published article: *Factual Hybridity: Games, Documentary and Simulated Spaces*, Media International Australia, no 104, August, 2002.

2   The more serious moral edification aspects of John Grierson's theories of documentary contain a certain suspicion of pleasure.

3   AI uses computer programs to model aspects of intelligent behaviour – mostly symbolic aspects, sometimes physiological. Emergence is the concept of some new phenomenon arising in a system that was not initially in the system's specification, enabling new global forms to arise from local interactions.

4   In Hale's Tours, audiences boarded a train simulation to watch footage designed to represent passing scenery. Another example of early simulation is the short lived Cinéorama, in which the audience stood in a wicker basket to watch a wide screen panorama from ten synchronised projectors to simulate being inside a hot air balloon flying over Paris.

5   *The Sims* has been hailed as the best selling PC/Mac game of all time, selling 6.3 million copies worldwide (Business wire: 21 March 2002). *The Sims Online* launched in early 2003 which intersects in very interesting ways with a number of the ideas highlighted in this paper. However, discussion of this remains outside the scope of this paper and will be taken up elsewhere.

Part III: Film

11. A Production Designer's Cinema: Historical Authenticity in Popular Films Set in the Past

Michele Pierson

The Australian film critic, Adrian Martin, put his finger on something when he suggested in a review of *Moulin Rouge!* (Baz Luhrmann, 2001) that the film was 'all set design but no real mise-en-scéne' (2001: A3, 5). Here we have one of those risky, 'what if' propositions whose very formativeness is their most productive quality. As is so often the case with this kind of writing (and not only film reviewing but academic writing too), there is less fun to be had in dismissing Martin's claim as obviously counter-intuitive than in asking: what *might* it mean? After the Academy of Motion Picture Arts and Sciences awarded Catherine Martin (Art Direction) and Brigitte Broch (Set Decoration) the award for best art direction at the 74th Academy Awards there would, of course, be those who would say that like the Academy, this remark merely registered the local and not so local gossip that *Moulin Rouge!* more strongly bears the imprimatur of its production designer than that of its director.

If production designers themselves are to have any say in the matter, however, it has to be said that there is not a production designer working today who does not insist that the role of the production designer is to realise the creative vision of the film's director. Or, as Vincent LoBrutto's description of the job would have it: 'the production designer researches the world in which the film takes place to capture a sense of authenticity and render the director's vision to celluloid reality' (1992: xi). Adrian Martin himself would most certainly have resisted any attempt to be drawn on speculation about the nature of the collaborative partnership between Baz Luhrmann and his production designer wife. His comment on the absence of 'real mise-en-scéne' in *Moulin Rouge!* is, in fact, more properly considered alongside the work of Siegfried Kracauer. For like Martin, Kracauer had also felt that some film-making choices inevitably place a strain on the relationship between production design and mise-en-scéne. Kracauer, however, understood this tension to be less a product of any one film's unique circumstances of production, than of a more general condition of certain types of film-making.

The more general condition of film-making that I am interested in thinking about here is the condition of setting films in the past. This condition had also interested

Kracauer in *Theory of Film: The Redemption of Physical Reality* (1960). My own approach to thinking about the way that popular films deal with the past engages in a critical interrogation of Kracauer's assumption that, because viewers of historical film are likely to remain 'conscious of the efforts going into [their] construction', the authenticity of these films' re-creations of the past will necessarily be in question (1978: 77). I want to suggest that the 'staginess' that Kracauer associates with films set in the past does, indeed, condition the way that viewers engage with them: just not necessarily in the way he suggests. Other conditions that impact on how the authenticity of a film is determined by audiences – conditions that have a still more general applicability – might be suggested.

One of way of understanding the tension between production design and mise-en-scéne that Martin identifies in *Moulin Rouge!* might be to see it as arising out of circumstances in which, instead of being integrated into the actual staging and filming of the action, the realisation of a number of aspects of production design has been deferred until post-production. The contemporary production designer is not only responsible for choosing locations and overseeing set design and décor, but also for deciding whether a set should actually be built or whether it should be created in whole or in part with computer-generated imagery (see Ettedgui 1999: 10). While these kinds of decisions are made in consultation with a director, any decision to delegate a substantial part of set construction to a visual effects supervisor will also have an impact on the kind of environment the director has to work with on-set. The extent to which the physical intangibility of this environment will mean that directors have less scope for control over the look of the film will depend, in part, on individual directors and their ability to make a not yet (fully) realised setting intellectually and emotionally tangible for actors and crew.

In cases where the nature of settings and/or the style of production design for a film is such that audiences too may be more or less aware of the conditions of their production – more or less aware of the physical intangibility of environments, objects, and even characters seen on-screen – some styles of performance may also be more effective than others at assuring audiences that these settings are still inhabited by and meaningful to characters played by actors. Martin was not the only viewer to complain that the acting in *Moulin Rouge!* 'comes in only two modes – star turns from Kidman and McGregor, and quirky, often tiresome eccentricities from everyone else'. Nor was he the only one to feel that, all things considered, McGregor also 'registers as the one completely convincing element in the movie' (2001: A3 5). Like other actors of his generation (but, perhaps, most notably Johnny Depp and Edward Norton), McGregor's performance style places less emphasis on virtuosity and craft (in the manner, say, of an actor like Kevin Spacey or the wonderfully histrionic Philip Seymour Hoffman), than on what can only be called 'sincerity'.

Lionel Trilling reminds us that the word 'sincerity' is typically taken to refer 'to a congruence between avowal and actual feeling' (1972: 2). What remains suggestive about his account of the historical 'rise' and 'decline' of sincerity – its slide into anachronism and eclipse by the more morally strenuous term 'authenticity' – is the idea that sincerity was brought into disrepute by a creeping instrumentality. Far from implying an 'unmediated exhibition of self', it came to insinuate the intervention of performance: or, in Trilling's words, the 'fulfilment of a public role' (9). In some sense, of course, all contemporary film actors are required to convey sincerity in their public role as actors. It is their job to convey the impression that public performance can still give expression to 'actual feeling'. Whereas an older generation of actors conveyed sincerity through a combination of learned technique and the refinement of individual gestures and mannerisms, today it is those actors whose performance styles are least clearly defined by a recognisable personal or 'emotional idiolect' that seem most sincere (see Naremore 1988: 197). It is younger actors' less studied style of performance that today communicates sincerity to their younger audiences (consider, for instance, the warm response that Eminem's performance in *8 Mile* (2002) received from both audiences and critics).

Naturally, it is also those actors whose publicity most consistently reports on their ambivalence about Hollywood and its star system who are the most strongly identified with this performance style. Reports of Norton's privacy, Depp's move to France, and McGregor's London residence, all work to place them at some personal remove from Hollywood. The casting of McGregor and Liam Neeson in *Star Wars: Episode 1 - The Phantom Menace (1999)* provides one of the more obvious examples of the way performance sometimes gets called upon to address the potential for tension between production design and mise-en-scéne under circumstances in which significant elements of the production design are disarticulated from the physical staging of the action. For much of the responsibility of convincing audiences of the emotional reality of the films' virtual sets and computer-generated characters falls on these actors' performances, and their ability to convey a sense of meaningful interaction between them. In allowing the actors in *Gladiator* (2000) to speak in their own accents, Ridley Scott also calculated that if there was a sacrifice to be made in terms of historical verisimilitude, it would be more than made up for by performances that would come across as less 'actorly' and therefore more sincere.

Moulin Rouge! and *Gladiator* are also both films set in the past: the first, a musical set in Paris in 1899, the latter an historical epic set in ancient Rome. Since films set in the past often require the re-creation of vistas, environments and material artefacts that no longer exist in the here and now, their settings have often been among the most recognisable as the work of design. As the example of *The Phantom Menace* makes clear, however, this is not a circumstance unique to period films. The settings in many science fiction and fantasy films, musicals, adventure and horror films also have the look of having been designed. Since the decision to leave the actual creation of sets or parts of sets to post-production is made as often (if not more often) by production designers and directors working within the genres of science fiction and fantasy, this is not a condition of filmmaking specific to films set in the past either. Kracauer's own grouping of historical with fantasy film is a reminder of this. It might still be argued, however, that both of these circumstances – the need to re-create the past for the present and the decision to re-create it in post-production – expand production designers' contributions to (if not exactly control over) mise-en-scéne.

All films that have what Charles and Mirella Jona Affron call a high degree of 'design intensity' have to try to resolve the problem of how to make sets that exhibit degrees of invention ranging from studied whimsy to the highly stylised and even the pictorial *feel* authentic to audiences (1995: 116). This is because audiences still want to experience films as authentic no matter how fantastic their settings and indeed their narratives might be. If, for the museum curator, determining the authenticity of an artefact involves verification of the circumstances in which it was produced, the term 'authenticity' means something quite different when it is used to describe a dimension of aesthetic experience. All films set in the past offer a number of solutions to the problem of providing audiences with a re-creation of the past that can be experienced as authentic, including (as I have already suggested) appealing to the sincerity of star performances. In a great variety of popular films set in the past – among them films such as *Moulin Rouge!, Gladiator, The Mummy* (Stephen Sommers, 1999) and *The Mummy Returns* (Stephen Sommers, 2001), *Sleepy Hollow* (Tim Burton, 1999), *Crouching Tiger, Hidden Dragon* (Ang Lee, 2000) or even something like *Kate and Leopold* (James Mangold, 2001) - the problem of how to make sets that have a high degree of design intensity look and feel authentic is one that is often addressed most powerfully and persuasively through production design.

With the possible exception of *Gladiator,* all of the films just listed are much more likely to be identified by audiences and critics according to genres such as the musical, fantasy-adventure, horror, sword-fight film or romantic comedy than as historical films. While scholarship on the historical film has long wrestled with the question of which types of films can or should be included in the category, the impulse of recent work in this area has been to recognise that all kinds of films, and not just bio-pics or films based on historical events, put history to use (see Landy 1996: 1-29). Some of this scholarship has been particularly concerned to stress the differences between the kinds of historical representations found in much popular cinema and those found both in scholarly historiography and in those forms of historical drama specifically concerned with re-creating past lives and events. In their introduction to a collection of essays on British historical cinema that includes discussion of costume dramas, *Carry On* films and examples such as *Zulu* (Cy Endfield, 1964) and Kenneth Branagh's *Henry V* (1989), Claire Monk and Amy Sargeant suggest, for instance, that their readers hardly 'need reminding that a "historical" film will often be a work of pure entertainment and pure fiction' (2002: 4). With their mix of exotic historical settings, visual effects and fantasy narratives, films such as Moulin *Rouge!, Crouching Tiger* and *The Mummy* certainly make entertainment and, in particular, the enjoyment of their inventive settings and effects a high priority.

For all this blatant invention and patent artifice, these films nevertheless make history an important site of subjective investment for audiences. But the kind of historical remembering that they enact is not *only* the stuff of historical actuality. Much popular cinema is only selectively and unevenly concerned with staging the kinds of historical representations that ask audiences to believe that 'this really happened like this' or that 'things really looked like this in the past'. These kinds of concerns may not have been entirely absent from the minds of Luhrmann, Martin and Broch when they embarked on the making of *Moulin Rouge!,* or even from those of the team of artists and designers who worked with Stephen Sommers to re-create ancient Egypt or Cairo in the 1920s for the *Mummy* trilogy. But all of these films just as obviously present audiences with a whole other set of criteria for engaging with their re-creations of the past.

That it is through their own production histories that many popular films set in the past most strongly impress upon audiences a sense of their real historical significance, is something on which both Vivian Sobchack, and more recently, Philip Rosen have commented. In her insightful and acerbic account of the historical epics that came out of Hollywood in the 1950s and 1960s, Sobchack makes the point that this cinema offered the historical 'eventfulness' of its own production – announced through the monumental scope of its production design and through the widespread promotion of the monumental expenditure required to realise it for the cinema screen – as its guarantee of authenticity, assuring audiences that no amount of labour or expense had been spared in the making (1990: 28). New releases of these old widescreen epics on DVD are, of course, being accompanied by extensive production notes that not only give details about the eventfulness of their original production, but also of their subsequent restoration. The production notes for a recent DVD release of *Spartacus* (Stanley Kubrick, 1960) take care, for instance, to point out that its restoration in the early nineties was the most extensive in history.

In his examination of the production history of historical epics such as Cecil B. de Mille's *Cleopatra* (1934), Rosen is particularly interested in the way research is used to authenticate the re-creation of the past. He argues that promotional assurances that producers have made every effort to make sure that sets, props, costumes – indeed every detail of the historical epic's elaborately rendered mise-en-scéne – has been thoroughly researched by a team of advising experts, offers audiences a de facto guarantee that the artefacts of the past seen on-screen are historically accurate (or as accurate as cinematic, and especially genre, conventions will allow). Since this type of promotional material also foregrounds the process of actually making these films and, in particular, the labour that goes into realising mise-en-scéne, this type of production discourse also makes an explicit appeal to audience appreciation of the real creative labour that has gone into their production.

Although Rosen's examination of popular films set in the past pays particular attention to the way in which the historical detail and production of their mise-en-scéne grounds them in a researched and 'documentable profilmic', his discussion of the musical *An American in Paris* (Vincente Minnelli, 1951) also addresses the question of how a film's mise-en-scéne can appear 'so overwhelming, so extravagant, so playful, so performative as opposed to referential that we call it spectacle', and still offer audiences an experience of the real (2001: 193). One answer to this question has already been given. As is the case whenever special effects are foregrounded for audience attention, those elements of mise-en-scéne that most strongly have the look of having been designed also most strongly invite appreciation of their creative realisation by production and visual effects designers. However, it is not only Rosen's argument that the 'showily artificial' settings in *An American in Paris* celebrate the virtuosity of their designers, but also that by grounding their origins in researched sources – in this case, impressionist paintings of the period in which the film is set – they still make history (in this case 'art history') the real site of their authentication.

Charles Tashiro, who along with the Affrons has written one of the few scholarly monographs on production design published in English, has also commented on the use of paintings in films set in the past. Tashiro's interest is more specific than Rosen's, focusing on those relatively rare occasions when films depicting a real historical event meticulously reproduce the mise-en-scéne of a historical painting that is already well known for its depiction of the same event (1996). For both of these writers, the self-conscious referencing of paintings in films performs two functions. On the one hand, the mise-en-scéne of the past acquires greater authenticity for audiences because it accords with the understanding they have acquired of it through contact with other modes of historical representation. And, at the same time, individual viewers' exercise of the (art) 'historical capital' necessary for identifying the self-referential nature of this kind of aesthetic choice itself provides the feeling of engagement they associate with the experience of authenticity (Pierre Sorlin cited in Tashiro 1996: 20).

Among the more popular films listed here, the production design for *Gladiator* is, perhaps, the least design-intensive. But even so, Ridley Scott and production designer Arthur Max have spoken at length about their sources of inspiration, citing not only the 'romantic vision of Rome' found in a number of nineteenth-century British and French paintings, but also films like Leni Riefenstahl's *Triumph of the Will*; recalling that '[w]e copied *them* [Nazi propaganda films] copying the Romans, which added an extra layer and another cultural interpretation' (Max cited in Magid 2000: 55). While discussion of the self-referential and even baroque nature of a popular cinema that consistently makes reference to its own history the most satisfying site of content for at least some of its viewers has certainly been taken up in other contexts, this aspect of popular cinema has less often been addressed within the context of the way these films depict the past (for an exception see Tashiro 1998 and Cartmell et al. 2001). Through the allusiveness of their production design and through promotion and discussion of their production in the popular and mass media – but perhaps most importantly through the commentary and bonus material that is increasingly packaged with DVD releases – many popular films also offer audiences identification of their detailed referencing of artworks, but especially other films and film styles, as one of their most satisfying sites of authentication.

Any one of the films listed here so far could be used to further illustrate this point. In an account of the making of *The Mummy Returns* in *Cinefex* – a publication that is neither a fan magazine nor a trade publication but is avidly read by both film fans and film professionals (but perhaps most significantly in this day and age, by film students) – every person contributing to the film describes their work in terms of the films that served as inspiration and model. If the direction for the film's matte paintings of London was to make it 'look like *Mary Poppins*', research for the film also included going back and looking at *Lawrence of Arabia,* at *Spartacus,* at 'all the great battle sequences from *Barry Lyndon*' (Fordham 2001: 127), which are also such important references for *Gladiator.*

It is a detail about an early sketch for one of the more fanciful settings in *The Mummy Returns,* however, which has the most to say about the 'historicity' of production design in many popular films set in the past. The sketch – of the main characters sailing toward a mythical pyramid – is credited not only with being reminiscent of the work of Ray Harryhausen, but of being 'the first real design that captured the period romance and epic sweep of that part in the movie' (Fordham 2001: 14). The really telling part of this anecdote concerns, not the referencing of Harryhausen, but the detail that to achieve the right look, the sketch was 'scanned and tinted sepia in Photoshop'. Sepia has, of course, come to function as the colour of history in all sorts of popular cultural contexts. Think, for instance, of the photographs that visitors to many living history museums and theme parks can have taken of themselves as mementoes of their experience: their modern selves transported back into the past through the magic of mise-en-scéne and sepia toning. As Robert Brent Toplin has also pointed out in his recent defence of Hollywood's treatment of history in the United States, 'the History Channel features this color icon in its brownish orange logo and in the background sets in its studio' (2002: 13).

While research on the use of colour in early cinema suggests that in this period of experimentation colour tended not to be used to signify temporal shifts, so much as to mark its own, highly unregulated appearance as a temporal event in itself, conventions for using colour to evoke the past developed rather quickly after the 1920s (see Hertogs and de Klerk 1997). In contrast to the use of Technicolor in the 1950s and 1960s to imbue epic cinema's spectacular mise-en-scéne with a special vividness and intensity, the practice of using black and white to signal temporal shifts in narrative has, for instance, long been conventional for more serious and/or melodramatic films. More contemporary popular cinema has developed its own system of colour coding for capturing the period romance of 'olden times'. If the colour of the past in *The Mummy* and *The Mummy Returns* is not exactly sepia, these films' palette of sand, gold and brown nevertheless extends to every aspect of their production design – from buildings, costumes and lighting to the many digitally created sets – washing everything in a golden brown hue that is not so very far from it either. This use of colour is even more obvious in *Kate and Leopold,* which plucks its time-travelling romantic lead out of a brown nineteenth century and hurls him into the living colour of modern times. Toplin gives another, less obvious but more widely cited example of the use of a modified sepia palette to colour the past, reminding us of Steven Spielberg's desire to give the opening scenes of *Saving Private Ryan* (1998) 'the appearance of an old newsreel' (13).

The association of sepia with history has its beginnings in the nineteenth century. When early photographs faded they lost their metallic lustre and took on a brown tinge. One way of thinking about the colour of the past in popular film, then, might be to suggest that to really give its settings historical authenticity, popular film not only remembers old films – through, for instance, the techniques of allusion, homage and pastiche – but also gives them something of the colour and grain of old techniques of photographic and cinematographic reproduction. In the opening sequence of *Moulin Rouge!,* it is not so much colour as the simulated flicker of early cinema that gives the film its period look. E. Elias Merhige's art-house film, *The Shadow of the Vampire* (2000), likewise insists that its film-within-a-film look like old film. *The Shadow of the Vampire* recreates the making of F. W. Murnau's *Nosferatu* (1922), casting John Malkovich as Murnau and Willem Dafoe as the actor-vampire Max Schreck. For early scenes depicting the shooting of the film, the rolling of the camera motivates a transition from colour cinematography to grainy black and white. But the 'real' *Nosferatu* (i.e. the version actually made by Murnau) has also been incorporated into the film: serving, at one moment, as an establishing shot of the ruined castle in which the film is being shot and, at another, as a glimpse of the film-in-progress. The latter occurs just after Schreck has sucked the living daylights out of one of the hapless crew under the cover of a momentary blackout during shooting. As Murnau sets about restoring order to the set, Schreck plays with a projector on which the film-in-progress is spooled. The film that Schreck glimpses – the film-within-the-film – is the real *Nosferatu*. For a brief moment, it fills the cinema frame, every scratch, every artefact of decades of wear and tear lovingly preserved.

Signs of the material deterioration of Murnau's film guarantees its authenticity for viewers in a way that no attempt to restore it to the time of the film's diegesis, when it was new, pristine, and still to be remembered, could have done. By inserting an old film where a new one should be, viewers of this arty, sometimes camp, and occasionally ponderous film, are invited to savour cinema's fragile materiality. But what of other films that re-create the past, not just through allusion to old paintings and films, but also by giving them something of the look of having been made at an earlier time: how might the terms in which these films lay claim to historical authenticity be understood? Even some of the films that appear to be the least concerned with whether or not their re-creations of the past accord with 'how things actually were' present audiences with a layered, multivalent imagining of the past that asks for their participation in making it *feel* authentic. To suggest that a wide range of popular films set in the past offer viewers the opportunity to participate in the exercise of a number of different modes of historical recognition and knowledge – in what might even be described as a form of popular historiography – is not to suggest that there might not also be reasons for being suspicious of a cinema that makes this exercise such a satisfying end in itself. It is, however, to again be reminded that under these conditions the authenticity of aesthetic experience is finally decided by audiences themselves.

Not even Eric Rohmer gets to circumvent audience desires to make these kinds of determinations without risking losing their interest. Earlier, I suggested that any time there is the possibility that audiences will become aware that significant elements of a film's mise-en-scéne are not actually present for actors, production design becomes an especially important site for addressing their desire for the film to look and feel 'right' or authentic. While art cinema audiences bring a different set of criteria to their viewing of more experimental works, any historical film that stakes its claims to authenticity on a singular vision of the past nevertheless still takes a risk. For *L' Anglaise et le Duc/ The Lady and the Duke* (2001), a film set during the period of the French Revolution, Rohmer had the idea of using scenic backgrounds painted in the style of the period to recreate outdoor scenes of Paris in the late eighteenth century. Live action footage of actors filmed before a blue screen were keyed into these backgrounds in post-production. Asked to comment on this decision, he replied: 'Yes. I don't much care for photographic reality. In this film, I depict the Revolution as people would have seen it at the time' (Ferenzi 2001). For viewers, though (and I mean viewers sympathetic to the spirit of creative experiment that this enterprise entails), the trouble with Jean-Baptiste Marot's paintings is that after the first few scenes, there is nothing more to discover in them: no surprise encounters with familiar but forgotten memories of other paintings, other films, await. Does the past recover in this gesture the quality of fundamental and unrecoverable difference from the present? Perhaps. But the film's conceit is to imagine that recourse to a 'highly visible artifice' is itself a sufficient condition for illuminating this truth. For all the obvious aesthetic and cultural conservatism of more popular, mass-market films, one of the things that they have going for them is that they long ago worked out that this kind of determination is not theirs alone to make.

Through the highly visible artifice of their own production design, many popular films create past worlds in which it is not so much the likeness of these worlds to historical actuality that is calculated to appeal to audiences, but the conventionality, familiarity and accessibility of their historical references. Not all viewers have the kind of (film) historical knowledge that might enable them to identify *The Mummy's* debt to Harryhausen, and fewer still may actually have seen the early films that provided the inspiration for the opening sequence of *Moulin Rouge!* But by filtering the colour and texture of old photographs, newsreels and films through their production design, these films also give the past an historical authenticity that is more broadly, popularly, accessible.

References

Affron, Charles and Mirella Jona (1995) *Sets in Motion: Art Direction and Film Narrative.* New Brunswick, NJ: Rutgers UP.

Cartmell, Deborah, I. Q. Hunter and Imelda Whelehan (eds.) (2001) *Retrovisions: Reinventing the Past in Film and Fiction.* London, Sterling, Virginia: Pluto Press.

Ettedgui, Peter (1999) *Production Design and Art Direction.* Woburn, MA: Focal Press.

Ferenzi, Aurélien Ferenzi (2001) 'Interview with Eric Rohmer', *Senses of Cinema,* no. 16, Sept-Oct. Accessed online at http://www.sensesofcinema.com/contents/01/16/rhomer.html, 31 July, 2003.

Fordham, Joe (2001) 'Warrior Kings', *Cinefex,* no. 86, July: 13-30, 127-9.

Hertogs, Daan and Nico de Klerk (eds.) (1997) *Disorderly Order: Colours in Silent Film.* London: BFI.

Kracauer, Siegfried (1978) *Theory of Film: The Redemption of Physical Reality.* London, Oxford, New York: Oxford University Press.

Landy, Marcia (1996) *Cinematic Uses of the Past.* Minneapolis: University of Minnesota Press.

LoBrutto, Vincent (1992) *By Design: Interviews with Film Production Designers.* Wesport, Conn. and London: Praeger.

Magid, Ron (2000) 'Rebuilding Ancient Rome', *American Cinematographer,* vol. 81, no. 5, May: 54-9.

Martin, Adrian (2001) Review of Moulin *Rouge!, The Age* 24 May: A3 5.

Monk, Claire and Amy Sargeant (eds.) (2002) *British Historical Cinema: the history, heritage and costume film.* London and New York: Routledge.

Naremore, James (1988) *Acting in the Cinema.* Berkeley, Los Angeles, London: University of California Press.

Rosen, Philip (2001) *Change Mummified: Cinema, Historicity, Theory.* Minneapolis and London: University of Minnesota Press.

Sobchack, Vivian (1990) '"Surge and Splendor": A Phenomenology of the Hollywood Historical Epic', *Representations,* 29: 24-49.

Tashiro, C. S. (1996) 'When History Films (Try to) Become Paintings', *Cinema Journal,* vol. 35, no. 3, spring 1996: 19-33.

Tashiro, C. S. (1998) *Pretty Pictures: Production Design and the History Film.* Austin: University of Texas Press.

Toplin, Robert Brent (2002) *Reel History: In Defense of Hollywood.* Lawrence, Kansas: University Press of Kansas.

Trilling, Lionel (1972) *Sincerity and Authenticity.* London: Oxford University Press.

12. The New Spatial Dynamics of the Bullet-Time Effect

Lisa Purse

The Matrix (1999) is a generic hybrid: an action film that engages with a number of concerns familiar from science fiction literature and science fiction film. Certainly since its inception science fiction as a genre has been directly concerned with human beings' social and physical relationships to and interactions with technology. In contemporary science fiction, current (and currently imagined) technological developments inflect these concerns in particular ways. Mark Poster observes that, following on from the prevalence of multi-channel television and an increasingly visual media culture, the 'effect of new media such as the internet and virtual reality [...] is to multiply the kinds of "realities" one encounters in society' (1995: 86). A recurring idea in science fiction, familiar from the literature of Philip K. Dick, for example, is that the reality we perceive may not be 'reality'; that it may be a simulation or perceptual trick, and, further, that such a simulation or 'false reality' may be under someone else's control. This idea has found new currency in cyber-culture and in the wider culture, with the developments in interactive virtual reality technology and the creation of different worlds and interactions over the Internet, alongside scientific developments in fields such as genetics. The ways our lives are mediated electronically have forced us to question our perceptual cognition. Richard Wright has identified a series of recent movies that reflect this concern, taking 'their inspiration from a media critique which sees the new information societies as having created and imposed on their populations a form of organisation structured by mediated forms of experience' (2000). These include *The Truman Show* (1998) and *eXistenZ* (1999), in which apparent reality is revealed as a television show and an inescapable game respectively. Such films explore our anxieties regarding our lack of control over the mediated realities existing in our everyday lives.

The Matrix is set in a future where sentient machines have conquered the earth and humans have been reduced to a 'power source', kept subdued in huge battery farms by a computer simulation into which they are plugged. A computer hacker, Neo, discovers that the everyday world he inhabits and perceives is in fact this computer simulation, the Matrix program. From this briefest of summaries, the two characteristically 'science fiction' concerns that underpin this narrative are clear: how technology is impacting on our human lives; and whether we can trust our perceptual cognition of our world.

The film addresses these concerns through both its narrative and its visual style. Both modes of address combine in the moments of 'bullet-time'. Bullet-time is achieved using a combination of conventional camerawork and special effects. The scene is initially shot using conventional cameras, with the path of the camera movement mapped out using computers. More than 100 still cameras are rigged up in a line along the path of the camera movement, circling the action. These take a series of still images that can then be animated, allowing the filmmakers the freedom to vary the speed of the camera movement in relation to the event taking place. Thus, during bullet-time, while an event plays out in slow motion, the camera appears to move around the action at a higher speed and in a different direction.[1]

Michele Pierson observes that 'all special effects represent a mode of visual display that privileges aesthetic novelty over realism' (2002: 156), and the reality is that, like so many other special effects that were new for a moment, one could argue that bullet-time is now just another step in the ongoing quest to find the next, newest, amazing effect. So in a sense, in trying to consider the dynamics of the bullet-time special effect, in its seminal debut appearance in *The Matrix* in 1999, we have to do a little time-travelling of our own, back to the first time we witnessed the bullet-time effect, watching *The Matrix* on a large cinema screen when the film was released. At the time, I was impressed by the newness and seamlessness of the effect, since I had not seen anything quite like it before. But there was something else about the effect which made it seem uniquely contemporary, a response perhaps to our cultural impulse towards the immersive or interactive spectacle. If bullet-time's novelty factor ensured audiences' rapturous responses, what was it that made bullet-time different and new in the context of other contemporary special effects? I am interested in how the spectator's conventional spatial relationship to the cinema screen, and to the action taking place in the filmic world, seems to work differently during moments of bullet-time. I want to consider how the term 'hypermediacy' might help to describe the impulse behind this special effect, and how temporal manipulation increases its impact. I also want to locate bullet-time in the context of our contemporary technological and media culture.

Action and spectacle cinema shows us the most spectacular images while trying simultaneously to convince us of their verisimilitude, through the use of state-of-the-art computer-generated images. Phillip Hayward and Tania Wollen observe how 'the illusion of the real has had to be made more convincing and the spectacular has had to be made more "realistic"' (1993: 2). But this is not simply a case of making the fictional appear seamlessly real. There is a continual striving for a higher level of immediacy of the spectacle, and a higher level of immersion in the moment. Tom Gunning has shown how these impulses were present in cinema at the turn of the nineteenth and twentieth centuries (which was also a time of great technological developments), in what he terms the 'Cinema of Attraction'

(1986: 2), but we can also link these impulses to contemporary concerns about our spatial and temporal positions in an increasingly technologised world. Sherry Turkle has described the current cultural context in terms of 'the story of the eroding boundaries between the real and the virtual, the animate and the inanimate, the unitary and the multiple self, which is occurring both in advanced scientific fields of research and in the patterns of everyday life' (1996: 23), and I have already mentioned a number of recent films that have reflected cultural anxieties regarding human beings' multiply-mediated existence. In our technologised environment, as in the film, the screen and the image it carries become a central metaphor for constantly mediated reality. The screen is both a surface on which images appear and a 'window' onto a different world, it is both a boundary and an avenue. Is it a coincidence, then, that *The Matrix* seems to be preoccupied with screens and surfaces? Not just the many computer monitors, but glass windows, mirrors, and reflective sunglasses and clothing. Smooth surfaces indicate non-permeable barriers, strength and self-containment, but such surfaces can also be transgressed, broken, or manipulated. As Neo sits waiting to be freed from the Matrix program, he stares at a reflection of himself in a cracked mirror, but the cracks suddenly appear to repair themselves. When Neo reaches out to touch the mirror to verify what he has seen, the mirror surface unexpectedly yields to his touch, becoming a gel-like substance which works its way up Neo's arm. Even those surfaces whose nature we think we know reveal unanticipated qualities.

The foregrounding of reflective screens and surfaces points to the film's thematic concerns with technology, interfaces, cyberspace, and the boundaries between the real and the virtual. But such foregrounding also links to the film's preoccupation with its own visual style. Within the film itself, commodities such as mobile phones and sunglasses are photographed – displayed – fetishistically; close-ups linger over their reflective surfaces and sleek lines. In a similar way, *The Matrix* self-consciously displays itself as a commodity, a special effects movie to be consumed and enjoyed. Combining generic characteristics from science fiction and action-spectacle genres, the film fits Jose Arroyo's description of current high concept action cinema, which 'strives to offer a theme park of attractions: music, colour, story, performance, design and the sense of improbably fast motion. The aim is to seduce the audience into surrendering to the ride' (2000: 22). But it is a ride in which display is central. Steve Neale has described science fiction film's use of special effects in terms of self-reflexive exhibitionism, making clear the fetishistic economy at work in special effects' visual display. He works from Christian Metz to draw our attention to the fact that, 'while there is always a degree of duplicity, of secrecy, of the hidden attached to the use of special effects, there is always "something which flaunts itself". This flaunting both caters to – and counters – the spectator's awareness, while ensuring at the same time that cinema will take the credit for the impact' (1990: 166).

Special effects broadly fall into two categories: those that are meant to maintain the verisimilitude of the image without being noticed, and those that are meant to be perceived as amazing effects in themselves. Thus, while watching *Titanic* (1997), the spectator is not expected to notice that the extras visible on the doomed liner's decks are, in some scenes, computer-generated. By contrast, the morphing technology on display in the rendering of the liquid-metal T1000 in *Terminator 2: Judgment Day* (1991) is intended to be visible, and to contribute to the spectator's amazed response to and pleasure in the film's action set-pieces. These two categories match what Jay David Bolter and Richard Grusin call 'the twin preoccupations of contemporary media: the transparent presentation of the real and the enjoyment of the opacity of media themselves' (2000: 21). Bolter & Grusin re-describe these twin preoccupations in the terms 'immediacy' and 'hypermediacy', which are extremely useful in accounting for the dynamics of special effects: 'The logic of immediacy dictates that the medium itself should disappear and leave us in the presence of the thing represented', while the logic of hypermediacy is 'to take pleasure in the act of mediation'. Significantly, 'the logic of hypermediacy can assert itself within the logic of immediacy' (2000: 6, 14, 155). So in the case of *The Matrix*, while the film spends much of its time creating and maintaining the immediacy of its fictional world, the bullet-time sequences are moments of intense hypermediacy, in which the act of mediation itself is the focus of the spectator's pleasure and amazement.

The way the film plays with the temporality of each special effects sequence also seems designed to focus intense attention and expectation on the act of mediation, the fetishized display of the special effect. As in other action and spectacle cinema, slow motion is used during the action sequences to emphasise the spectacular nature of the event shown, giving the spectator plenty of time to take pleasure in the image and the movement of the action. In this type of cinema, slow motion is normally employed in one or two shots within an action sequence, for the full duration of the shot. However, during certain moments in *The Matrix*, slow motion is used rather differently – manipulated, if you like. I want to look at two such moments in detail to assess how slow motion might function to emphasise the act of mediation.

First, I want to consider the explosion which follows Neo and Trinity's gun battle with a SWAT team in the lobby of a government building. They are trying to rescue Morpheus, who has been captured by the agents who police the Matrix program. To facilitate the rescue, Neo and Trinity place a bomb in the lift of the building, and sever the cables which hold the lift in place. The lift crashes to ground level and the bomb explodes into the lobby area. When the lift door is punched out and somersaults into the lobby with the explosion billowing out behind it, we expect to see the whole movement at the same speed, for the duration of any given shot during the sequence. But here the bomb explosion starts in real time, then in the middle of the shot the action is slowed. The following shot starts at this slower speed, so that we see the lift door's movement into the lobby in slow motion, and then *within that same shot* the scene converts back to real time to show the end section of the explosion. The speed at which the action is presented has changed unexpectedly and unusually in the middle of two shots in the sequence, in a way that surprises the spectator and therefore draws particular attention to the level of visual presentation, as well as to the verisimilitude of the effect.

Later, Trinity has to leap out of an ailing helicopter as it is about to slam into the side of a building. She grabs onto a rope which Neo is holding, and makes the jump. Here, different slow motion speeds are used to present the action, and moreover, in one particular shot, slow motion is used at the same time as real time in the same shot. In the first shot of this sequence, Trinity leaps out of the helicopter in slow motion, hanging onto the end of the rope. There follow two shots of Neo in real time, struggling to maintain his grip on the rope Trinity is suspended from. A fourth shot from behind Neo depicts Trinity moving through the air away from the helicopter, in slow motion. The fifth shot is from above, as the helicopter crumples into the side of the building. This shot is in slightly faster slow motion and rather surprisingly the side of the building ripples out from the site of the helicopter's impact as if it were a fluid. But strangest of all, in shot six, Neo turns to watch the helicopter in apparent real time, while simultaneously in the background of the same shot the helicopter's impact is shown at a speed which is apparently slower than real time. What is happening here? Clearly, there is a certain amount of play with the temporality of the action in such sequences, which recalls the way in which temporality was manipulated to enhance the affect of the cinematic spectacle in the early cinema of attractions, as Tom Gunning describes:

> the very moment of display can be manipulated into a scenario of suspense unique to the aesthetic of attractions. Founded on the moment of revelation, the cinema of attractions frequently redoubles its effect of appearance by framing the attraction with a variety of gestures of display [...]. Beyond enframing (and therefore calling attention to) the act of display, it also performs the important temporal role of announcing the event to come, focusing not only the attention but also the anticipation of the audience.

(1996: 77)

Gunning explains that framing gestures could occur within the film, such as the announcing gesture of the magician delivering his magic trick, or outside the diegesis, in the way the film was presented. He gives the example of early film exhibitors Smith and Blackton, who would freeze the first frame of their film *The Black Diamond Express* while Blackton spoke over the image, warning the audience that the train would shortly come to life and rush toward them. The suspense created by withholding the moving image 'redoubles the basic effect of an attraction, cathecting curiosity through delay and creating a satisfying discharge by unleashing the suspended rush of time' (1996: 78). This account seems to fit the use of slow motion in *The Matrix*, since the film tends to suspend moments during each big special effects sequence to intensify the 'wow-factor' before letting them play out. But as we see from shot six in the helicopter sequence, the temporality of the spectacle also appears to be manipulated *within* the diegesis. How else could Neo turn to look in real time at a helicopter crash which was unfolding in slow motion? Such moments of ambiguity – between the implication that Neo is able to see in something other than real time, and the film's extra-diegetic decisions to present some moments in slow motion for spectacular ends – remind us how much this film's themes are linked to its visual presentation. While slow motion is used to cathect the spectator's attention and appreciation, and focus his or her anticipation of what might happen within and after the effect, the use of slow motion in this shot is also suggestive of the narrative's thematic transformation of Neo; the film's ability to manipulate the spatial and temporal dynamics of its visual narration mirrors Neo's own developing ability to manipulate the spatial and temporal dynamics of the Matrix program. This thematic emphasis, which crosses the boundary between the extra-diegetically determined visual narration and the dynamics of the diegesis, is even more evident in the bullet-time sequences.

Bullet-time not only uses slow motion but also a mobile camera to pronounced spectacular and thematic effect. It slows down the action while simultaneously allowing the spectator to contemplate the action in a spatial way. During bullet-time, the camera moves into and around the space of the action, a movement unusual enough to underline the spectator's awareness that he or she is witnessing a special effect, thus priming the spectator for a more focussed admiration of the technology and effect on display. Having gestured towards the temporal dynamics of the bullet-time effect, I now want to focus on the effect's spatial dynamics. It is first important to place bullet-time in the context of the traditional presentation of special effects set-pieces in action cinema. Most action sequences follow a pattern, of fast editing, close-ups and cross-cutting to make the spectator feel he or she is 'in the thick of it', contrasted with long shots which take in all of the action as a spectacle in itself, and in particular allow the spectator to recognise and enjoy the special effects which work to ensure verisimilitude in the sequence. These moments of display, of hypermediacy, when the camera pulls back to allow the spectator to contemplate the special effect in all its computer-generated glory, are the moments at which the spectator is usually most distant from the action. In addition, at such points the two-dimensionality of the image is re-asserted, as the spectator is asked to appreciate not just the verisimilitude of the special effect but its composition and design. An example of this is the final chase sequence in *Mission: Impossible* (2000) where Ethan Hunt, played by Tom Cruise, is being dragged through the air by a train in the Channel Tunnel, while a helicopter pursues him. Close-up shots of Ethan's face, hands, the helicopter cockpit's interior, and so on, are intercut with wide-angle shots which display from a distance the totality of the scene – and its special effects – for the spectator.

In *The Matrix*, the most heightened moments of hypermediacy – the bullet-time sequences – are points at which the spectator is *not* asked to step back in this way. By contrast, in bullet-time's defining camera movement, the spectator is drawn fully into the diegetic space, disrupting the conventional spatial relationship between the spectator, the screen, and the filmic world. I want to illustrate this by considering one of the examples of bullet-time in more detail, the bullet-time moment that occurs during the subway sequence in which Neo and Agent Smith confront each other and fight. As these combatants face each other, pieces of trash skid on air currents across the floor of the deserted subway station. This part of the sequence gets underway with a series of conventional static shots, in a shot / reverse-shot pattern familiar from the face-to-face confrontations common to many action films, in particular the Western, and taken to stylistic extremes by spaghetti westerns. A further couple of static shots serve to establish the nature of the action, as both Neo and Agent Smith draw their weapons. However, once the two characters have started moving, the camera becomes mobile. The next three shots begin to draw the spectator into the filmic world's spatial coordinates. In the first shot Neo starts to run forward, and the camera dollies forward with him. The next shot (from Neo's point of view) shows Agent Smith running towards the camera, and then – rather surprisingly – jumping over the camera. Similarly in the following shot, Neo runs along the wall towards the camera and then disappears over the camera. Both shots give the spectator a clear sense of being placed within this filmic world, not attached to or aligned with one or other of the characters, as is often the case, but spatially separate from them within the diegesis. The spectator is drawn into the filmic space more fully by the next shot, which utilises bullet-time to allow the camera to move around the filmic space in one seamless movement, that is, without using cuts to vary the camera's relationship to the action. As the characters meet and spin round in mid-air, struggling to avoid the bullets from their respective guns, their actions are slowed down. Simultaneously, thanks to the special effects, the camera dollies round the characters in the opposite direction. The camera – our 'window' onto the events taking place – no longer feels like a fixed point or two-dimensional plane in relation to the action; instead it probes into the three-dimensionality of the diegesis. In this shot the camera does not follow the characters' movements exactly; in fact, the arc of the camera moves in a contrasting direction to the arc of the characters. We can observe, therefore, that rather than the camera tracking a character or object's movement, or presenting a character or object's point of view, the camera here is detached, able to plot its own path through the filmic space.

But this 'freedom' to contemplate the characters' bodies-in-motion from every angle has other significant effects. In this way bullet-time works to further emphasise the three-dimensionality of the filmic space, and creates a sense of the camera's autonomy, so that the spectator has, for a moment, an increased sense of accessibility to the filmic world. What is different about bullet-time is the way this special effect pushes the spectator into the three-dimensionality of the diegesis, appearing to break the conventional spatial relationship between the spectator and the two-dimensional image-plane, between the spectator and the space of the filmic world: we are no longer external witnesses of the action. This creates a sense of momentary immersion in the film's fictional universe – thematically mirroring the characters' immersion in the artificial world of the Matrix program. In some ways this impulse towards an immersive immediacy defines not only bullet-time but the cultural context in which *The Matrix* exists. As Margaret Morse has noted, 'The cinematic apparatus has now been largely subsumed into an electronic culture of video and computer-assisted imagery based on principles of envelopment and temporal simultaneity rather than distance and sequential unfolding' (1999: 64). There are a number of contemporary technologies which similarly engage with these notions of envelopment and temporal simultaneity: the three-dimensional worlds of computer games through which you can move an avatar, and choose the angle from which you see the action; the continuing project to make virtual reality environments as immersively seamless as possible; the interactivity with different cyberspaces available in modern technological interfacing. Moreover, I would suggest that the disruption of the conventional spatial relationships between the spectator, the flat cinema screen, and the fictional world it depicts, which I contend defines bullet-time, references the way the distance between user and interface has become increasingly fluid in contemporary culture.

The bullet-time effect flaunts the verisimilitude of the image. Revolving around the body is a way to guarantee the seamlessness and apparent 'reality' of what we are seeing, while we simultaneously register its constructedness as a spectacle. However, it is also a way of allowing the spectator to think that he or she can see *everything*. In this sense, bullet-time's underlying impulse is not new. If *The Matrix* is concerned with our fragmentary, alienating existence in an increasingly mediated world, then it may be that its filmic strategies also exist to reassure the spectator that he or she can still occupy a position of wholeness, of mastery. Barry Keith Grant has noted that 'the [science fiction] genre's reliance on special effects is itself an enactment of science fiction's thematic concern with technology' (1999: 21). Scott Bukatman has identified 'the sublime' in the spectacles science fiction films offer us, and suggests that such transcendental spectacles relate clearly to our anxieties about technology:

> *The presence of the sublime in the deeply American genre of science fiction implies that*
> *our fantasies of superiority emerge from our ambivalence regarding technological*
> *power [...] The might of technology, supposedly our own creation, is mastered through*

a powerful display that acknowledges anxiety but recontains it within the field of spectatorial power.

(1999: 265)

Bukatman continues, 'the language of consumption and the display of spectacle grounds the spectator/visitor and hides the awful truth: that an environment that we made has moved beyond our ability to control and cognize it' (1999: 265).

Bullet-time is, in its very dynamics, an explicit expression of the need to see everything, to see the whole. It is an expression both of the film's mastery over the visual – its ability to *show* everything – but also the spectator's mastery of the visual – his or her ability to *see* everything. This impulse to reassure is also evident, barely hidden, in the film's narrative trajectory: if at the start of the film Neo learns that the world he perceives is just a computer simulation, the rest of the film concerns his reassuring journey towards mastering that perceptual world, towards becoming The One. It is fitting, then, that the moments at which Neo displays his growing ability to control the spatial and temporal dynamics of the Matrix program are expressed through a special effect, bullet-time, that offers the spectator an omniscient view of the space, time, and movement of the action. Thus the film invokes a fantasy of omniscience which is as relevant for the spectator as for the film's characters. And if bullet-time allows the spectator a mastery over the visual, it is also fitting that this special effect draws the spectator into the three-dimensional spatial coordinates of the film's world. The ultimate mastery of the visual is not just to see all that can be seen, but to be *in* the spectacle itself.

References

Arroyo, Jose (2000) 'Mission: Sublime' in Arroyo, Jose (ed.), *Action/Spectacle Cinema, a Sight and Sound Reader*. London: British Film Institute, 21-25.

Bolter, Jay David & Grusin, Richard (2000, 2001) *Remediation: Understanding New Media*. Cambridge, Massachusetts, London: The MIT Press.

Bukatman, Scott (1999) 'The Artificial Infinite: On Special Effects and the Sublime' in Kuhn, Annette (ed.), *Alien Zone II: the Spaces of Science Fiction Cinema*. London, New York: Verso, 249-275.

Grant, Barry Keith (1999) 'Sensuous Elaboration: Reason and the Visible in the Science Fiction Film' in Kuhn, Annette (ed.), *Alien Zone II: the Spaces of Science Fiction Cinema*. London, New York: Verso, 16-30.

Gunning, Tom (1986) 'The Cinema of Attraction: Early Film, Its Spectator, and the Avant-Garde'. *Wide Angle*, Vol 8, Nos 3-4, Fall 1986, 1-14.

Gunning, Tom (1996, 1999) '"Now You See It, Now You Don't": The Temporality of the Cinema of Attractions' in Abel, Richard (ed.), *Silent Film*. London: The Athlone Press, 71-84.

Hayward, Philip & Wollen, Tania (1993) 'Introduction: Surpassing the Real' in Hayward, Philip & Wollen, Tania (eds) *Future Visions: New Technologies of the Screen*. London: BFI Publishing, 1-20.

Morse, Margaret (1999) 'Body and Screen'. *Wide Angle* Vol 21, No1, January 1999, 63-75.

Neale, Steve (1990) '"You've Got To Be Fucking Kidding!" Knowledge, Belief and Judgement in Science Fiction' in Kuhn, Annette (ed.), *Alien Zone: Cultural Theory and Contemporary Science Fiction Cinema*. London, New York: Verso, 160-8.

Pierson, Michele (2002) *Special Effects: Still In Search Of Wonder*. New York and Chichester, West Sussex: Columbia University Press.

Poster, Mark (1995, 2000) 'Postmodern Virtualities' in Featherstone, Mike & Burrows, Roger (eds) *Cyberspace, Cyberbodies, Cyberpunk: Cultures of Technological Embodiment*. London, Thousand Oaks, New Delhi: SAGE Publications, 80-95.

Turkle, Sherry (1996) *Life on the Screen: Identity in the Age of the Internet*. London, New York: Weidenfeld & Nicolson.

Wright, Richard (2000) 'The Matrix Rules'. *Film Philosophy* Vol 4 No 3, accessed online at http://www.mailbase.ac.uk/lists/film-philosophy/files/wright.html

Notes

1   More information about this effect can be accessed at

http://whatisthematrix.warnerbros.com/cmp/sfx-bullet_walk.html

13. 'I was dreaming I was awake and then I woke up and found myself asleep': Dreaming, spectacle and reality in *Waking Life*[1]

Paul Ward

Introduction

The relationship between film and dreaming is complex and multilayered. Much has been written that directly compares the cinema viewing experience with the dream state; indeed this is one of the underlying strands of much psychoanalytic film theory, the psychic mechanisms through which spectators relate to the sounds and images on the screen (see for example: Ellis 1982: 38-61; Baudry 1976). There are also films that represent some form of utopia (or dystopia) and, by so doing, invoke thoughts of dreams, nightmares, and similar visions (Howells 2003).[2] But there are few films, in my view, that actually capture the twisting (il)logic and 'uncanny' textures of the dreaming state as well as Richard Linklater's animated feature *Waking Life* (2001). Obviously, the film is 'about' dreaming – or, rather, about the difference between dreaming and waking life – so its 'dreaminess' is figured at a thematic as well as an aesthetic level. My contention is that it is the foregrounded relationship between the dream state and the waking state, and how they are figured by the specific tropes of this film, that make it such an effective representation. I want to explore some of the ways in which this recent form of animation offers a specific type of *spectacle*.

Firstly, I will outline some problems encountered when considering animation's representation of the real. At the most basic level, there is a paradox in the sense that animation is generally thought of as an 'unrealistic' mode of representation, so how – and, more to the point, why – would it mimic reality? More recently, it has become clear that the dividing line between 'live action' and 'animation' has become less easy to draw, and the role that computer-generated imagery (CGI) plays in blurring this particular line is central to much discussion of contemporary moving-image production (see for example Cubitt 2002, Ndalianis 2000). Therefore, the notion of the real, waking world and the dream world – and the differences and overlaps between them – is something that requires careful attention.

Once I have sketched these broader debates, I shall move on to discuss rotoscoping as a process, before looking more closely at Bob Sabiston's 'Rotoshop' technique, used in *Waking Life*.[3] Rotoscoped animation has a closer than usual relationship with live action, giving it the potential to create an 'uncanny' or eerie impression.

One of the key points of this chapter is that it is precisely this uncanniness that points to and underscores the ability of rotoscoped imagery to represent *a different order of reality*. This is something I explore elsewhere in more general detail (see Ward, 2004). Here, I want to examine how rotoscoping offers an ideal vehicle for looking into the 'realism' and 'plausibility' of dreaming. Thus, in the final part of this essay, I will pursue some links between the two via Walter Benjamin's concept of the 'optical unconscious'.

Animation and the real

Many recent live action films use computer animation in order to shore up their verisimilitude. In other words, the animation is invisible in the sense that no one recognises it *as* animation; the use of computer animation to render the magnitude of crowd scenes in *Titanic* (1997), for example. The animated imagery in such examples is *co-opted* by the more dominant frame of live action. Another prime example is the recent furore over the character of Gollum in *The Lord of the Rings* trilogy – is he being played by an actor, or generated by a computer? As we shall see in relation to my arguments about the rotoscoping used in *Waking Life*, it is more accurate to recognise that what we are looking at is a case of not one or the other, but *both*.[4]

So, animation is often used to 'add to' the startling verisimilitude of live action films. Another paradox is at work with films that *are* recognised and 'understood' as animation – the *Toy Story* films (1995 and 1999), *Final Fantasy: The Spirits Within* (2001) and the like – where the CGI is admired for its ability to mimic with amazing accuracy the surface details of phenomenal reality. 'Look how *real* this looks! (though I know, *really*, that it isn't real)' is arguably what passes through viewers' minds. And this form of disavowal – 'I know this *isn't* real, but there is something about it that seems/feels/looks really real' – is central to what I am exploring in relation to *Waking Life* and its peculiar take on reality and dreaming. Yet, with *Waking Life*, the engagement with – and mimicking of – the textures of phenomenal reality is less firmly 'anchored' precisely because the point of departure for the visuals is that they are dreamt (or *are* they?) by the protagonist.

Andrew Darley has explored precisely this paradox (1997, 2000) and I have written about video games and animation using Darley as a reference point (Ward 2002). The key debates around animation and realism, and documentary representation specifically, are examined in another of my essays (Ward, forthcoming). The most important point to be made here is that there is some discrepancy between what Darley refers to as the 'surface play' of the 'new media' artefacts he analyses, and the narrative structures, such that the surface or 'phenomenality' of these artefacts is foregrounded, their relative in/authenticity made *part of* the self-conscious spectacle. However, viewed historically, such focusing on the comparative in/authenticity of specific signifying practices is hardly a 'new' phenomenon. The playing out of 'digital versus analogue' scenarios – as seen in films like *The Matrix* (1999), *Dark City* (1998), *Existenz* (1999) – where the 'real world' is threatened in some way by a dream/fantasy world, can therefore be seen to have precedents in media history (see Rodowick 2002). Such points are useful because they force us to remember that 'new' developments must always be seen in their full historical context, and that new media are always likely to 'remediate' existing media, rather than replacing them outright (see Bolter and Grusin 1999). However, it is characteristic of remediation that there is a period where what Darley refers to as 'surface play' is foregrounded, and various paradoxes – 'I know this is not real, but it seems real' (and vice-versa?) – are played out. The computer rotoscoping seen in *Waking Life* is an example of such 'surface play', but it is a particularly interesting case, because one can argue that it simultaneously covers over *and* reveals the underlying reality of the image (which is to say, the digital live action footage, which records the profilmic events). It is this oscillation between revelation and obfuscation – a playing with surface and depth – that characterises *Waking Life* and its peculiar form of spectacular realism.

Rotoscoping and realism

The convergence and overlap between media forms is figured, quite literally, by the rotoscope technique, where 'live action' is refigured by animation. Live action footage is 'drawn over', a frame at a time. In *Waking* Life, the protagonist, Wiley Wiggins, tries to work out if he is asleep or awake; my argument is concerned with the way that this dreaming/waking life metaphor is a useful one for those investigating the dialectic between live action and animated forms, and the relative levels of realism/spectacle we attach to them. The fact that Wiley Wiggins cannot fully determine whether he is dreaming or awake is mirrored by our perception of the film – what is this: animation? live action? a bit of both? His 'uncertainty' directly reflects our own, regarding the ontological status of what we are experiencing. He is convinced at certain points of the 'reality' of his experiences, but then he awakes, suggesting that what we have just seen was 'not real'. At the same time, even the parts of the film that Wiley 'believes in' are shot using outlandish and spectacular computer rotoscoping techniques. Before looking in more detail at *Waking Life* itself, I would like to make a few introductory points about the rotoscope as a general animation technique.

The rotoscope was patented in 1917 by Max Fleischer, and was most famously used in the *Out of the Inkwell* and *Betty Boop* cartoons of the early decades of last century (Langer 2003; Crafton 1993; Frierson 1993). These films exhibit an eerie type of movement, which is at one and the same time 'realistic' *and* 'unrealistic': 'realistic' in the sense that the movements of Koko the Clown or Betty Boop[5] strikingly mimic those of a real person (unsurprisingly enough – the animators *had* traced a real person's live action movements, after all); 'unrealistic' because such strikingly real movement is strangely at odds with the 'cartoonal' world. One of the rotoscope's initial uses outside of entertainment was for military training films, where the complexities of dealing with ordnance were made clearer via the tracing of live action footage (see Crafton 1993: 158). This points to one of the fundamental characteristics of the rotoscope's refiguring of live action: it makes things *simpler*. Line, colour, texture – all are in some sense simplified when compared to the photographically 'real'. Yet, therein lies the haunting and problematic thing about rotoscoped animation – it has a very close relationship with live action, yet is 'not quite' live action. Or, more accurately, rotoscoped material is 'more than' live action; it is in a strange way revealing *more* of the real than the apparently real photographic imagery that acts as its basis. The movements are 'too real' to be proper 'cartoony' animation (with all its squash and stretch), yet they are at the same time 'unreal' in the way that they move, the convergence of live action and animation making for a strange *appropriation* of the real. So, what needs to be recognised is that rotoscoped animation is more often than not invoking its 'realism' in a highly self-conscious way.

This is something that Joanna Bouldin has argued in relation to Betty Boop (Bouldin 2004). She suggests that 'the real', though attenuated in animated films, is never entirely banished; and that the rotoscope technique offers some of the more compelling examples of 'realism' in animation. The fact is, Bouldin argues, that rotoscoped animation is predicated on the 'evidence' of the real person, captured in the live action footage. Far from depicting an unreal figure, divorced from the real, the rotoscope manages to 'amplify' the real person 'underlying' the animated layer. In this respect, the rotoscope 'thickens' (to use Bouldin's term) the presence of the bodily, corporeal person. At the same time it renders them ghostly, spectral – so it is no coincidence that the rotoscope's eeriness is often talked about as 'surreal' or 'uncanny' (Langer 2003). Similarly, the connections between rotoscoped imagery and 'dreaminess', and the related concepts of morphing, daydreaming and the vicissitudes of memory are manifold (see Bukatman 2000).

Animation and dreaming: *Waking Life*

The themes addressed in *Waking Life* centre on the apparent reality of a dream state. When Wiley Wiggins is not blankly listening to someone philosophising, he is more often than not talking about why his dreams seem so real. The apparent reality of a dream state is something that Wendy Doniger O'Flaherty has examined at length (1984). There are times when someone, while dreaming, recognises this state and says to themselves, 'This is only a dream'. O'Flaherty points out that this is a paradox and goes right to the centre of how we define and understand reality and the relative realisms of specific representations. For, the 'reality' of a dream is precisely that: it is a *dream*. To conclude otherwise robs it of its particular 'realism'; something akin to *not* suspending disbelief while watching a film. (Which can be fun, or a pain, depending on with whom one is watching.) At the same time, however, to say 'This is only a dream' *does* recognise the specific ontological status of what one is experiencing. The sticking point is the word 'only', as this implies that the events that are being described as 'dream' are being compared, 'unfavourably', with an alternative – that is, the 'real' world of actuality, one's waking life. The thought processes inevitably go: 'Things are happening, they are weird, bizarre, unsettling – this is *only* a dream' (or, more forcefully, 'this *must* be a dream').

The comparing of the 'really real' with the 'dreamt real' sounds like a strange thing to do, but one is in actuality comparing physical reality with metaphysical reality, material with psychic reality. Such an exercise draws out some of the contradictions and fissures inherent in our experience of the world. And it is because of the *plausibility* of certain things we experience and see in our dreams that they can appear to have a 'reality' that spills over into our apparent waking life. O'Flaherty (45-6) outlines Freud's discussion of latent and manifest content in dreams: if one fears robbers in a dream, then the robbers are *not* real, but the fear of them *is*. It is not hard to discern here that such real *affects* (awakening from a *frightening dream*, to find that one is *actually frightened*) can lead to a blurring of *manifest* content (the frightening thing in the dream) and *latent* content (the fear itself). The manifest content can be equated with the experience of phenomenal or surface reality – the obvious and apparent reality that surrounds us – and the latent content can be equated with underlying relations, feelings, associations.

The seeming conflation of manifest and latent contents leads to the commonly cited features of dreams: that they are 'bizarre', 'weird', and that they consist of odd, abrupt shifts in tone, characters who morph into someone (or something) else, and other tropes such as condensation, synecdoche, symbolism and metaphor. Needless to say, these are all characteristic of animation too (Wells 1998: 68-126). However, as Bert O. States argues, there are problems with the way that dreams are described as 'bizarre'. He takes issue with the simple comparing of the dreamt with 'how things are' in waking life. *Of course* dreams are going to seem 'bizarre', the deck is already stacked against them in that they are being measured against the 'norm' of waking life:

> To say that dreams exhibit less common sense, efficiency and reliability than waking thought seems rather like saying that objects in a vacuum fail to obey the rules for falling bodies in the open atmosphere, and ignoring the conditions responsible for the 'failure'.

(States 2000)

The 'unrealism' of much of what happens in *Waking Life* is what leads Wiley Wiggins to question the 'reality' of his surroundings; ergo – he must be dreaming. Yet, dreams have a reality of their own. As does animation. As Linklater himself puts it:

> *this film uses dreams as a kind of operating system for the narrative, the hitch for most of the ideas. The realism of (live-action) film would have cancelled out the ideas [...]. This style of animation allows you to see a different state of reality.*

> (quoted in Silverman 2001)

In other words, the state of dreaming and the state of animation are inextricably linked, and linked in their ability to show a different 'state of reality'. As with Benjamin's 'optical unconscious' we are given 'access' to something that is not ordinarily, straightforwardly 'there', but that needs to be *uncovered* and made clear.

In *Waking Life* many scenes revolve around the bizarre and uncanny atmosphere of events. The film begins with its putative protagonist arriving in town by train. After making a phone call to try to bum a lift – all the time being watched rather *too* intently by a woman – Wiley walks out of the station and is hailed by a man in what can only be described as a 'boat-car'. There is another passenger already in the car (this is actually Linklater himself, who crops up again later in the film), who remains silent, but the driver more than makes up for this with his constant barrage of talk. 'Ahoy there! [...] this vessel is see-worthy, as in "see" with your eyes [...] we are in motion to the ocean!!' After a short journey, with Linklater silent and the boat-car's driver offering a non-stop harangue, we have the following exchange:

Driver: So, where do you want out?

Wiley: Er, who me? Am I first? Erm, I dunno, really anywhere's fine.

Driver: Just just just gimme an address or something, OK?

Linklater: Tell you what, go up three more streets, take a right, go two more blocks, drop this guy off on the next corner.

Wiley: Where's that?

Driver (looking ominously over his shoulder): Well, I don't know either, but it's some-where, and it's going to determine the course of the rest of your life. [Bursts into demented grin] All ashore that's going ashore! [mimics hooting of ship's horn].

As soon as they drop Wiley off, he crosses the road and finds a piece of paper in the middle of the road. Stooping down to pick it up, he reads 'Look to your right'. As Wiley does so, he sees a car come careering towards him. At the point of impact, Wiley awakens.

Here, it is not just the 'it was all a dream' pay-off of the sequence that makes us think about the dreaming theme. The oddness of the behaviour of the people, and the bizarre aesthetic of the interpolated rotoscoping [6] – shimmering, wobbling – has a 'dreamlike' quality. The indeterminacy of things – for example, the boat-car – also emphasises the dreaminess. It is neither one thing nor the other, it is between the two and yet at the same time both, and it is this uncertainty that is characteristic of Wiley's dreaming/waking dilemma. It is also characteristic of the 'spectacle' that is on offer here: a self-consciously 'odd' image, which takes the rotoscoped material and amplifies it, by virtue of the extra flexibility that the software allows. The animation is simultaneously 'smooth' *and* somehow 'jerky'. The uneasiness felt while viewing such material stems from the uncertain ontological status of the imagery: in other words we are unsure what we are looking at. The live action footage has been overlaid by the Rotoshop technique, but it is still *there*, underneath the animated layer. Thus, the imagery itself has a neither-one-thing-nor-the-other status. This is a phenomenon that Alan Cholodenko (1991), following Derrida, would term an 'undecidable'. The simple either/or binarism is short-circuited, and we are left uncertain as to the status of what we are viewing. Cholodenko takes the notion of the 'frame' in *Who Framed Roger Rabbit* (1988) as a point of departure for his analysis, but the rotoscope can be seen to function in exactly the same way. It 'serves to mark the unaccounted for operations of the repressed but irrepressible trace, mark of the other' (212). Tropes like the 'frame' and, as I am suggesting, the rotoscope

are hybrid or composite figures of the 'both/and', of the hama [this is Derrida's term, meaning 'at the same time'], which takes the form of 'X and not X at the same time'.

(*ibid.*)

The dreamlike oddness of the events and the way they are figured is suggestive of just such an 'undecidability', as is the general theme of not being able to determine (or decide) whether what one is experiencing is *really* real, or merely a *dream*-real.

A key aspect of dreaming that is figured in the boat-car sequence, and one that Wiley discusses with various characters at other points in the film, is the idea of waking up and yet still, ultimately, being in a dream state. This is something that O'Flaherty discusses in her work on dreaming, and the notion of 'infinite regress' in dreaming is also part of Hofstadter's compelling work (1980). As noted earlier, there are many instances of a dream being recognised *as* a dream, and the dreamer in some way drawing a comparison between what is happening in the dream and their reality, to the extent that they 'try to wake up'. This phenomenon, metadreaming, or dreaming that one is dreaming, is in many ways the 'central' theme of *Waking Life*. The notion of 'recursion' or 'infinite regress' in the dream world is, at one and the same time, highly seductive and very frightening. What if one never wakes up? What if, *a la The Matrix*, we are in perpetual sleep, but are 'fed' dreams to keep us 'happy'? And, as implied throughout this discussion, and in *Waking Life*, how can we tell the difference?[7]

This representing of a dream-state means we have to address the ways in which dreaming can have its own 'reality'. If it is real enough for Wiley Wiggins to be uncertain, or rather, be fooled by how real it seems (and we accept, as the film seems to, that he is not simply delusional), then we must engage with these issues. Simply put, they take us to the heart of our understanding not only of mediated representations (like films, TV programmes, computer games, and animation), but also the apparently 'unmediated' thing that is our experience of the real world of actuality. The difficulty lies in the fact that the world of dreams and the world of actuality are often seen as diametrically opposed when in fact they should be seen as dialectically linked. This is something that we can explore via Benjamin's concept of the optical unconscious.

Waking Life, rotoscoping and the 'optical unconscious'

As Susan Buck-Morss points out about Benjamin's *Arcades Project*, it is underpinned by a theory of 'modernity as a dream world, and a conception of collective "awakening" from it as synonymous with revolutionary class consciousness' (253). In other words, people are 'enchanted' by the specific conditions of capitalism, and modern life is very much analogous to a dream state.

> *Underneath the surface of increasing systemic rationalization, on an unconscious 'dream' level, the new urban-industrial world had become fully reenchanted [...] the 'threatening and alluring face' of myth was alive and everywhere[...]. It appeared, prototypically, in the arcades, where 'the commodities are suspended and shoved together in such boundless confusion, that [they appear] like images out of the most incoherent dreams'.*

(254)

It is not too much of a leap to see that animation has a peculiarly strong link to this way of conceptualising modern life. The 'boundless confusion' of many animated cartoons, and the 'incoherence' of much animation suggest that they are a rich resource for those of us interested in exploring this area. Esther Leslie talks of Benjamin's notion of an 'optical unconscious' which *switches a space consciously discerned by people for an unconsciously discerned space inspected by the camera eye. A 'new region of consciousness' is summoned by film, contracted only in conjunction with technology. The harmony between humanity and machinery [...] emerges [...] through the ways that the apparatus obliges viewers to see the world.*

(2002: 105)

Leslie goes on to note that Benjamin discusses enlargements, slow motion and other filmic devices that 'render [...] more precise what was already visible but unclear' (*ibid*). My point here would be to stress that the rotoscope does precisely this too: it takes a pre-existing live action record of something and renders aspects of it 'more precisely'. It takes us beneath the phenomenal surface and reveals something of the real relations underpinning things. At the same time, however, the rotoscope has that peculiar characteristic, whereby it makes clearer, yet at the same time blurs, obfuscates, (literally) covers over. This is the paradox I alluded to earlier, that places rotoscoped imagery in the realm of the 'undecidable'. And yet, the uncanny feeling that the 'ghostly' aspect of rotoscoping engenders – the feeling that the real, live action person is *there*, underneath – makes a reading of the *social* dimension of rotoscoped imagery, and the dreaming which it is representing here, a distinct possibility.

From the point of view of technology and technique, therefore, it can be seen that *Waking Life* offers a good example of such an 'optical unconscious': the 'dreaminess' of the images, as experienced by us and the main character in the film, are figured by the rotoscoping. It is also vital to remember though that Wiley Wiggins spends the entire film trying to discern whether he is asleep or awake, and what might be the implications of not being able to discern this with any certainty. In this respect, *Waking Life* 'self-consciously' engages with the very philosophical questions that troubled Benjamin (and Marx before him) about the problems of dreaming, waking, the phantasmagoric, and the real. It is a film about dreaming and reality, and the unique spectacle that results shows that the animation techniques used are a perfect vehicle for such complex and contradictory subject matter.

References

Askwith, Ivan (2003) 'Gollum: Dissed by the Oscars?' *Salon.com*, accessed online 22 July 2003: http://www.salon.com/tech/feature/2003/02/18/gollum/?x

Baudry, Jean-Louis (1976) 'The Apparatus: Metapsychological Approaches to the Impression of Reality in the Cinema' *camera obscura* No. 1, 104-28.

Bolter, Jay David and Richard Grusin (1999) *Remediation: Understanding New Media.* Cambridge, Mass: The MIT Press.

Bouldin, Joanna (2004) 'Cadaver of the real: Animation, Rotoscoping and the Politics of the Body' *Animation Journal*, 12 7–3

Bukatman, Scott (2000) 'Taking Shape: Morphing and the Performance of Self' in Vivian Sobchack (ed.) *Meta-Morphing: Visual transformation and the Culture of Quick-Change*. Minneapolis and London: University of Minnesota Press, 225-249.

Buck-Morss, Susan (1989) *The Dialectics of Seeing: Walter Benjamin and The Arcades Project*. Cambridge, MA, MIT Press.

Cholodenko, Alan (1991) 'Who Framed Roger Rabbit, or The Framing of Animation' in his (ed.) *The Illusion of Life: Essays on Animation*. Sydney: Power Publications, 209-242.

Crafton, Donald (1993) *Before Mickey: The Animated Film 1898-1928*. Chicago: University of Chicago Press.

Cubitt, Sean (2002) 'Digital Filming and Special Effects' in Dan Harries (ed.) *The New Media Book*. London: BFI, 17-29.

Darley, Andrew (1997) 'Second-order realism and post-modern aesthetics in computer animation' in Jayne Pilling (ed.) *A Reader in Animation Studies*. London: John Libbey, 16-24.

Darley, Andrew (2000) *Visual Digital Culture*. London: Routledge.

Ellis, John (1982) *Visible Fictions Cinema, Television, Video*. London: Routledge.

Frierson, Michael (1993) 'Clay Comes Out of the Inkwell: The Fleischer Brothers and Clay Animation' in Pilling (ed.) *A Reader in Animation Studies*, 82-92.

Hofstadter, Douglas R. (1980) *Godel, Escher, Bach: An Eternal Golden Braid*. Harmondsworth: Penguin.

Howells, Richard (2003) 'Keep on Dreamin': Utopia and the Sociology of the Hollywood Movie', paper presented to the International Association for Media and History Conference, University of Leicester, 16-20 July, 2003.

Langer, Mark (2003) 'The Rotoscope, the Double and the Uncanny', paper presented to Animated 'Worlds' Conference, Surrey Institute of Art and Design/Animation Research Centre, Farnham, 9-11 July 2003.

Leslie, Esther (2002) *Hollywood Flatlands: Animation, Critical Theory and the Avant-Garde*. London: Verso.

Morris, Sue (2002) 'First-Person Shooters – A Game Apparatus' in Geoff King and Tanya Krzywinska (eds.) *ScreenPlay: cinema/videogames/interfaces*. London: Wallflower Press, 81-97.

Ndalianis, Angela (2000) 'Special Effects, Morphing Magic and the 1990s Cinema of Attractions' in Sobchack (ed.) *Meta-Morphing*, 251-271.

O'Flaherty, Wendy Doniger (1984) *Dreams, Illusions and Other Realities*. Chicago: University of Chicago Press.

Rodowick, David (2002) 'Dr. Strange Media, or How I Learned to Stop Worrying and Love Film Theory', unpublished version of Professorial inaugural lecture, delivered 4 February 2002, Kings College London. Accessed online 18 November 2002, at: http://www.kcl.ac.uk/humanities/cch/filmstudies/digital-culture/StrangeMedia/

Silverman, Jason (2001) 'Animating a Waking Life', *Wired News*. Accessed online 19 June 2003 at: http://www.wired.com/news/culture/0,1284,47433,00.html

States, Bert (2000) 'Dream Bizarreness and Inner Thought', *Dreaming* 10(4). Accessed online 22 July 2003 at: http:///www.asdreams.org/journal/articles/10-4 states.htm

Ward, Paul (2002) 'Videogames as Remediated Animation' in King and Krzywinska (eds.) *ScreenPlay*, 122-135.

Ward, Paul (2004) '"Rotoshop" in Context: Computer rotoscoping and animation aesthetics', *Animation Journal*, 12, 32-52

Ward, Paul (forthcoming) 'Animated Realities: the animated film, documentary, realism', publisher to be confirmed.

Wells, Paul (1998) *Understanding Animation*. London: Routledge.

Notes

1   The title for this essay comes from the Laurel and Hardy short *Oliver the Eighth* (1934). In this film Ollie is in danger of having his throat cut in the night by a mad widow (she has already dealt the same fate to seven other Olivers). The plan is therefore that Stan should stay awake while Ollie sleeps. Stan, predictably, falls asleep, leading to the following exchange:

Ollie: What are you trying to do? Do you want me to get my throat cut?

Stan: No.

Ollie: Well, then don't go to sleep!

Stan: Well, I can't tell when I'm asleep.

Ollie: That's why I want you to stay awake – so that you can *see* that you're not asleep.

Stan: Well I couldn't help it. I was dreaming I was awake, and then I woke up and found myself asleep.

Interestingly enough, the whole of this 'mad widow' sequence turns out to be a dream that Ollie was having. If only he'd stayed awake, he'd have been able to *see* he wasn't asleep....

2   For an interesting discussion of how film theory that invokes dreams and dreaming relates to videogaming, see Morris (2002).

3   'Rotoshop' is the nickname given to Sabiston's software. (See also Note 5, below).

4   The debate over precisely what *kind* of performance Gollum constituted – acting or computer trickery – went as far as the Academy Awards, where Gollum was presented with an award for Best Digital Performance. See Askwith (2003) for a discussion of some of these issues.

5   Although the character of Betty Boop herself was not routinely rotoscoped, her movements were in at least one of her cartoons – *Betty Boop's Bamboo Isle* (1932) – and other characters in the series were animated using the technique. See Bouldin (2004) for more details

6   'Interpolated' rotoscoping is a feature of Sabiston's software. The animator/rotoscoper does not have to trace each and every frame of the live action footage; the program automatically 'interpolates' certain frames, which gives the Rotoshop material its characteristic look.

7   Another interesting animated film that explores this theme is the *Kid's Story* sequence of the *Animatrix* set of short films (2003).

14. *Cannibal Holocaust* and the Pornography of Death

Julian Petley

In recent years there has been a good deal of discussion of 'mock-documentaries'. These have been described as fictional texts which 'look' like documentaries and 'make a partial or concerted effort to appropriate documentary codes and conventions in order to represent a fictional subject' (Roscoe and Hight 2001: 2). In some cases the intention is purely playful and comic, as in *This is Spinal Tap* (1984), but in others, such as *Bob Roberts* (1992), there is a clear desire to mount a critique of documentary practices themselves. As Brian Winston has argued:

> *Given the ideological power of the realist image in claiming to be trustworthy, it is clearly legitimate to use a faked documentary form to force the audience, as it were, to confront its credulity in such images and its prejudices about what they might represent.*

(2000: 37)

Curiously, none of the recent books which discusses the mock-documentary and its techniques actually mentions, let alone analyses, the most scandalous attempt to pass off fiction as fact, namely the 'snuff' movie, in which, apparently, people are actually killed purely for the delectation of the camera, and hence of the cinema-going public. The scandal first erupted with the release of the film *Snuff* in 1975, and, although this was soon revealed to be an obvious and opportunistic fake, rumours about the existence of 'snuff' movies stubbornly refuse to go away, being periodically fed by the alleged discovery of the real thing. Thus, for example, on 6 April 1993, the *Independent* reported that Trading Standards Officers had 'seized copies of a snuff movie at a children's fair in Birmingham', whilst the *Mail* worked itself into a frenzy over 'snuff films on sale with *Peter Pan* at children's comic fair'. Dr Mike Hilburn, chairman of Birmingham Trading Standards Committee, was quoted as stating that one movie 'contained absolutely disgusting scenes of a man being hacked to death, decapitated and disembowelled. I have never seen anything like this before, and I have no doubt that the scenes were genuine'. Given that no movie actor has ever been known to die for the camera, the scenes, inevitably, were entirely fictional. More specifically, they came from an Italian feature film directed by Ruggero Deodato and entitled *Cannibal Holocaust* (1979).

The aura of 'snuff'

I have already explained at some length elsewhere (Petley 2000) why I believe that the commercially made 'snuff' movie is an entirely imaginary creature, and other sceptical examinations of the myth can be found in Johnson and Schaeffer (1993) and Kerekes and Slater (1995). Although this is most emphatically not – *pace* Black (2002: 68) – to deny the possibility that real murders may have been filmed or otherwise recorded by their perpetrators for purely private purposes. My earlier contribution to this subject suggested that gullible and hyped-up press reports about the existence of commercially produced 'snuff' films are major contributory factors to the apparently widespread belief that such a genre actually exists. However, what I want to examine here are the formal cinematic strategies which can lead viewers, and are indeed *intended* to lead viewers, to believe that the images of death which they are witnessing on screen represent the 'real thing'. In what follows I will be concentrating largely on *Cannibal Holocaust*; this is partly because it has so frequently stood accused of being a 'snuff' movie, but it is also on account of the curious fact that, although it is a cinematic mock-documentary *avant la lettre*, it nonetheless provides an excellent demonstration of many of the sub-genre's key aesthetic strategies and devices.

Even in this case, however, extra-textual factors played a significant role in creating the aura of 'snuff' around Deodato's film. Thus, in January 1981, a French magazine, *Photo*, published an article entitled 'Grand Guignol Cannibale' which suggested that people may actually have been killed during the making of *Cannibal Holocaust*. Four weeks after it opened in Italy, on 8 February 1980, the film was banned under an ancient law, originally drafted in order to outlaw bull-fighting, which prohibited the wounding or killing of animals for entertainment purposes. Deodato fought the ban, but it was three years before the film re-appeared in Italian cinemas. Meanwhile, in Britain, *Cannibal Holocaust* was in the process of becoming one of the earliest and most notorious victims of the 'video nasty' panic, being repeatedly demonized by the press, seized by the police and found guilty by the courts under the Obscene Publications Act, even though the version distributed here was a relatively tame one shorn of the most extreme footage. Apparently irrevocably banned under the Video Recordings Act 1984, the film was condemned to a *samizdat* existence in Britain, but, as we have already seen, its notoriety was kept alive by the occasional high-profile seizure. And even though, in 2001, the British Board of Film Classification (BBFC) did finally pass *Cannibal Holocaust* for distribution on video and DVD, they cut it by five minutes and 44 seconds, in the process largely obliterating many of the features analysed below. (For full details of the cuts see Slater 2002: 110 or visit the BBFC website.)

If you meet this man, cross the road

Cannibal Holocaust's roots lie in the 'Mondo' (or 'shockumentary') cycle sparked off by Gualtiero Jacopetti and Franco Prosperi's *Mondo cane* (1962); indeed, Deodato chose Riz Ortolani as the composer for *Cannibal Holocaust* specifically on account of his score for that first 'Mondo' movie. Its more recent ancestry can be traced to the cannibal cycle launched by Umberto Lenzi's *Il paese del sesso selvaggio* (*Deep River Savages*) (1972), a cycle to which Deodato's also contributed *Ultimo mondo cannibale* (*Cannibal*) (1976). Although rendered exotically 'other' by being long-banished from Britain by the combined efforts of the police, courts, Trading Standards Officers, Mary Whitehouse, journalists and the BBFC, the cycle actually plays to exactly the same fascination with the tropical 'exotic' as the Tarzan, Indiana Jones, Lara Croft and Sheena films, not to mention television programmes such as *Survivor* and *I'm a Celebrity ... Get Me Out of Here!*

Like all films which have become the object of intense controversy, *Cannibal Holocaust* has become enshrouded in myth in almost every respect; thus it is a good idea to preface this analysis of the film as a mock-documentary with a clear outline of its plot.

At the start of the film, we learn that a documentary team working for the American broadcaster BDC-TV has failed to return from filming in the jungles of South America. The team consists of Alan Yates; his girlfriend, Faye Daniels; Jack Anders; and Mark Tommaso. They have worked together before, and are famed for their raw and shocking documentaries. The company organizes a search party, led by New York University anthropologist Professor Harold Monroe. Once in the jungle, Monroe's group makes contact with the Yacumo people, who greet them with fear and suspicion. They discover that the Yacumo, who are not cannibals, believe that Yates' team had cast an 'evil spell' over the jungle and its peoples; as Monroe's guide Chako suggests, their unusual behaviour is actually part of a 'religious ceremony to chase evil spirits out of the jungle – white men's spirits'. However, once convinced that they mean no harm, the Yacumo guide them to the Tree People or Yamamomo, who indeed are cannibals. As Monroe puts it, speaking into his cassette player just before his first meeting with them, the Yamamomo and their enemies the Shamatari or Swamp People are 'two cannibal tribes', each of which 'considers the other fair game to be hunted – and then eaten'. Again, it takes time for the Yamamomo to establish a relationship of trust with the search party, but, once this has been achieved, they lead the group to a grisly totem: the skeletal remains of the documentary team, festooned with cans of film... Monroe returns with these to New York, where, with his help, the television company plans to edit the footage into a programme entitled *The Green Inferno*. Before he starts work, however, a company executive shows him one of the team's previous works, a 'Mondo'-esque compilation of atrocity footage called *The Last Road to Hell*; after the screening she informs a visibly shocked Monroe that: 'Just to give you an idea how Alan and the others worked, everything you just saw was a put-on [...] Alan paid the soldiers to do a bit of acting for him'. As Monroe examines the footage he brought back, he learns more of the team's methods, and comes to understand why both the Yacumo and Yamamomo initially received his search party with such fear and suspicion. Because, in pursuit of dramatic footage, Yates' team had set fire to a Yacumo village, intending in the finished film to represent this as a raid by the Yamamomo. Then, in the course of their search for the latter, the male members of the team had raped a Yamamomo girl. This led to the Yamamomo wreaking a terrible revenge, but one which, professionals to the very end, the team members had managed to capture on film. When faced with the filmed evidence of their crew's behaviour, BDC-TV executives cancel the proposed broadcast and order all of the footage to be destroyed.

Not altogether unsurprisingly, the film attracted charges of racism in those countries in which it was actually released, such as France. Thus Jean Roy in *Cinéma 81* insisted that it was 'a racist and fascist film which has been conceived as such in order to make a buck out of everything that is degrading' (1981: 126), whilst François Géré in *Cahiers du Cinéma*, complained of 'a racism the like of which, I must say, I had not seen in a long time'. Admitting that it was difficult not to abandon himself to the only desire the film excites, that of censorship, Géré concluded that all one can say of Ruggero Deodato is to repeat what the English said of Mussolini in 1940: 'If you meet this man, cross the road' (1981: 63).

Even leaving aside the complicated anthropological debate about whether or not cannibalism actually exists, it has to be admitted that *Cannibal Holocaust* does indeed represent the peoples of the South American jungle in the most regressive and reprehensible terms – indeed as 'savages', with the full gamut of the negative, colonialist connotations the word implies. It is also impossible to 'redeem' the film in the manner attempted by Mikita Brottman (1998), whose reading of it as a moral fable in which the film-makers induce a cannibalistic frenzy amongst the Yamamomo, after which Monroe restores a non-cannibalistic social order, is based on a conflation of the Yacumo and the Yamamomo.

Mercenary media

The other charge levelled against the film is that it exploits precisely what it purports to condemn. Thus Alain Garsault in *Positif* stated that '*Cannibal Holocaust* would deserve only a contemptuous silence were it not for the enormous hypocrisy of its authors', adding that rarely had this familiar technique 'been employed with such obvious and such total bad faith' (1981: 65). This, I would argue, is actually a much more complicated matter than that of the film's racism, and consideration of it will take us to the heart of *Cannibal Holocaust*'s status as a mock-documentary.

On one level, *Cannibal Holocaust* does indeed contain a critique of mercenary media voyeurism and sensationalism. The film-makers' own comments on the atrocities which they stage for the camera indicate that their motives are entirely commercial and ignoble: 'Keep rolling – we're gonna get an Oscar for this!' shouts one of them in the climactic scene. And when they discover a real atrocity – a girl impaled on a pole – Alan has to be reminded that he is being filmed so that he can replace his gloating expression with one of apparent shock and horror. Nor are the television executives much better; after watching the footage which clearly shows the team burning the Yacumo village and brutalising its inhabitants (a scene which Alan describes at the time as 'beautiful'), one of them has the gall actually to praise its 'authenticity', and, when Monroe protests, retorts: 'Come on, Professor, let's be realistic. Who knows anything about the Yacumo civilisation? Today people want sensationalism. The more you rape their senses, the happier they are'. Similarly the projectionist of the 'found' footage states admiringly that: 'Their ratings were fantastic – higher than most of the big comics. And did they know how to play an audience!' And before she sees the very worst of the footage, the executive is aghast that Monroe no longer wants to be involved in the programme, telling him: 'We're talking about the most sensational documentary to come along in years, and you want just to shelve it, to forget about it as if it had never been found?' The film's bleak view of the values of contemporary television workers is also communicated by the scenes in which Monroe, in between examining the footage he brought back from the jungle, interviews members of the team's families: absolutely no one has a good word to say about any of them.

On the other hand, however, the film does lay itself open to the charge of hypocrisy by representing the film crew and the broadcaster for whom they work as clearly American and not Italian, even though, at the time of the film's release, the excesses of 'TV-realità' were already a cause for concern in Italy. Indeed, Deodato has stated that his poisonous picture of television reporters and executives was inspired by his revulsion at the sensational way in which Italian television news had reported the deaths and injuries caused by Red Brigade terrorist attacks in the 1970s (Fenton, Grainger and Castoldi 1999: 19).

Contradictory modes

However, simply to dismiss *Cannibal Holocaust* for revelling in what it apparently condemns, is, I would agree with Neil Jackson, to ignore the 'provocative potential of the film's contradictory modes' and, in particular, of its 'attempts to pass off much of its narrative as recorded, unscripted document', mimesis as actuality (2002: 34). For indeed, as Raymond Lefèvre puts it: 'the film begins like *Tintin au Congo* and ends like *Le sang des bêtes*' (1981: 39).

There can be few films which display such concern with validating the apparently indexical status of their images. Thus, for example, an opening title states: 'For the sake of authenticity, some sequences have been retained in their entirety'. And, at the end, just in case anyone is wondering how they came to see images which had apparently been destroyed, a closing title discloses that: 'Projectionist John K. Kirov was given a two month suspended jail sentence and fined $10,000 for illegal appropriation of film material. We know he received $250,000 for that same footage'. An early segment of the 'found' footage carefully establishes the fact that the film crew had two cameras, thus satisfactorily accounting, in diegetic terms, for those scenes in which we see team members actually filming.

Meanwhile, the 'found' footage itself is an absolute compendium of visual devices which one associates with the documentary mode at its most immediate: shaky, hand-held camerawork, 'accidental' compositions, crash zooms, blurred images, lens flare, inaudible or intermittent sound, direct address to camera, scratches and lab marks on the print, and so on. (In respect of *Cannibal Holocaust*'s 'realist' elements it is interesting to note that Deodato had worked as Roberto Rossellini's assistant on a number of films, including *Viva l'Italia!* (1960), *Anima nera* (1962), and *L'età del ferro* (1964)). The projection of the 'found' images again gives rise to an overt concern with validating the nature of what is visible on screen and audible on the soundtrack. Thus as the first of the footage runs, the projectionist helpfully adds that: 'The negative needed special treatment because of the humidity. The quality isn't the best, but it's pretty good considering the lousy conditions they were shooting in'. The scene continues:

Executive: Unfortunately two reels were light-fogged and we had to throw them out.

Projectionist: I've put a piece of black leader between one sequence and another.

Executive: Good, that's where we'll put the interviews with the families and the one where you [the professor] talk about your search for them.

Projectionist: This first segment is silent. [Noise of projector on soundtrack]. Evidently they didn't always use their mikes, though they were attached right to the camera just above the lens, like a gun barrel, see? [A camera held by one of the team is clearly visible at this point].

Projectionist: Remember, this is a very rough cut, almost like watching rushes. A lot of this stuff will be thrown out during the actual editing.

Projectionist: Here we are – should be some sound coming in now. No, no, not yet. Here. [Projector noise gradually fades out].

Executive: How much of the material is without sound?

Projectionist: Less than half. Every so often I've laid in some stock music to juice things up.

However, the paradox of these various devices is that, whilst they are meant to testify to the verisimilitude of what is being shown on screen, they also, at the same time, operate self-reflexively, drawing attention to the process of filmic representation itself and demonstrating that even the most 'realist'-seeming text is in fact an artificial construct. From here, it is surely but a short step to thinking critically about how *Cannibal Holocaust* is *itself* constructed – particularly in the light of its own jaundiced representation of the media, as outlined earlier. Indeed, it could be argued that the film actually contains its own auto-critique, and that to reject the entire enterprise as merely hypocritical is to miss the point.

Just to complicate matters a little further, however, the 'documentary' visual markers serve equally to *disguise* the fabricated nature of the pro-filmic event; as Kerekes and Slater note: 'The ever reliable pop start or film hiccup [...] occur always at the most technically advantageous moment – that is, when Faye's head is about to be lifted from her shoulders or Jack is about to have his chest split asunder' (1995: 49). Equally, in the scene in which the team discover the body of a girl impaled on a pole – a scene which is frequently cited when *Cannibal Holocaust* is charged with being a 'snuff' movie – we clearly see Tommaso circling the body in order to film the grisly spectacle from every possible angle. However, we ourselves are treated to only part of what is clearly meant to be this shot in the montage of the 'found' footage, since to have shown the body in close-up from the rear would have given the game away by revealing that the actress (in fact, the film's costume maker) is sitting on a bicycle seat attached to the pole. Indeed, even the full frontal close-up shot is conveniently obscured by lens flare, as this too might have shown how the effect was achieved. One's perception that this scene, though certainly convincing, is faked is based partly on the knowledge that commercial film-makers simply do not kill people – even 'savages' – for the delectation of the camera, and partly on extra-textual information such as the interviews with Deodato in Fenton, Grainger and Castoldi (1999; 21) and on the EC Entertainment DVD of the film.

The twitch of the death nerve

Much more controversially, however, the film interweaves its scenes of faked human carnage with scenes of the all-too-real killing of animals, scenes which, as Jackson observes, 'transcend the representational parameters of the fictional text' (2002: 41). Here we really do witness, to borrow a Mario Bava title, 'the twitch of the death nerve' – often in unflinching close-up. This technique is clearly intended to intensify, by a process of association and osmosis, the verisimilitude of the scenes in which humans are apparently mutilated and killed. Thus the film crew's guide Miguel (or rather, the actor playing him) cuts the throat of a muskrat, a Yacumo cuts off the top of the head of a monkey and squeezes out its brain, and the actor playing Alan shoots a small pig. The most extended of such scenes is the killing, disembowelling and eating of a turtle. From the way this scene is filmed it is obvious no trickery was involved; in particular, the initial decapitation of the turtle by the guide Felipe (although, again, it is the actor who performs the deed) is filmed in one shot precisely to emphasize that what we are seeing is 'real live death'. The only purpose for which montage is used in this sequence is not to obscure a fake turtle being substituted for a real one at the apparent moment of death, because this clearly did not happen. Instead, it is brought into play simply to maximize the number of angles from which the spectator can view the creature's still pulsating innards. One is also left wondering, incidentally, whether it is 'Faye Daniels' or the actress portraying her who throws up at the sight of this extremely unpleasant scene. Whatever the case, however, in *Cannibal Holocaust* the real deaths of the animals fulfil exactly the same function as the real death of the rabbit in Renoir's *La règle du jeu* (1939), which, as Vivien Sobchack has pointed out:

> *Exceeds the narrative code which communicates it. It ruptures and interrogates the boundaries of narrative representation. It thus has a "ferocious reality" which [the death of the character André Jureau] does not. It stands as an indexical sign in an otherwise iconic/symbolic representation [...] The rabbit's death violently, abruptly punctuates narrative space with documentary space.*

(1984: 293)

Significantly, in a subsequent scene, Felipe (but, here, not the actor playing him) is bitten on the foot by a deadly snake. The action, which climaxes in Anders hacking off Felipe's leg in a vain attempt to save him, is filmed and edited in much the same 'realistic' manner as the death of the turtle – except in one crucial respect. For whereas the actual killing of the turtle was presented in a single shot, here, a combination of montage, whip-pans and camera flare neatly disguises the moment at which, just before Anders' machete makes contact with what is supposed to be Felipe's leg, one is safe to assume prosthetic effects and fake blood were brought into play during the pro-filmic event. The juxtaposition of these two scenes is the clearest illustration of *Cannibal Holocaust*'s aesthetic strategy in which, as Jackson points out: 'actual and simulated mutilation of the body are presented through identical stylistic modes in order to equalize their perceptual effect' (*ibid: 42*).

The fact that the scenes of animal killing in *Cannibal Holocaust* serve to make the scenes of human death and injury more convincing does not, of course, serve to justify their staging in the first place. However, this is not the only device used by

Deodato to blur the boundary between the representation of fictional and actual death.

As noted earlier, *The Last Road to Hell* was described by a BDC-TV executive as a 'put-on'. However, its textual characteristics, plus a certain amount of extra-textual knowledge gleaned from genuinely documentary scenes in various 'Mondo' movies, lead one to believe exactly the opposite. Thus Deodato not only borrows from the codes and conventions of the documentary in order to blur the conventional boundaries between the fictional and the factual, but he also presents actual documentary scenes – which, in all their brevity and artlessness, are actually far more disturbing than any of the orchestrated horrors, however convincing, elsewhere in *Cannibal Holocaust* – as fakes. Here Mikita Brottman is entirely accurate when she states that:

> *"The Last Road to Hell" is a testament of the actual transgression of all those rules that "The Green Inferno" merely pretends to break, particularly those of voyeurism and the public appropriation of what is essentially a private moment – the moment of death. The real "genuine" footage slips by quickly, briefly, undramatically, and with little attention drawn to it; the fake "genuine" footage, on the other hand, is announced elaborately, exotically, and melodramatically.*

(1998: 149)

Hence her wholly justified, if inelegant, conclusion that: '"The Last Road to Hell" is a fleeting and crucial glimpse of the unimaginable reality that *Cannibal Holocaust* (falsely) disguises itself as' (*ibid: 150*).

The pornography of death

It is, I would argue, not simply the manner in which *Cannibal Holocaust* deliberately mingles fictional and factual modes of representation which accounts for its troubling, not to say scandalous, qualities, but, more specifically, the way it crosses conventional barriers between fictional and factual modes of representing death.

As Catherine Russell has observed: 'Death remains feared, denied, and hidden, and yet images of death are a staple of the mass media [...]. Such is the paradox of the absence of death from daily lived experience on the one hand and its omnipresence in the media on the other' (1995: 1). In this, she is echoing Geoffrey Gorer's famous essay 'The Pornography of Death', in which he observed that, whereas during the nineteenth century, death as a natural process was frequently and openly discussed, and sex was largely unmentionable outside the context of pornography, in the twentieth century exactly the opposite came to be the case, with fictional violence playing an analogous role to the sexual imagery which was such a concomitant of nineteenth-century prudery. As Gorer put it: 'While natural death became more and more smothered in prudery, violent death has played an ever-growing part in the fantasies offered to mass audiences' (1965: 173). But while it is indeed the case that death in our society has come to achieve a status at once spectacular and taboo, it is, *pace* Russell and Gorer, only in *fictional* works of one kind or another that its representation is omnipresent, whilst documentaries and news programmes are far more sparing in terms of both the amount and the nature of the images of the dead and dying which they offer us.

Death in fictional feature films is not only amply represented but is often exceedingly visible. Safely contained by narrative, in iconic and symbolic signs and structures, cinematic fictions offer a mediated view of death which softens its threat. Furthermore, for extra-textual reasons, we know that, as Russell puts it: 'Death in fiction film always belongs to the regime of the fake, marking the very threshold of the "illusions of reality" and the myth of "total cinema": the pathos and irony of representation' (1995: 19). For this reason, she argues that:

> *The representation of violent death in film constitutes a special crisis of believability, a threshold of realism and its own critique. Enacted death, bodily violence, and corporeality (such as surgical operations) are privileged points at which realism makes a firm break with the real, as the bullet-ridden corpse is at once the height of artifice and of horror.*

> (*ibid*: 23)

Thus the extent to which a fictional film can claim to be presenting death 'realistically' is obviously limited and relative. Furthermore, as Sobchack points out: 'The representation of the event of death is an indexical sign of that which is always in excess of representation, and beyond the limits of coding and culture [...]. Nonbeing is not visible. It lies over the threshold of visibility and representation (1984: 287). In this respect it is significant that at the climax of *Cannibal Holocaust* (exactly as in *The Blair Witch Project* (1999)), as the sole surviving film-maker dies and their still-operating camera drops to the ground, capturing in close-up the moment of the film-maker's death before running out of film, the end of life becomes synonymous with the end of cinematic representation.

It is for this reason that Sobchack argues that the most effective cinematic signifier of death is violent action inscribed on the *living* body, because it is this which most effectively signifies the transformation from being to not-being. In this she is echoed by Russell when she argues that:

What Linda Williams has described as "the frenzy of the visible" in the context of hard-core pornography compensates for the invisibility of female sexual pleasure. The frenzy of violence likewise opens up the possibility of resistance in its excessive over-compensation for the unrepresentable, unknowable, and invisible event of death.

(1995:18)

The representation of death in non-fiction films is obviously constrained, too, by the limits of signification, but it is also constricted by the various taboos surrounding 'real' death in our society and thus has always to be ethically justified. Witness, for example, the avoidance of footage of bodies, and, in particular, of people jumping to their deaths from the World Trade Center on September 11, or the considerable heart-searching about 'how much' to show on British television of the footage of the dead during the invasion of Iraq in 2003 (for an extended discussion of the latter see Petley 2004). As Sobchack puts it:

When death is represented as fictive rather than real, when its signs are structured and stressed so as to function iconically and symbolically, it is understood that only the simulacrum of a visual taboo is being violated. However, when death is represented as real, when its signs are structured and inflected so as to function indexically, a visual taboo is violated, and the representation must find ways to justify the violation.

(1984: 291)

In this respect, it is interesting to note that Deodato himself felt constrained to justify the scenes of animal killing in *Cannibal Holocaust*, firstly on pragmatic grounds (the animals were eaten by the extras), and then by criticising the very taboo identified by Gorer:

When I was a child I lived in the country, and it was normal to see a chicken, a rabbit or a pig being killed. Today my daughter sees it and she becomes distressed. Even when there was a dead person in the family, in previous times all the family used to watch over the corpse; today when somebody dies their body is hidden straight away. Before, death was a natural fact, and now it has become a taboo.

(Fenton, Grainger and Castoldi 1999: 16)

The documentary which represents 'real live death' has not only to justify its cultural transgression but also to make visible its justification for doing so. This it does by means of certain signifiers, such as 'the camera's stability or movement in relation to the situation which it perceives, in the framing of the object of its vision, in the distance that separates it from the event, in the persistence or reluctance of its gaze' (Sobchack: 292). These signify 'the manner in which the immediate viewer – the filmmaker with camera – physically mediates his or her own confrontation with death, the way s/he ethically inhabits a social world, visually behaves in it and charges it with a moral meaning visible to others'(*ibid*). Furthermore, such signifiers are the means by which the spectator gauges his or her *own* ethical stance in relation to the filmed death:

> *It is the codification of visual behaviour as it acts to circumscribe the sight of death and bear (bare) its traces that allows both filmmaker and spectator to overcome, or at least to circumscribe, the transgression of what in our present culture is a visual taboo. It allows both filmmaker and spectator to view death's 'ferocious reality', if not from a comfortable position, then from an ethical one [...]. This activity constitutes a moral conduct: the conventionally agreed upon manner and means by which a visually taboo, excessive, and essentially unrepresentable event can be viewed, contained, pointed to, and opened up to a scrutiny that is culturally sanctioned.*

> (*ibid*)

Voyage au bout de l'abominable

It is precisely these carefully erected and culturally sanctioned distinctions between fictional and factual modes of representing death that *Cannibal Holocaust* violates and tramples on at every turn. And it is for this reason, I would argue, that the film is still capable of generating such opprobrium and outrage in a cinematic culture far more suffused with images of carnage than was the one into which it was born. It is this, too, which makes *Cannibal Holocaust* such a different kind of film from the superficially (and suspiciously) similar *The Blair Witch Project*. Admittedly, *Blair Witch* goes beyond its predecessor in the sense that, not content with utilising various documentary codes and conventions in order to create a plausible 'reality effect', it also brings into play, to the same end, the 'video look' and various extra-textual resources such as web-sites, a television documentary, and DVD extras (Roscoe 2000). However, in the last analysis it is little more than a clever *jeu d'esprit*, and completely lacks the lasting ability of *Cannibal Holocaust*, this 'voyage au bout de l'abominable' as Raymond Lefèvre (1971: 41) called it in homage to Céline, to provoke, scandalize and shock. Of course, this is not necessarily a positive, let alone progressive, attribute, but any film which can give rise to sustained and serious reflection on matters such as media sensationalism and voyeurism, fictional and factual representational codes and conventions, and attitudes towards death and its representation in modern societies, and which does so in a way that gets under the skin of the censorious, must surely have something going for it!

References

Black, Joel (2002) 'Real(ist) horror: from execution videos to snuff films', in Mendik, Xavier and Schneider, Steven Jay (eds.), *Underground U.S.A.: Filmmaking Beyond the Hollywood Canon*. London: Wallflower, 63-75.

Brottman, Mikita (1998) *Meat is Murder! An Illustrated Guide to Cannibal Culture*. London: Creation. A slightly different version of the chapter on *Cannibal Holocaust* in this book appears in Brottman, Mikita (1997) *Offensive Films: Toward an Anthropology of Cinéma Vomitif*. Westport, Conn.: Greenwood Press.

Fenton, Harvey, Grainger, Julian and Castoldi, Gian Luca (1999) *Cannibal Holocaust and the Savage Cinema of Ruggero Deodato*. Guildford: FAB Press.

Garsault, Alain (1981) *Cannibal Holocaust*, in *Positif*, 243, June, 65.

Géré, François (1981) *Cannibal Holocaust*, in *Cahiers du Cinéma*, 326, July-August, 63.

Gorer, Geoffrey (1965) 'The Pornography of Death', in Gorer, Geoffrey *Death, Grief and Mourning in Contemporary Britain*. London: The Cresset Press, 169-175.

Jackson, Neil (2002) '*Cannibal Holocaust*, Realist Horror, and Reflexivity', in *Post Script: Essays in Film and the Humanities*, 21, 3, 32-45.

Johnson, Eithne and Schaeffer, Eric (1993) 'Soft core/hard gore: *Snuff* as a crisis in meaning', in *Journal of Film and Video*, 45, 2-3, summer-fall, 40-59.

Kerekes, David and Slater, David (1995) *Killing for Culture: an Illustrated History of Death Film from Mondo to Snuff*. London: Creation.

Lefèvre, Raymond (1981) *Cannibal Holocaust*, in *Image et Son*, 361, May, 39-41.

Petley, Julian (2000) 'Snuffed out: nightmares in a trading standards officer's brain', in Mendik, Xavier and Harper, Graeme (eds.) *Unruly Pleasures: the Cult Film and its Critics*. Guildford: FAB Press, 205-219.

Petley, Julian (2004), 'Let the atrocious images haunt us', in Miller, David (ed.) *Tell Me Lies: Propaganda and Media Distortion in the Attack on Iraq*. London: Pluto, 164-175.

Roscoe, Jane (2000) 'Mock-documentary goes mainstream', in *Jump Cut*, 43, 3-8.

Roscoe, Jane and Hight, Craig (2001) *Faking It: Mock-documentary and the Subversion of Factuality*. Manchester: Manchester University Press.

Roy, Jean (1981) *Cannibal Holocaust*, in *Cinéma 81*, 270, 125-26.

Russell, Catherine (1995) *Death, Closure, and New Wave Cinemas*. Minneapolis: University of Minnesota Press.

Slater, Jay (2002) *Eaten Alive! Italian Cannibal and Zombie Movies*. London: Plexus Publishing.

Sobchack, Vivien (1984) 'Inscribing ethical space: ten propositions on death, representation and documentary', in *Quarterly Review of Film Studies*, fall 1984, 283-300.

Winston, Brian (2000), *Lies, Damn Lies and Documentaries*. London: British Film Institute.

15. Beyond the Blair Witch: A New Horror Aesthetic?

Peg Aloi

Following the runaway commercial success of the low-budget 'fake documentary' *The Blair Witch Project* (1999), a number of American independent film-makers attempted to imitate the film's unique production elements and recreate its raw but subtle visual aesthetic. Despite its containing no trace of what might be called cinematography, art direction, or traditional narrative structure, the film does possess a signature 'look' (resulting from the use of hand-held cameras and the setting of key action sequences off-camera or in total darkness) and 'feel' (urban dwellers interact with nature while a threatening occult force manifests, associated with a given location's history). It may be argued that *The Blair Witch Project* is one of the finest horror films of all time, and certainly one of the most original, ground-breaking American independent films of the last decade. For what seemed the first time in years, a commercially viable horror film took a 'less is more', psychological (as opposed to visceral) approach to horror, and audiences worldwide were fascinated and outraged in equal measure. The accompanying web-based publicity campaign generated rumors of the film's 'authenticity' (i.e. that the 'found footage' was indeed real), prompting some audience members to visit the film's location in search of 'what really happened.' The film's visual and aural stylings (filmed as it was by actors with virtually no film-making experience) have also impacted shifting trends in the horror genre, inspiring a range of imitative works in film and even in television reality shows such as MTV's *Fear*. This chapter explores the new horror aesthetic emerging in contemporary cinema: one that favors implied authenticity over seamless artificiality; as well as the evolving contexts and implications surrounding what we think of as 'horror.' I will refer throughout to three films that I feel constitute the most significant representations of this burgeoning school: Eduardo Sanchez and Dan Myrick's *The Blair Witch Project*; Brad Anderson's *Session 9* (2001); and Larry Fessenden's *Wendigo* (2001).

Low-budget horror cinema is not a new phenomenon, although it has taken on a fashionable mantle recently, with a film industry very enamored with digital video and its possibilities. Their camp or kitsch value aside, such films can make a strong immediate impression, or achieve 'cult' status over time, simply because they succeed as examples of the genre.

In his essay 'The Pragmatic Aesthetics of Low-Budget Horror Cinema', Thomas M. Sipos writes:

The bulk of horror's finest films, its most influential, effective and innovative works, have been low-budget efforts produced by film-makers who were forced to cut corners [...] [and who] put their technical compromises to artistic effect, their pragmatic choices to aesthetic service.

(Sipos 2001)

In this gentleman's club we can include film-makers whose work may seem very different in intent and realization, but who all have the creative use of a low-budget aesthetic in common. There is Roger Corman's *Masque of the Red Death* (1964), Jacques Tourneur's *I Walked With a Zombie* (1943) and *Curse of the Demon* (1957), Robin Hardy and Anthony Shaffer's *The Wicker Man* (1973), and Bill Gunn's *Ganga and Hess* (1973). Perhaps the most influential and ground-breaking is George Romero's 1968 masterpiece, *Night of the Living Dead*. As Sipos describes it:

Night of the Living Dead's grainy, high-contrast black and white images, its harshly reverberant soundtrack, and its rough, handheld camera work convey an urgent documentary sensibility, conferring an immediacy to its story and an intimacy with its actors. It's as though we're watching real people in live combat, much as the Vietnam conflict appeared to audiences of its day.

(Sipos 2001)

Sipos' reference to contemporary news footage underscores the uncanny authenticity of the simulated news broadcasts contained within the film, and suggests a symbolic paralleling between the flesh-eating ghouls and their victims and the Vietnamese and American soldiers. Romero's later films also suggest a metaphorical reading for zombies: consumerism and 'mall culture' are the targets in the sequel, *Dawn of the Dead* (1979). A Romero historian, Paul Gange, writes that all of Romero's artistic choices in *NOTLD*, including the grainy film stock, the portrayal of gore, and even the chosen genre, were

always a budgetary rather than an aesthetic consideration [...] and the decision to take a direct, visceral approach to the gore was purely an attempt to make the film noticeable; [...] it wasn't a political or artistic statement or anything else that critics have read into it.

(Gange 1987: 21-22)

Gange also states that Romero had never wanted to use black-and-white film, but simply could not afford colour stock (21). But because of this financial limitation, he achieved the look that inspired the zombie-as-social-metaphor readings, and created an artful *mise en scene* which relied upon composition instead of colour, and his use of black paint for blood and animal parts for human entrails more or less revolutionized horror special effects. Romero's signature look has been widely imitated and credited as inspiration to many filmmakers since, as seen in works such as Herk Harvey's *Carnival of Souls* (1962) or Sara Driver's *You Are Not I* (1982). Certainly Romero's portrayal of lurching, ravenous flesh-eating ghouls has had many imitators, most notably Alan Ormsby with his low-budget black comedy *Children Shouldn't Play with Dead Things* (1972). Sipos argues that *NOTLD* emerged as a classic of the genre 'precisely because many of its pragmatically motivated technical limitations serve aesthetic functions' (Sipos 2001).

Although it would be reasonable to expect that Romero's film would spawn an aesthetic revolution in horror, this did not immediately occur. Ten years after its release, Romero offered another pioneering glimpse at a common horror stock character with his low-budget, subtle vampire story *Martin* (1978). Though it had a lukewarm critical reception at first, it is now regarded among Romero's finest works. In the meantime, American-made horror films were an amalgam of 1960s-style B-quality fluff, disaster films, and a few sophisticated stories based on novels such as Thomas Tryon's *The Other* (1972) or Ira Levin's *The Stepford Wives* (1975). Major aesthetic changes to the genre did not occur until 1978, but these changes had mostly to do with sophisticated technology, not artistic concerns *per se*. Critic Philip Brophy argues that the American cinema of the 1970s

> *heralded a double death for Genre in general, as theoretically and critically it became a problematic which more and more could not bear its own weight, and, in terms of audiences and commerciality, it was diffused, absorbed and consumed by that decade's gulping, belching, plug-hole: Realism.*

> (Brophy 1985)

Following this 'death,' Brophy posits a rebirth of horror cinema during a crucial two-year period in 1978 and 1979, with the release of Carpenter's *Halloween* (1978), Scott's *Alien* (1979), Cronenberg's *The Brood* (1979) and Romero's *Dawn of the Dead* (1979). He even suggests budding horror fans might become budding cinephiles, as these new films might encourage a return to the artists' earlier 'classics': 'The historical door of the Horror genre was reopened, allowing discovery of Romero's *Martin*, *The Crazies* (1973) and the classic *Night of the Living Dead*, as well as Cronenberg's *Rabid* (1977) and *Shivers* (1976)' (Brophy 1985). However, as audiences grew used to sophisticated, colourful effects in films, not to mention increasing amounts of graphic footage of war on the nightly television news, made 'acceptable' by the Vietnam coverage of the 1970s, they might well have seen these 'classics' as quaint or archaic. If, as Brophy states in his introduction, horror is a genre 'which mimics itself mercilessly, because its statement is coded within its very mimicry,' then his assessment of the way contemporary horror films 'recklessly copy and redraw their generic sketching' would seem to suggest that the genre lends itself over time to entrenched models of aesthetics, narrative and production methods. Brophy argues that the two main elements defining modern horror's form are (the increasing use of) 'special effects with cinematic realism and sophisticated technology, and an historical over-exposure of the genre's iconography, mechanics, and effects'. Or, as he later puts it: 'The contemporary horror film knows that you've seen it before; it knows that you know what is about to happen; and it knows that you know it knows you know'.

For Brophy, then, horror cinema circa 1985 is caught up in an artistic dilemma: innovation of style, story or form becomes impossible because of expectations intrinsic to the genre. Audiences and film-makers are involved in a satisfying, mutually assured fakery: film-makers use genre conventions to allow the audience a reasonable opportunity for a willing suspension of disbelief. But increasingly, throughout the 1980s, the conventions of horror aesthetics began to stray from their roots in surrealism and German Expressionism, and had to capitulate to the new trends engendered by '70s realism and '80s sensationalism. Even so-called 'arty' popular horror films of the 1980s (Tony Scott's *The Hunger* [1983], or Alan Parker's *Angel Heart* [1987], for example) offered grisly, if beautifully photographed, scenes of violence. But even as this trend towards 'realistic' violence grew, so did another: self-referential irony. A blackly humorous element began to creep in, and the more excessive the violence and gore, the more tongue-in-cheek the film's tone, including Sam Raimi's *Evil Dead* films and the popular sequels to *Halloween* and *Nightmare on Elm Street* (all of which eventually spawned the *Scream* and *Scary Movie* parodies). With American horror increasingly unable to take itself seriously, new life had to be infused into the genre. Since 'more' had become the operative concept (more gore, more violence), perhaps 'less' might be a good place to start. Enter the *Blair Witch*? Not quite yet. First, there was the Dogme collective in Scandinavia.

The three films discussed in this essay have garnered their share of Dogme references from critics. Richard Scheib wrote that '*Session 9* is reflective of the new aesthetic that seems to have settled on the horror film after *The Blair Witch Project* – and which in turn was influenced more than a little by Lars von Trier, Thomas Vinterberg and their Dogma school of minimalist purity' (Scheib, 1999). It has been argued by more than one critic that *Blair Witch* is, in effect, a Dogme film (Parker, 1999), although it did not seek any such validation. The nature of horror films, with their reliance upon artificiality of design and supernatural motifs, would seem to be outside the realm of narratives suited for Dogme, the 'rules' of which preclude the use of genre. Nevertheless, several Dogme films released so far have been violent or disturbing in their own right, most notably *The King is Alive* (2000) and Thomas Vinterberg's *The Celebration* (*Festen*, 1998), which includes an arguably-supernatural scene portraying the ghost of the protagonist's deceased twin sister.

The notion of minimalist purity is worth noting as we trace the evolution and impact of the new horror aesthetic. This spare approach to aesthetics goes hand-in-hand with the 'fake documentary' conceit, which seems eminently suitable for horror, since it allows for audience speculation that what are normally accepted as 'supernatural' stories could in fact be 'real.' Paradoxically, however, the 'less is more' approach of *Blair Witch* relegates horror to the realm of the psychological, and not the 'actual' realm suggested by the presence of blood and gore. In his essay on language and the *Blair Witch* phenomenon, James Keller states: 'While the violent history of the Blair Witch may be a complete fabrication, it is at least as real as any other legend of the supernatural, all of which exist only in the retelling of the pertinent tales' (Keller, 1999). But this minimal manifestation of evil may well have a sensationally gory predecessor. Although Myrick and Sanchez have denied it ('If we stole from anything, we stole from *COPS*' [Collura 1999]), a number of critics have speculated that they were more than a little inspired by Italian director Ruggero Deodato's *Cannibal Holocaust* (1979), the subject of the previous chapter. This film was not widely known until critics began pointing out similarities to *Blair Witch*: most notably the 'found footage' framework and the notion that the 'film-makers' died during the process. The fake documentary format allows for a provocative narrative context, and also primes the canvas for acceptance of low-budget production values.

Now audiences have become inured (if reluctantly) to hand-held camerawork in horror films, this aesthetic may become as entrenched as the dramatic camera angles and chiaroscuro lighting of early horror. Certainly the trendy acceptability of this visual style has allowed fledging filmmakers a niche in a marketplace which might have shut them out a decade ago. The implementation of a 'new' simpler aesthetic is also clearly an effort to hearken back to a 'simpler' horror cinema. Tellingly, Sanchez and Myrick's company, Haxan Films, is named for an obscure 1922 Swedish silent film, *Haxan: Witchcraft through the Ages*. Clearly the film-makers wished to make known their love of classic horror cinema. That they were able to create a box office record-breaker, and a new horror classic, with less money than what most Hollywood productions spend on sugarless gum, is astonishing.

Anderson and Fessenden, independent filmmakers also working within budgetary limitations (although both already had critically acclaimed films to their credit before beginning work on *Session 9* and *Wendigo*) probably would not have found the critical and audience acclaim they did with these films if *Blair Witch*'s raw aesthetic, controversial but intriguing, had not paved the way. Comparisons have been made between the three films by critics because of similarities in subject-matter, setting and aesthetic choices. For the Dogme artists, production limits were self-imposed, artistic, political, even philosophical; for Sanchez-Myrick, Fessenden and Anderson, budget was key. But it still came down to the same thing; location, location, location.

The 'look and feel' of these three films depends to a large extent upon their chosen locations, selected for reasons of financial accessibility and practicality, but also for their inherent suitability for the film-makers' aesthetic vision. The Dogme 95 rules, known as the 'Vow of Chastity,' do not allow artificial or exotic locales to be used (Vinterberg, von Trier 1995). Likewise, the three American narratives being discussed here were written (or in the case of *Blair Witch*, constructed and improvised) to take place in a precise, but decidedly unexotic, location. In each case, there is an overwhelming sense of 'rightness' – and 'realness' – to these locales. The Blair Witch could not conceivably have lived anywhere other than in that patch of woods in Maryland. The Wendigo had to manifest in an area rich in Native American folklore, where urban tourists and local hunters could clash, like upstate New York. The ninth session of *Session 9* had to be recorded in a grand old Victorian mental hospital in Danvers, Massachusetts (formerly known as Salem Village). The choice of these locations was specific, sensible, organic; which is the precise manner in which the Dogme film-makers are asked to work.

The film-makers seem well aware of the similarity of their working styles to their Dogme counterparts. Daniel Myrick said of *Blair Witch*: 'It was all an aesthetic, versus trying to create reality, because it had to look real' (Broom 1999). The idea of what is 'real' and how such a question informs aesthetic choices seems crucial for all of these film-makers. Larry Fessenden, who uses Super 16mm film and authentic forest locations in New York's Catskill region, had lofty design aspirations which hearken back to horror's roots:

> *I'm sort of tributing the German Expressionists. I'm saying, look, can the audience participate in creating this monster? That's part of the Wendigo and part of the process of enjoying the film. I wanted to sort of allow that in a deconstructionist way, so the audience could see something that wasn't real.*

(Kipp 2001)

In one interview Brad Anderson admits that *Session 9* was conceived of as 'a little DV project – a little Dogme movie. We were gonna shoot it on little digital cameras, just sneak into the place and shoot it.' Then he laughs and says: 'The whole *Blair Witch* curse kind of felt like it was gonna fall on us. Like that kind of whole thing had already been done before. So we figured we'd do it as a really straightforward movie' (Chase 2002). In another interview, Anderson describes the impetus for his foray into horror:

The seed for the film came out of that location [...]. I'd often see this place driving down Route 93, looming there on the hill. It always occurred to me that this would be the most appropriate place to do a good horror movie.

(Orange 2001)

Ed Sanchez said of *Blair Witch* that the location came first in the creation of their narrative. 'We needed a reason for them to be out in the woods; originally it was about a satanic cult, then the witch legend came through' (Aloi 1999a: 3). For these film-makers, then, the location IS the film, and it is ultimately the wooded location that inspires the story's underlying 'legend' and its supernatural content. In her essay on gender in *The Blair Witch Project*, Deneka C. MacDonald writes: 'A figure whose image plays an integral role in her literary presentation, the "witch" is typically fused with her "forest"' (MacDonald 2001). Dan Myrick says local mythology played a part: 'The Northeast, there's a lot of witch folklore out there... [so we asked ourselves] what would logically be out there? But it's really just a set-up to get three kids in the woods so we can fuck with them' (Aloi 1999a). As Keller puts it, 'the division between fiction and reality dissolves whenever the issue of myth and legend is broached [...] [such] tales, just like the Blair Witch, have only a textual reality' (1999). In other words, since we never 'see' the Blair Witch in the film, she may be anything we imagine her to be, just as she would be if we had only read about her. The 'tale' of making the film, the ordeal the actors faced, may be added to the already complex layer of texts surrounding this production: the 'fabricated texts' of the original film, the television specials, the dossier, the CD, and so on – and the 'real texts' acknowledging the whole *Blair Witch* phenomenon, including online discussion groups, accounts of fans who travelled to Burkittsville to 'get the real story,' and the meta-cinematic sequel made by Joe Berlinger, *Book of Shadows: Blair Witch 2* (2000). All of these texts taken together, a virtual explosion of literature, images and hype, add up to the sort of cultural spectacle one normally associates with big-budget blockbusters; this may be what led to the unusually pervasive crop of mean-spirited criticism that greeted Berlinger's film, in which a group of *Blair Witch*-savvy young adults make their own film in the woods.

Sanchez and Myrick' s rag-tag production team were experienced hikers and outdoorsmen. This ensured safety on what was a notoriously-unorthodox film shoot: the actors/photographers had almost no contact with the film-makers on a daily basis, and were referred to written notes left in agreed-upon locations. They were kept to a grueling schedule, hiking progressively longer distances each day, while their food rations and rest periods were decreased dramatically. While never in danger of actually being lost, the actors were nevertheless getting more exhausted by the day. Coaching the actors during the actual shoot was unnecessary: they were thoroughly immersed in as realistic a scenario as could safely be arranged. This was guerilla film-making, raw and mercenary, inventive and effective, and also surprisingly affordable. Knowing what they could afford to spend on videotape and film, the film-makers had only to let the actors/photographers keep the cameras running. The monumental task of editing the footage to create a comprehensible fictitious chronicle shows what a leap of faith these film-makers were making with their young cast. The actors brought back the 'real' footage; but the film-makers had to selectively determine what audiences might ultimately accept as being 'true.'

While shooting films always carries its share of risks, the 'true story' of working on low-budget productions is fraught with difficulties engendered by lack of resources. Brad Anderson was able to gain backing from USA Films and had a budget of just under $2 million. The bulk of his funds went towards transferring the initial video footage to film, demonstrating his commitment to crafting a specific aesthetic above all else. His location, the abandoned Danvers State Hospital, was deemed unfit for human entry just after the production wrapped; Anderson described the shoot as 'arduous'. He describes the intensity of the actors' experiences, the uncanny and sometimes-frightening psychological effects of working in this unusual location. Studio executives thought the film had been shot on a soundstage. He received memos saying: 'We were so amazed at the way your production designer made the chipped paint on the wall look so realistic,' and: 'How did she get the floors to look so decrepit?' Anderson says 'That's the Hollywood mentality: why go there to the real thing when you can just replicate it on a soundstage in Burbank?' (Chase 2002). In saying this Anderson is also echoing the Dogme edict that artifice of setting should be forbidden to cinema; but he shows disdain for comfortable, well-funded Hollywood-style shoots as well.

The Dogme directors may formally eschew aesthetic concerns, but their seemingly cavalier attitude towards *mise en scene* is belied by the sheer visual beauty of their films. In straining at the seams of technical minimalism, a refreshing new aesthetic is born. At least the new indie horror directors are not intentionally rejecting aesthetics out of hand as being too formal or unnecessary. The use of natural light in some Dogme films is inventive and occasionally pointed out as being too clever or pre-ordained; such as the candlelight ghost sequence in *The Celebration*, or the lovemaking scene in *Mifune* (1999) where a lamp is knocked from a table to the floor, providing a backlit effect. Both films were photographed by Anthony Dod Mantle, who went on to film Harmony Korine's *julien donkey-boy* (1999) and Danny Boyle's zombie thriller *28 Days Later* (2002). Fessenden and Anderson both have DPs they have employed more than once; Fessenden refers to Terry Stacey as 'a real rock 'n roll kind of DP' who understood his desire to 'pay attention to the environment and get a shot of that cool tree' because 'that's very much a part of the movie' (Kipp 2001).

The creative utilization of natural light in contemporary horror films becomes all the more intriguing when considering the history of the horror aesthetic. Spooky organ music aside, the black and white horror classics were almost wholly dependent upon lighting to create tone and mood. Lighting is the element that shapes a representation of a monster or monstrous human or monstrous psychological force that is striking and memorable; hard to shake off because we cannot fully see what it is, or it is revealed to us with such dramatic effect that it speaks to our most private fears. Some of the foremost examples of filmic lighting in the horror genre have occurred in famously low-budget productions, such as Tourneur's afore-mentioned films, or the use of natural shadows, flashlights, torchlight and car headlights in *Night of the Living Dead*. The three contemporary film-makers discussed here, Anderson, Fessenden and Myrick/Sanchez, not only utilize natural and non-cinematic lighting to dramatic effect; but often the presence or absence of light is itself key to the narrative. The campers in *The Blair Witch Project* cannot see who or what is near their tent because their flashlights are inadequate. They eventually decide not to light a fire at their camp, despite the cold, believing its illumination will draw their stalkers to them. In *Wendigo*, the darkened forest takes on a surreal quality and Fessenden uses effects that suggest the characters' perception of the forest shifts at night. In *Session 9*, the character who is afraid of the dark (Jeff) ends up trapped in the basement as the electrical generator fails, and he runs screaming down a tunnel as the lights wink out faster than he can outrun them. It is daytime, and yet his irrational fear makes the scene play as if it is midnight. In making light and dark so crucial to story, these film-makers pay homage to the genre's most significant visual element, even as they reinvent it by using a minimalist aesthetic.

Early 1970s film audiences were charmed by the soft, grainy look of American art-house films, an effect crafted in part through the use of natural light and realistic locations. This aesthetic also spread to the horror genre, notably in Daniel Mann's *Willard* (1971), William Friedkin's *The Exorcist* (1972), and *Ganga and Hess* (1973), and some might argue that Roman Polanski's *Rosemary's Baby* (1968) heralded a new look and tone for American horror cinema. But in terms of low-budget affairs, none was more shocking or reviled, and ultimately influential, than Wes Craven's *Last House on the Left* (1972), a work that featured natural settings and lighting, and realistic violence. Craven was inspired by the immediacy and power of the Vietnam television coverage and experimented with different 16mm film stocks to get the right amount of graininess (Szulkin 1997: 49). He based his screenplay upon Bergman's *The Virgin Spring* (1960), a medieval tale of rape, revenge and redemption (Szulkin: 35). But the film's literary ambitions were lost upon audiences and critics; it was lambasted for its newsreel-style crudity, gratuitous sexual brutality and misanthropic message. Although Craven's film was so hated by critics and audiences alike that he was moved to actually give away the only full print of the film to a fan (*Films in Review* publisher Roy Frumkes)

(Szulkin 157), he continued to work in horror and emerged some years later with the wildly popular *Nightmare on Elm Street* series (from 1984).

With this series, Craven shifted the realm of violence and death into the realm of dreams, creating a world in which characters' fear of their own nightmares determined the actual level of danger to which they were vulnerable. This is an ingenious commentary upon the horror genre, since, as has been discussed by countless theorists (E. Ann Kaplan, in her 1983 book *Women and Film*, for example), the ritual of cinema is markedly similar to the experience of dreaming. We are immobilized in a dark room in which images we cannot control (and yet are actively, imaginatively involved in creating) are spooled before us, challenging us to believe in them and perhaps to be frightened of them. Sanchez and Myrick understood this, with their filming of key action sequences in total darkness.

But increasing the genre's psychological depth ever so slightly did not negate the fact that 1980s horror films had become little more than titillating showcases for gory effects. Fessenden has commented upon the need for the horror genre to reinvent itself: 'Recently, horror movies have fetishized serial killers and clinically gruesome effects, as we become possessed by the arbitrariness of violence and our ability to recreate it in the movies. This is a slump. But the genre can rise again from the proverbial grave' (Kipp 2001). But breaking out of this rut has proved difficult for Hollywood; even Craven, following the successful *Scream* (1996) and *Scream 2* (1997), finds himself doing little these days beyond attaching his name to forgettable, formulaic 'Wes Craven Presents' films such as *Dracula 2000* (2000) or *They* (2002). Roy Frumkes, the afore-mentioned fan who acquired Craven's *Last House* outtakes, said that Craven feels that '*Last House*'s raw power transcends any of the work he has done in Hollywood' (Aloi 1999b).

For independent filmmakers to try to sell a horror film that does not follow the tried and true, if banal and unoriginal, 1980s-style formula, is difficult in a demographic-obsessed market in which horror is already a limited genre. To shatter the mold of the contemporary horror film, and still market such a product *as* a horror film, is daring indeed. Dan Myrick said about *Blair Witch*: 'We wanted people, from the beginning to the end of the film, not to have any clue while watching the film that it was a piece of fiction' (Broom 1999). So it was an intelligent commercial move, if a morally questionable one, to set rumors and fake facts in place months before the film's release, right down to listing the actors as 'deceased' on the Internet Movie Database website, and putting up missing persons flyers in Park City, Utah, during the Sundance festival. And though it is debatable whether such success can ever be duplicated (the Haxan team were very adamant in turning down any offers to direct the sequel, although a 'prequel' is in development), what the young Orlando upstarts did was to infuse the horror genre with life, boldness and vision. They proved that the horror genre had life in it to be renewed.

In recent years the horror genre's foray into digital video has become very popular internationally, particularly in Japan, with recent films such as *The Ring* (1998), *Audition* (2000) and *St. John's Wort* (2001) attracting huge fan bases around the globe. These Japanese films also feature a narrative emphasis upon video and computer technology and culture. *The Blair Witch Project* is clearly commenting more or less directly upon video culture. A review on the Internet Movie Database calls the film 'an organic criticism of a generation raised on television (Internet Move Database 1999). That the film purports to be a 'found' text which offers evidence and an explanation of what happened to the 'missing' film crew downplays the idea that this uncut footage had to be edited. Some audiences may believe the reel is played as it was filmed, unexpurgated, as a way to discover the 'truth.' Ironically the 'real' film-makers, in order to craft their narrative, had to edit more than 100 hours of raw footage (Aloi 1999a). It is tempting to describe this process as one of 'discovery,' of finding truth within a mystery (what really happened in the woods?), similar to what audiences are asked to believe, since the 'real' film-makers did not fully know what had transpired during the shoot until they themselves viewed the footage. Audiences are constantly reminded of the artificiality of cinema while viewing this film: the 'realness' quotient of *Blair Witch* is stymied by jerky camera movement and unscripted, awkwardly repetitive dialogue which, despite being completely natural, nevertheless occasionally has a false ring to it, for audiences weaned on seamless, Hollywood-style narratives. But by shattering expectations of what horror film could be, Myrick and Sanchez, along with Fessenden and Anderson, have effectively created a new genre (and perhaps acquired a new audience) alongside their new aesthetic, inspired by their own idiosyncratic love of cinema and their ability to critique the contemporary culture in which they are willing participants.

In an article he refers to as his 'secret discussion of horror', Larry Fessenden states: 'What I like about horror films is that combination of metaphor and heightened reality. The focus on fear, the most potent and influential of human emotions, draws attention to the elemental forces at work in life's interactions' (Fessenden 2001). *Wendigo* portrays what happens when we let the wild man/werewolf lay dormant too long; a comment upon our increasingly-technological culture. Fessenden's earlier films in what he has called a trilogy deal with two other potent horror archetypes: *Habit* (1997) is about vampires and *No Telling* (later redubbed *The Frankenstein Complex*) (1991) updates Mary Shelley to the era of corporate-backed animal experimentation. *Wendigo*'s commentary upon the modern dichotomy of nature/technology is seen from the opening frame: Miles, an 8-year-old boy played by Erik Per Sullivan, is sitting in his parents' car, en route to a weekend in the country. He plays with two plastic figures: a werewolf, and a futuristic robot. As Fessenden puts it: 'These are in constant conflict: our most base, animalistic, man-nature kind of mythology thing (if ya read yer Joseph Campbell) and the futuristic dream that we'll be robot people who will be enhanced' (Kipp 2001). This archetypal image sums up the central theme: when humans allow their connection to the realms of mythology and nature to be eclipsed by technology and the stress of contemporary living, an unbearable tension is created and must be released.

Similar themes of repression and release can be seen in the *Blair Witch* and *Session 9* narratives; Heather, Mike and Josh do not know what fear truly is until they spend a few days in the woods, cold, hungry, and sleepless; the asbestos workers in Danvers do not fully confront their inner demons until they have spent a few days in the crumbling mental asylum, poisoned, harassed, and sleepless. In all three cases, the narrative suggests that nothing becomes 'real' until the characters are removed from the comforts and routine of the everyday. The status quo is challenged. Similarly, the typical aesthetic and narrative devices of what has passed for 'horror' in recent years is likewise challenged and reimagined, inspired in part by the film-makers' desire to honor the genre's history and staying power.

Fessenden says he chooses to work with horror because

> *it's the most subversive and psychologically raw genre of film [...] Horror also suggests a world unknown, which at least opens the mind to spiritual issues. There is an aesthetic in that, an aesthetic of mystery, darkness, but also of transcendence. My interest is to bring that aesthetic – the gothic aesthetic – into the everyday modern scenario, and also to use the genre to reflect current psychological and social concerns.*

(Fessenden 2001)

And so there we have a thoroughly modern filmmaker speaking of the Gothic aesthetic – which is the birthplace of horror literature in the late 19th century, and the finishing school of horror cinema that has its origins in the early 20th century. Film-maker and scholar John Gianvito suggests that, to some observers, the resurgence of the Gothic in visual culture is a sign of *fin de siecle* anxiety in an era that finds us closer than we have ever been to the brink of extinction: 'The Gothic experience is about stepping into darkness, into that which is forbidden, repressed [...] it resides in a deeper desire to give a shape, a face, to one's greatest fears and thus gain some control over them' (Gianvito 1997: 50). The *Blair Witch* 'documentarians' sally forth to create a film and stumble, lost, into a dark primal place where no help comes; they die. The family from the city sets out for a relaxing country weekend and find threatening phantasms, brutality and needless death. The anxious workers just want to get the job done, and instead wind up haunted, betrayed, broken, dead. What could be more Gothic? These filmmakers take on that most ancient and modern of human fears, but rather than give it a shape (an antlered god? a crumbling asylum?) or a face (a witch? a serial killer? a sadistic film crew?), they give us darkness, dust, ashes, shadows, trees, disembodied voices, the unknown. Less, not more. Not a New Gothic. A New Horror.

References

Aloi, Peg (1999a), interview with Daniel Myrick and Eduardo Sanchez. 'The Witches Voice: Witches and Pagans in the Media'. 11 July. http://www.witchvox.com/media/blairwitch interview.html

Aloi, Peg (1999b) 'Last House on the Left.' *The Boston Phoenix*. Arts section, 3. May 20. Broom, Tracie (1999) 'Witch Doctors.' *The Metropolitan*, online version, 19 July 1999. http://www.metroactive.com/papers/sfmetro/07.19.99/blairwitch-9927.html Date of access: 15/12/02.

Brophy, Philip (1985) 'Horrality: The Textuality of Contemporary Horror Films.' (reprint) *Screen* Vol. 27. London, UK. Cited from original publication in *Art & Text*, no.11, Melbourne, 1983/5, http://media-arts.rmit.edu.au/Phil_Brophy/Horrality.html. Date of access: 15/12/02.

Chase, David (2002) 'Sessions with Brad.' *Fade In Magazine*, fall www.fadeinmag.com/ANDERSON/interview/brad.html. Date of access: 17/12/2002.

Collura, Scott (1999) 'The Cannibal and the Witch.' *If Magazine*, online edition: Volume 2, Issue 6. 20/9/99. http://www.ifmagazine.com/common/article.asp?articleID=322. Date of access: 17/11/2003.

Espe, Erik (2002) Review of *Session 9*. http://www.esplatter.com/reviewsotos/session9.htm. Date of access: 1/02/2003.

Fessenden, Larry (2002) 'Horror Movies.' 2002. http://www.glasseyepix.com/html/vamp.html. Date of access: 1/02/2003.

Gange, Paul (1987) *The Zombies That Ate Pittsburgh: The Films of George A. Romero*. New York: Dodd, Mead & Co.

Gianvito, John (1997) 'An Inconsolable Darkness: The Reappearance and Redefinition of Gothic in Contemporary Cinema.' *Gothic: Transmutations of Horror in Late Twentieth Century Art*. Ed. Christopher Grunenberg, et al. Cambridge, MA: MIT Press.

Glucksman, Mary (2001) 'Monster Movie', *Filmmaker Magazine* (online edition), 21/2/2001. www.filmmakermagazine.com/archives/ online_features/monster_movie.html. Date of access: 07/01/2003.

Internet Movie Database (1999) (no author credited) Review of *The Blair Witch Project*. http://www.imdb.com/Sections/Genres/Horror/. Date of access: 17/12/2002.

Kaplan, E. Ann. (1983) *Women and Film: Both Sides of the Camera*. New York: Routledge Press.

Keller, James. (1999) '"Nothing That is Not There and the Nothing That Is": Language and the Blair Witch Phenomenon.' *Studies in Popular Culture*, vol. 22, no. 3. http://www.pcasacas.org/SPC/spcissues/22.3/keller2.html. Date of access: 11/19/2003.

Kipp, Jeremiah (2001) 'Wendigo Blues: An Interview With Larry Fessenden.' http://filmcritic.com/misc/emporium.nsf/84dbbfa4d710144986256c290016f76e/d1381d2e453e313 688256a37007d4779?OpenDocument. Date of access: 07/01/2003.

MacDonald, Deneka C. (2002) 'Trespasses into Temptation: Gendered Imagination and *The Blair Witch Project.' Americana: The Journal of American Popular Culture*, vol. 1, issue 1. http://www.americanpopularculture.com/journal/articles/spring_2002/macdonald.htm. Date of access: 11/10/2003.

Orange, B. Alan (2001) 'That's Just Crazy' (review of *Session 9*). http://www.movieweb.com/columns/orange/rev_session9.html, 28/07/2001. Date of access: 15/12/2002.

Orange, B. Alan (2001) Interview with Brad Anderson and David Caruso. http://www.movieweb.com/columns/orange/int_session9_roundtable.html. 23/7/2001. Date of access: 03/01/2003.

Parker, Sabadino (1999) Review of *The Blair Witch Project*. http://www.popmatters.com/film/reviews/b/blair-witch.html. Date of access: 23/8/03.

Scheib, Richard (2001) *Session 9* review. http://www.rottentomatoes.com/source-973/?letter=s (The Science Fiction, Horror and Fantasy Film Review Database). Date of access: 11/01/2002

Sipos, Thomas (2001) 'The Pragmatic Aesthetics of Low-Budget Horror Cinema.' http://www.communistvampires.com/articles/pragmatic.htm. Date of access: 23/11/02. Originally published in *Midnight Marquee* 60, summer/fall 1999, and *Halloween Candy*, 1stBooks Library, 2001.

Szulkin, David (1997) *Wes Craven's Last House on the Left*. Surrey, England: FAB Press.

Vinterberg, Thomas and von Trier, Lars (1995) 'The Vow of Chastity.' Dogme 95 website: dogme95.dk. Date of access: 03/01/2003.

16. Spectres and Capitalism, Spectacle and the Horror Film

Mike Wayne

Within film studies, discussion of the horror film has been dominated by the genre's most popular sources of fear: monsters, vampires and psychotics. Ghosts, as a specific strand within the horror film, have attracted somewhat less critical interest, although possession, often demonic, rather than the residue of something once human (the ghost 'proper'), has figured within studies of the genre (Creed 1993, Krzywinska 2000). Methodologically, critical approaches to the horror genre have been dominated by psychoanalytic explanations, usually Freudian and Lacanian in orientation. Here the horror is conceptualised as the fear that subjects have towards their own constitutive 'lack' and the fetishistic substitutions they set in play in language and cultural representations generally to disguise and ameliorate this 'lack'. The lack or absence is understood within psychoanalytic traditions as the absent phallus, the nexus point for sexual and social power struggles. The 'social', however, tends in most cases to recede to a faint point on the horizon and instead sexual and intrapsychic processes dominate. Even where the social does figure (and it is usually weighted overwhelmingly towards questions of gender), it is not conceived as having any substantive dynamics outside the sexual/intrapsychic dynamics generated from the volcanic activity of the unconscious.

From a Marxist perspective, the most important 'lack' in psychoanalytic approaches is the lack of a *materialist* understanding of the social world. The Marxist cultural critic Raymond Williams once noted that the problem with capitalism is not that it is too materialistic, but that it is not materialistic enough (Williams 1989:185). What Williams is mobilising here is a rather different sense of the word materialism from its common usage. Normally 'materialism' refers to an excessive investment in material things, such as money and consumer goodies. Of course, capitalism does encourage this 'materialism', but at the same time it represses that deeper materialism comprised by the web of social relationships· and interdependencies that constitute the production and reproduction of human life, including consumer goods. And in this sense, capitalism is *not* materialistic enough because it actively frustrates our sense of sociality. The social becomes pale, thin; it starts to dematerialise before our eyes, and it becomes, in short, *spectral* or ghost-like (Wayne 2003: 183-219). One only has to consider how inadequate are the responses to capitalism's destruction of the natural environment on which all human societies depend, to get a sense of how impoverished our sense of collective responsibility has become, even as we stare into the abyss. The spectre then within the horror film offers us a way of getting to grips with this lack in our own social and body politic. I will identify three modes by which the spectre can be understood as a sign of the ghostly, dematerialised quality of life under capitalism. Firstly the spectre can be understood as a sign of a general waning of sociality, our capacity specifically for intersubjective communication with and recognition of others. Secondly, the spectre can be understood as a sign of the repression of particular social groups. Thirdly, the spectre can be understood as a sign not of the *effects* of capital on society in general or on particular marginalized social groups, but as a sign of capital itself, its particular logic of accumulation and the impact that has on the body (this is figured through possession narratives). But before we do that, I will first locate the figure of the spectre in relation to some broader Marxist cultural critiques of the 'society of the spectacle'. We shall see some hopefully fruitful overlaps and differences between the terms 'spectacle' and 'spectres'.

Spectacles and Spectres

Since its introduction into the English language from Old French in the fourteenth century, the word 'spectacle' (derived from Latin) has retained its original meaning of 'a show'. But not any old show. The term implies some organisation of the visual field that is *out* of the ordinary. Many of the debates and different conceptualisations of the term 'spectacle' turn on this relationship to, and conceptualisation of, the everyday or the norm. In the debased and overused lexicon of marketing today, the extraordinary qualities of a visual display are routinely promised as a means of filling our leisure time (and extracting our disposable income). In this conception, spectacle offers something wondrous and (often technologically) novel, dependent on an existing standard of 'ordinariness' to differentiate its own spectacular qualities while also returning us after the spectacle to that norm which has somehow been both marked by the 'rupture' of the spectacle and unchanged by it.

As a promise and as a rupture, there is (or was?) something latently revolutionary about spectacle. Thus within Marxist cultural theory of the 1920s and 1930s, a nascent mass culture was seen as a potential resource for rupturing the habitual relations of spectators to the world around them (Leslie 2002), denaturalising what was taken for granted and encouraging a series of aesthetic/perceptual shocks to promote social and political awareness. Hence Eisenstein's montage of attractions, Brecht's alienation effects and Benjamin's profane illuminations, which sought to release the utopian energies stored up in the everyday detritus of early consumer capitalism. In such cultural practices, elements of the mass media were conceived as potentially subversive stimulation. But with the commercialisation and conglomeration of the mass media, such optimism for the untapped radical potential of spectacle largely waned and in its place there emerged after the Second World War a more negative assessment of the spectacle.

The locus classicus of this position is the work of Guy Debord, who coined the notion of a 'society of the spectacle' (Debord 1983). Here the onlooker, observer, audience or spectator implied or addressed by the mass media is reduced to a passive agent rather than the active agent envisaged by Brecht, Eisenstein and other avant-gardists. Mass media spectacles offer only a unilateral monologue, not a genuine dialogue between spectacle and spectator; they are riven with manipulations and undeliverable promises. However, it is important to understand that the 'spectacle' in the sense used by Debord is not just a question of the media. It is rather the convergence between the commodity relations of advanced capitalism and the organisation of the senses, particularly though not exclusively the visual field (Debord 1983: 34). This broader critique of our social relations could encompass, for example, sport, politics, corporate identities (Kellner 2003) or our entire built environment. Thus in his study of nineteenth-century Paris, Walter Benjamin explored all the fragments of urban life that were synthesised into the spectacle of an emerging consumer capitalism. He noted, for example, the way mirrors could be used to expand the interior spaces of cafes and shops, making them lighter and brighter and how this was part of a general libidinalization of sight, of looking at others and the self in countless reflections, and all merging with the commodities on display. This narcissistic use of mirrors appropriates an older pre-capitalist image and channels it into the 'magic' of the marketplace. 'One may compare the pure magic of those walls of mirrors which we know from feudal times with the oppressive magic worked by the alluring mirror-walls of the arcades, which invite us into seductive bazaars' (Benjamin 1999a: 541). In this broader conception of spectacle, 'the real' and the spectacle merge; the everyday becomes the site of myriad commodity spectacles (each contradictorily proclaiming its extraordinary quality), the appearance-forms which disguise the deeper real relations of commodity capitalism and the exploitation and asymmetrical power relations on which it is built. Media spectacles are thus not quite the 'escapist' rupture with the ordinary that they present themselves as, because the ordinary and everyday tissue of experience under capitalism is *already an escapist fantasy*.

Debord describes the spectacle as 'the autonomous movement of the non-living' (4), and there is certainly one dimension of spectrality in the horror film, most commonly the haunted house, where the dominance of the 'non-living', the world of commodities, is vividly demonstrated. The relationship between the commodity and death or dead things is something which was posited in the rhetorical strategies of both Benjamin and Marx himself, as he tried to grasp a process by which people lose control over their own labour and its products. The imperative of capital accumulation acquires a life of its own and this thrusts the real human subject (labour turned into a mere commodity) into a new kind of (living) death.

Thus the dominance of the commodity form not only sees the 'non-living' acquire life, but the living acquire a death-like existence, or in a related (and within the horror genre, very popular) development, the dead haunt the living as a rebuke to their dematerialised mode of life.

The spectre, a term which entered the English language from French in the early seventeenth century, has some interesting overlaps and differences with spectacle. Like spectacle, a spectre is something visually arresting and out of the ordinary. But the sense of rupture it evokes is different in that a spectacle is presumed to have natural or human derivation, whereas the spectre passes over into the supernatural, escaping (or severely testing) rational explanation of known laws and matter. Yet even here there is an ambiguity, since the spectre (like other strange phenomena) often provokes rationalistic explanations grounded in natural, social or psychological laws. Just as the spectacle in some discourses is associated with the distraction or concealment of the real, so the spectre is associated with a certain insubstantial, phantasmatic quality. But here is a crucial difference. The spectacle is associated with a *public* show which may then be critiqued as a collective distraction from the real, but the not-real component of the spectre often overlaps with a sense of it being a subjective projection/misrecognition by the individual, or if given within a film an unqualified status of actually existing it usually 'exists' for a few select individuals (*Ghostbusters* [Ivan Reitman 1984 US] is an obvious exception). Thus while spectacles are public displays, spectres are often (but not always) displays for the private or individual gaze.

However, paradoxically, the *publicness* of the public spectacle, its quality as a means for engaging the public as socially connected collectives, is profoundly compromised by its commodification, as Benjamin and Debord argued. Conversely, the spectacle of the spectre is a fleeting, secret, half-glimpsed rupturing of the ordinary appearance-forms of the spectacle; and what is often half glimpsed in the private gaze of the characters (un)lucky enough to see the spectre, is precisely that genuine (if phantasmatic) publicness or collective social being, fragmented and atomised by the appearance-forms of capitalism's commodity relations and images. The spectre (this return of the repressed) has some ghostly affinities with the older Marxist/avant-garde cultural and theoretical practices. It works, however, from a more compromised interior space *within* the spectacle and, overtly at least, it is more grounded in the irrational – this, however, gives the horror genre its peculiar force since much of what we take to be rational masks the deep irrationality of capitalism. The private gaze onto a repressed public/collective relation marks a point of tension within popular forms still largely grounded in individualised modes of storytelling but increasingly having to 'process' raw social material from a systemic, collective and global system (Jameson 1992).

The Horror of the 'Public' Sphere

The term 'public sphere' has been closely associated with the work of the communications philosopher Jürgen Habermas. The public sphere refers to those social mechanisms – in which the media are crucial – for forming 'publics' that can critically engage in dialogue, debate and understanding of the society around them. In *The Structural Transformation of the Public Sphere* (originally published in the early 1960s) Habermas argued that the emerging property relations of capitalism were instrumental in forming a public sphere independent of European states still strongly influenced by the traditions of absolutist feudal rule. An emerging print media helped form and informed a new kind of subject: a reading public that would eventually start to hold rulers to some form of account. Habermas' account is Marxist enough to construct a narrative of dialectical reversal, whereby, as capital grows and expands, and as it transforms into monopoly capitalism and establishes new connections with a state which now bends to and supports capital, the public sphere of informed citizens is hollowed out and replaced by a sphere of privatised fantasies, where the collective dimensions of social life become ever more ghostly.

The Hong Kong horror film *The Eye* (Oxide and Danny Pang 2002) takes us into a consideration of this deadening of our subject-to-subject relations. In the film, a young women, Mun (Angelica Lee), who has been blind since age two, has a corrective operation to restore her sight. Unfortunately, her new corneas have come from a Thai village women who had second sight. As a result, Mun begins to see not only the normal everyday world she has been longing to see, but also a shadow world of ghosts. Mun's possession of the new eyes is unlike other possession narratives in which the subject's possession by a ghost deadens their subjectivity. Quite the contrary, Mun is not so much possessed as possessing new organs which are in effect unbearably sensitive to all the miseries, injustices and pain of other people in time and space. Her new organs of sight (and we often share her point of view, so that we too learn to see again) are like Benjamin's optical unconscious (1999b: 229-230), penetrating the realm of appearance-forms to glimpse our repressed sociality. It is ironic that the horror film as pop culture dedicated to the irrational, actually thematises the same concerns that have preoccupied a rationalist philosopher such as Habermas. In *The Philosophical Discourse of Modernity,* Habermas formulated a philosophy of communicative reason which critiqued what he called subject-centred reason which kills off 'dialogical relationships' and 'transforms subjects, who are monologically turned in upon themselves, into objects for one another. And only objects' (1987: 246). We may add that subject-centred reason (individualism at the level of philosophy) also makes other subjects *invisible*. To see what is usually unseen (and to hear what is usually unheard) is to be made aware that there is something ghostly, thin and faint in our social interrelationships. In seeing ghosts, such as the young boy who lived in the same block of flats and who committed suicide because he lost his report card, Mun is the antithesis of the monologically turned-in subject (even the boy's parents were not attuned to his problem). By contrast, Mun's cognitive and affective senses have broken through our normally contracted, foreclosed and privatised intersubjectivities (the near absence of diegetic noise in many places in the film heightens this sense of the isolation of everyday living).

In one scene Mun is in her bedroom and begins to see (again we are located in her point of view) its familiar features and objects rapidly alternate with a different room. It is as if her new organs of seeing are literally breaking down the four walls of her private self and extending their cognitive and emotional reach in time and space. And yet the ambivalences of the horror film are all too evident, for it is precisely this *extension* of her intersubjective awareness that constitutes the horror to be escaped. Thus while the horror of seeing ghosts suggests a critique of our phenomenal life under capitalism (and the shrunken nature of our public sphere), it is precisely those normal, everyday modes of blindness which provide welcome relief and escape from such painfully heightened modes of super-natural seeing. Horror films often construct a *frame,* say a geographical boundary (the haunted house for example) as well as a temporal frame (a before and after in the narrative), in which the spectacle of horror ruptures everyday modes of seeing, while at the same time the protagonists' escape from the frame provides a route back to some normality, which quietly represses the truth alluded to in the rest of the film; that this everyday life is the *real* horror. In *The Eye* the frame of horror is thus the eye operation itself, and it is hardly surprising when Mun elects to reverse the operation and return to her literal blindness to parallel our own metaphorical blindness in the reified world of capital. In this, *The Eye* is significantly different from *The Sixth Sense* (M. Night Shyamalan, 1999 US) where the boy Cole Sear learns in the end to be reconciled to his power to see ghosts. The fact that he is pre-pubescent is significant, for the horror film's conventional use of the young in this regard does in fact code a sociological truth; namely that children often are extraordinarily open and unencumbered (the way they will talk to strangers, for example) by social codes and conventions that will later turn them into more monologically inward subjects. The process of socialisation then is one in which a subjectivity is constructed in which earlier potentialities for a more extensively attuned orientation to the world around us, are hacked back and walled up within private, competitive, indifferent and anxious 'self contained' individuals (Cushman 1995). Ironically, while rationalistic discourses that permeate the news and information media often reproduce monologic inwardness against the public sphere they are supposed to foster, the irrational register of the fictional horror genre manifests a symptomatic anxiety about the fate of such subject-to-subject relations.

The Problem of the Intelligentsia
'All men are intellectuals', Gramsci once famously noted (we can forgive him the

gender specificity) 'but not all men have in society the function of intellectuals' (1971: 9). The intelligentsia are the growing fraction within the social division of labour who work with knowledge, whose central role is the production and dissemination of knowledge. Fredric Jameson argues, in relation to conspiracy films, that within popular narrative frameworks still largely grounded in individual agency, the category of the intellectual (understood within a Marxist framework) 'endows the individual protagonist with collective resonances, which transforms policeman or journalist, photographer or even media figure, into a vehicle for judgements on society and revelations of its hidden nature' (1992:39). There is some similarity between the conspiracy and the ghost-orientated horror film; indeed one may go so far as to say that they offer explorations of the two poles of the class structure; the conspiracy film sends its investigator into the sprawling (usually secret) operations of the powerful at the top of society, while the horror film usually sends its investigator (if it has one) to the bottom or margins of society.

Because ghosts have an affinity with or often haunt those on the margins of society, the poor, children and adolescents, their presence is registered at the level of urban legend, of oral history, of rumour and half-muttered whisperings. Thus the intellectuals – academics, scientists, and journalists – have to cross into this marginalised world in order to track down their ghostly subject. But their complicity with their position in the class structure often remains a point of contention within the narrative itself. *Candyman* (Bernard Rose 1992 US) opens with an aerial shot of the American city, the spectacle of the built environment here shown with its grid-like structure, boundaries, borders and divisions. The class divisions of Chicago's geography is an explicit reference point for the film, whose main character, a doctoral student of anthropology, can see the black working-class slums from her plush condominium. She crosses these class and racial borders to investigate and rationalise the urban myths of the Projects and specifically the myth of Candyman, a black ghost who eviscerates victims with his hook hand. On the one hand the film recognises the forgotten social crime – still effective at a collective level – which gives rise to the ghost. Candyman derives from a man who was the son of a black slave. Educated, an artist and painter, he fell in love with the white daughter of a powerful landowner and was hacked up, smeared with honey and stung to death by a swarm of bees for his trouble. But the film is politically ambivalent, emphasising Candyman's irrational violence, not least towards the poor black inhabitants of the Projects. This spirit has come not to unite the dispossessed but to slay them if they dare summon him by saying his name five times while looking in a mirror (cue foolish adolescents who do just that).

A similarly ambivalent structure of haunting, where the spectre is poised between having an affinity with particular marginalized groups and preying on them, is evident in Nakata Hideo's *Ring* (1999 Ja), the first instalment of the popular Japanese horror trilogy. Here the axis of social tension runs along the lines of generation and gender. Children, teenagers and women are pushed to the margins of power and recognition in a patriarchal and traditional Japanese society. As with *Candyman*, the outsider position of the investigator (here a journalist) is partly ameliorated by her gender. In this film the ghost or curse of Sadako derives from a telepathic and telekinetic woman from the 1950s who was hounded by the media and eventually betrayed and killed by her father, a disgraced academic who had an affair with Sadako's mother. The novel twist in *Ring* is that it is not only urban myth that keeps the curse alive but also the technological means of video recording and dissemination. The media apparatus which hounded Sadako in the past is now the means by which Sadako's ghost enacts her revenge – although now through the more privatised (and potentially 'underground') mode of consumption which video technology allows. Those who watch the dreaded video – a brief avant-garde text – must pass it on to someone else to watch within seven days or die a horrifying death. The cryptic avant-garde nature of the video is significant in giving it the status of a counter-spectacle inassimilable to the mainstream. The private television screen (through which the spectre of Sadako crawls) has a similar function to the bathroom mirror to which those who dare whisper the name of Candyman. The mirror in Benjamin's analysis of Paris functions as a mediating point in a dialectic between public space and private fantasy. But it worked to turn public space into a private fantasy. Conversely, the mirror and television screen in *Candyman* and the *Ring* films reflect back the private space of the inhabitant(s), but also provide the portal through which a now repressed injustice in the collective/public space of history breaks through. These reflecting screens provide the means of resolving the formal problem of bringing the private/individual gaze and spectral collectivity together into some kind of narrative relationship.

But the condition of escaping the curse in *Ring* is also significant. It offers a way out if the private gaze of the watcher is partially de-privatised by passing the tape on and expanding the circle of watchers ever-outwards in a kind of secret infiltration of the pseudo-public sphere or society of the spectacle. The perfect image of the ghost as the bad conscience of society (and its media) is found in *Ring 2* (Hideo Nakata 1999 Ja) where a television journalist betrays a teenager by not viewing the video after saying he would. After her inevitable death, the journalist tries to erase his videotaped interview with the girl before her death. But instead her image goes into a manic series of repetitive head movements before freakily turning to stare at the watching journalist who subsequently ends up in a mental asylum.

Possession

Thus far we have seen that the spectre can be read as a sign or trace of a repressed sociality or, what is only a symptom of the same thing, a repressed group within society. The spectre thus testifies to the deadening of our capacities for intersubjective recognition on which solidarity and collective life depends. But the spectre can also function as a sign of the deadening of our interior life as subjects subjected to the rule of capital. Possession narratives, in which the autonomy, independence and ethical and moral responsibility to others is at stake, convey this aspect of life under capital.

Under capitalism it is not labour (and its products) in all its diversity and specificity that is registered by economic 'value'.

> As [...] use values, coat and linen, are combinations of special productive activities with cloth and yarn [...] [but] as values, the coat and linen, are, on the other hand, mere homogenous congelations of undifferentiated labour.

(Marx 1983: 52)

Under capitalism, use value, which registers the particular qualities of things, is dominated by value, which is concerned only with the quantative question: 'how much'. As Marx also writes: 'In order to act as [...] a mirror of value, the labour of tailoring must reflect nothing besides its own abstract quality of being human labour generally' (Marx 1983: 64).

The figure of the ghost, then, becomes a way in which we can imagine the abstraction and homogenisation, the sheer equivalence which capital works on the human body and its labours and products, mental and physical. One of the most startling representations within modern cinema of this ghostly abstraction and its indifference to an authentic materiality is to be found in the film *Fallen* (Gregory Hoblit, 1998 US) starring Denzel Washington. He plays a New York cop, Hobbs, on the trail of a serial killer, but it gradually emerges that the killer is a demon, called Azazel, who inhabits the bodies of human beings, turning them into killers before, when they are caught or killed, leaving the body and entering another. Alternatively, the demon can pass from body to body simply by touching someone else. In one scene, the demon, which has decided it wants to taunt and set up Hobbs for the murders it is committing, enters the police station to reveal itself to Hobbs. The horror of this scene resides in the ease with which Azazel can infiltrate the police station, embodying itself in Hobbs' own colleagues. The scene also generates unease because what Hobbs knows, he cannot tell, for his knowledge is impossible to translate into a realm of effective public action (a characteristic splitting between what we know and what we can *do* with that knowledge is typical of advanced fetishistic capitalism). Throughout the film, there are constant references to the possibility of police corruption, to the possibility that someone on the inside might be setting Hobbs up and so forth. There are also repeated indications that police corruption is a given, difficult to tackle and politically dangerous. But what Hobbs finds out so much dwarfs even this possibility that it becomes literally unspeakable. For the problem goes much deeper than merely an institutional malaise. As Hobbs chases the demon out of the station, Azazel merely passes from one body into the next out in the busy street. It is a climactic moment in the film and one in which the scale of the horror (once again seen only by the individual gaze, despite the public space of the action) and Hobbs' powerlessness as a police officer, becomes shockingly evident.

What is significant about the imagery in *Fallen* is that the urban space where the masses live provides the demon with his realm of life, death, movement and reproduction. For those tempted to read the film as an allegory of AIDS, any hint of eroticism and sexuality is evacuated from the demon's movement from one body to another. It is also significant that it is to the mountains outside the city that Hobbs tries to lure the demon in order to kill it. For the demon can only survive outside the body for one breath; a place without bodies to enter is the place where the demon can die. The demon, like capital, is both utterly dependent on possessing a body and at the same time utterly indifferent and hostile to the body it enters.

If human labour, practically conceived as homogeneous, uniform and abstract (without the detail of specificity), is the substance of value, time is its measurement, the means by which the magnitude of value is expressed in the price or exchange value of the commodity, give or take fluctuations in supply and demand around the mean price. It is the average socially necessary time required for the production of labour (with particular skills) and the labour of production, required to make a given product, which measures, quantifies and (via competition) equalises labour and the amount of 'value' stored in the commodity. As Marx writes in *The Poverty of Philosophy*:

> [...] the pendulum of the clock has become as accurate a measure of the relative activity of two workers as it is of the speed of two locomotives [...] Time is everything, man is nothing; he is at most, time's carcase. Quantity alone decides everything; hour for hour, day for day.

(1967: 151)

Here, in the imagery of the carcase, Marx comes very close to explicitly linking the spectre of capital and the law of value with possession. The carcase metaphor evokes the live human body as eviscerated by value relations, as a husk, a shell. Emptied of bodily substance, labour is possessed by time, time conceived under the quantative law of value; the body is time's host. Although the body is alive and has to be alive in order to be valuable to capital so that it can have some agency as labour power, the body is also dead, a carcase.

In *Fallen* the demon Azazel uses the 1960s Rolling Stones song 'Time is on my Side' as his signature tune. It is a key moment in the film, one that begins to shift Hobbs' investigation away from the psychopathological to the metaphysical, when he discovers that he is trapped in some urban cyclical time loop. His own predicament of the good cop being framed for murders he did not commit replays what happened to a good cop back in the 1960s. The sense that time is indeed on the side of capital is precisely what Benjamin meant by 'homogeneous, empty time' (1999b: 252). There is a close relationship between the emptying out of the subject by the homogeneous force of capital, and the increasing sense of the pliability of time (loops, cycles, rewinds, gaps) which calls forth modifications in the temporal structure of classical narrative films. In such films as *The Mothman Prophecies* (Mark Pellington 2002 US), *Donnie Darko* (Richard Kelly, 2001 US) and *Dark City* (Alex Proyas 1997 US) visions of the subject swing (sometimes within the same film) from one dwindled to insignificance by the loss of time's 'objective' structure (it was never objective, it just felt that way) to omnipotence as the subject accumulates (mimicking capital) the powers of temporal manipulation. This splitting of the subject is deeply embedded into bourgeois history, culture and philosophy. Switching between impotence and omnipotence, the bourgeois model of the subject completely misses the real collective ties that bind and the ethics of mutuality and reciprocity implicit in them.

I have argued that the spectre within the horror film represents the dematerialisation of our social relations. Our capacity for subject-to-subject relations in time and space are subsequently frustrated and crippled. The media specifically, and the intelligentsia generally, have a key role in reproducing this stunted intersubjectivity or in challenging it. Our capacities for intersubjective relations are nothing less than our capacities for recognition of the other, for dialogue, negotiation and ultimately sharing our material and cultural resources.

References
Benjamin, Walter (1999a) *the Arcades Project*, translated by Howard Eiland and Kevin McLaughlin. Massachusetts: Harvard University Press.

Benjamin, Walter, (1999b) 'The Work of Art in the Age of Mechanical Reproduction' in *Illuminations*. London: Pimlico.

Creed, Barbara (1993) *The Monstrous-Feminine, Film, Feminism, Psychoanalysis*. London: Routledge.

Cushman, Philip (1995) *Constructing The Self, Constructing America*. Massachusetts: Perseus Publishing.

Debord, Guy, (1983) Society *of the Spectacle*. Detroit:Black and Red.

Gramsci, Antonio (1971) *Selection from the Prison Notebooks of Antonio Gramsci*, edited by Quintin Hoare and Geoffrey Nowell Smith. New York: International Publishers.

Habermas, Jürgen (1987) *The Philosophical Discourse of Modernity*. Cambridge: Polity Press.

Habermas, Jürgen (1996) *The Structural Transformation of the Public Sphere*. Cambridge: Polity Press.

Jameson, Fredric (1992) *The Geopolitical Aesthetic: cinema and space in the World System*. London: BFI.

Kellner, Douglas (2003) *Media Spectacle*. London: Routledge.

Krzywinska, Tanya (2000) *A Skin For Dancing In: possession, witchcraft and voodoo in film*. Trowbridge: Flicks Books.

Leslie, Esther (2002) *Hollywood Flatlands, Animation, Critical Theory and the Avant-Garde*. London: Verso.

Marx, Karl (1967) *Essential Writings of Karl Marx*, edited by David Caute. London: Panther.

Marx, Karl (1983) *Capital Vol. 1*. London:Lawrence and Wishart.

Wayne, Mike (2003) *Marxism and Media Studies: Key Concepts and Contemporary Trends*. London: Pluto.

Williams, Raymond (1989) *Problems in Materialism and Culture*. London: Verso.

17. Looking On: Troubling Spectacles and the Complicitous Spectator

Michele Aaron

According to psychoanalytic film theory, cinema, indeed any visual representation, depends upon the spectator's acceptance of an illusion as a form of reality. The relationship between illusion and reality, between the spectacle and the real, is a fascinating subject of considerable history with film studies, and, since '9/11' and its spectacular convergence of disaster movie and actuality, an ever hotter topic. My concern in this chapter, however, lies not so much with the qualities or politics of the illusion but with the spectator's acceptance of it, fake as it is. As psychoanalytic film theory makes clear, there exists a kind of contract between the spectator and the spectacle, a tacit agreement underlying this acceptance. It works something like this: 'I'll forget that you're fake, as long as you help'. In other words, we suspend our disbelief, we 'forget' we are watching a contrived fabrication, a film, provided that we are encouraged to do so. This is a two-way process; it requires an artful forgetting on both sides of the screen, for the spectator but also for the spectacle itself. As Christian Metz states of the spectacle: 'I watch it, but it doesn't watch me watching it. Nevertheless, it knows that I am watching it' (1982: 94). Thus the relationship between these two, between the spectacle and the spectator is revealed as '[an] active complicity which works both ways' (Metz 1982: 94).

There is much more at stake in this art-full forgetting than just a good night out at the multiplex. Indeed, this process is usefully described by Metz as a 'fundamental disavowal' (1982: 94), and can be seen as performing an important psychological function for the spectator, an exercise of self-consolidation rooted in fetishism. According to Freud's theory of fetishism, it is with more than a little anxiety that the small child, that is the small male child, notices that his mother has no penis and realises that he too could lose his or have it taken away. A thought too horrible to bear, the child finds ways to pretend that this threatened castration does not exist. In place of the absent penis, he installs a fetish; he covers over the original lack with a cherished alternative. Regardless of one's feelings about psychoanalysis and its gender trouble, or about the gross simplifications of my description, this presents us with a neat paradigm both for understanding the machinations of human behaviour when confronted with something troubling, and, more specifically, for explaining how fetishism connects to the spectacle.

Film, as Kaja Silvermann puts it in line with Metz, 'covers over the absent real with a simulated or constructed reality' and in so doing, she adds, 'makes good the spectating subject's lack, restoring him or her to an imaginary wholeness' (1988:

10). In this way, the cinematic spectacle, with all its appeals to authenticity, stands in for reality thereby reassuring the spectator that nothing is amiss. This fetishistic process fortifies the spectator's sense of self and, crucially, depends upon the spectator supporting the cover-up. The spectator willingly 'buys' this, this substitution of the spectacle for the real, thereby disavowing the absence of reality, and, as I will come to argue, his or her complicity in the cover-up.

What needs to be emphasised is that disavowal is a defensive mechanism: it staves off that which is threatening; it allows one to indulge in fantasy without suffering the consequences. The necessary and necessarily safe distance between the spectator and the dangers suggested by and within the cinematic spectacle, be they emotional, psychological, or even ethical, is maintained through disavowal. But what I want to do is challenge the spectator's removal and innocence with regard to the spectacle, and argue instead not simply for the spectator's complicity in its creation and endurance, but for the spectator's complicity in its often disturbing content. I turn then to a set of films that make a clear case for this, that are contra-disavowal. They deliberately break that cinematic contract between spectator and screen in two key, and not unrelated, ways: firstly, by aggravating the act of 'artful forgetting' at the heart of the spectacle-real dynamic, and secondly, by pushing the limits of what can be accepted by the spectator, indeed, what is accept-able. These two are interrelated in that, as will become obvious, it is the film's self-reflexivity, its anti-forgetting strategy, that renders the material so difficult to take.

Peeping Tom (Michael Powell, 1960), *The Eyes of Laura Mars* (Irvin Kershner, 1978), and *Strange Days* (Kathryn Bigelow, 1996) represent a certain trajectory of the heavily self-conscious or self-reflexive mainstream film that has seen its numbers swell in recent years as the tropes of postmodernism proliferate on the big and, with the popularity of reality television, little screen. Basically, self-reflexive narratives draw attention to themselves as texts, as artificial, mediated (re)presentations. They can do this in a variety of ways that impact upon the text's form and content. They might be about visual arts, about performance, about film-making. They might contain the machinery of their production: showing people making or watching shows or films. They might point out the devices of the medium or the signifiers of cinema, say, or of viewing, with recurrent images of cameras or of eyes. They might be about the pleasures of looking, or the fear of it, the lure of voyeurism or the dangers encountered. They might, in some cases, knowingly reference or borrow from other texts. Each of the selected narratives revolves around visual images and their production and use. *Peeping Tom* focuses on film, *The Eyes of Laura Mars* on photography and *Strange Days* on a form of video. The murder plots of each make their relationship to the pleasures and dangers of looking especially fraught.

It is not just that these films are about image-making or image-watching (so many films are) or that they suggest that both are entangled with dangers and delights (so many films do), but that they firmly incorporate the spectator into their narratives while heavily restricting the reassurances on offer. Each film merges the gaze of the image-maker, the image-viewer and the spectator, and does so in the most publicly and personally violent of situations. That it is also the gaze of the murderer, potential victim and spectator that is merged, means spectatorial implication becomes loaded with sadomasochistic intent. In *Peeping Tom*, Mark stabs women with the blade attached to the tripod of his camera, the victim watches herself being killed in a mirror attached to the front of the camera. We, the audience, simultaneously, watch the action through the cross hairs of the camera lens. In *The Eyes of Laura Mars*, Laura, via extra-sensory perception, ESP, witnesses the murders of other women, and then at the climax of the film, 'sees' the murderer pursuing her. In the futuristic *Strange Days*, 'playback' technology allows videoed events to be 'enjoyed' as lived experience via special headgear. The playback-spectator's vision fills the screen as subjective narration for the similarly all-seeing film spectator.

Artful reminders

Primarily, these highly self-reflexive films inhibit the spectators' ability to do that 'artful forgetting' by consistently reminding us that we are watching a film. We cannot suppress our status as spectators for the films are all about spectatorship. The radical charge of this spotlighting of the spectator's experience (as the films' self-consciously merged-perspectives make evident) is a fundamental *avowal* of the real. However, this radical charge is not a given in all self-reflexive films. Indeed, film studies' theorisation of self-reflexivity has found it capable of encompassing extreme functions, to be either conservative or transgressive. On one hand, self-reflexivity's demystification of fantasy has been regarded as a ploy to seduce the viewer further into the spectacle, and ideology, of, for example, the musical (see Feuer 1986: 159-74).[1] On the other, directors such as Jean-Luc Godard and Louis Malle have been seen to enlist its ability to dismantle the codes of classical cinema and, as a result, they have been distinguished for their radical practices (see Hedges 1991: 13). Certainly one must ask whether the self-reflexivity of *Peeping Tom*, *The Eyes of Laura Mars*, and *Strange Days* further seduces the spectator into an ideological spectacle, or whether it dismantles the traditional codes of mainstream cinema.

What self-reflexivity's radical function depends upon, and what discussions of it negotiate, is the spectator's distance from the effects of the text. Self-reflexivity is positioned against the self-protecting function of fetishism, of disavowal: it reveals what should be covered up. It would seem, in this way, to be fundamentally interventionist. Yet, this situation is easily recouped for more conservative ends.

Talking about the musical, Jane Feuer found the key purpose of its self-reflectivity, as she calls it, to perpetuate the 'myth of spontaneity' (1986: 159-74) and its attendant pleasures of fantasy, through naturalising artificiality itself. This is achieved through masking the artificiality of the spontaneous performance in two main ways. Either by concealing the technology that accompanies it or through overwhelming, or distracting from, the sense of contrivance with the depiction of characters' innate energy and/or sincerity (see also Dyer 1986: 175-89). So, for example, in *Singin' in the Rain* (Gene Kelly and Stanley Donen, 1952) we have a scene in which Gene Kelly's character sings a love song to Kathy on an unused stage set, and his exuberance outshines the camera lights he manipulates.

In the horror genre, within which we could locate my group of films, self-reflexivity similarly serves to emphasise the pleasures particular to the genre, in this case, the creation of fear, and does so through implicating the spectator. Carol Clover, questioning the frequency of, and obsession with, images of eyes in horror films, sees the goal of this form of self-reflexivity as the promotion of fear through audience identification and implication, and sees *Peeping Tom* as a '*horror* metafilm: a film that has as its task to expose the psychodynamics of specularity and *fear*' (1992: 169, original emphasis).

In reminding spectators that they are watching a film, they are made aware of themselves as spectators. This awareness can allay fear, for in exposing its own artificiality, the risk-laden experience is made safe: unreal and distant. Alternatively, self-reflexivity can seem to accentuate the horror by bringing it closer to home, by drawing the spectator in. Self-consciousness in the film breeds self-consciousness in the audience. If terrible things happen to the viewers depicted in the film itself then one's status as viewer seems especially fraught. Both of these positions argue for the spectator's implication but to opposing ends, so what gives a self-reflexive horror film its radical edge? How and why might we distinguish *Peeping Tom*, *The Eyes of Laura Mars*, and *Strange Days*?

For Feuer, the musical used self-reflexivity to strengthen rather than undermine the spectacular-ness of the spectacle. The devices of the medium were exposed in order that the devices of the character appeared that much more powerful, honest and natural in their singularity. In *Peeping Tom*, *The Eyes of Laura Mars*, and *Strange Days* such qualities are, understandably, absent. However, the visual excesses of the monsters or gore which saturate the horror genre, could be seen as a kind of spectacular displacement of the reality check of self-reflexivity, but this visual excess is also lacking from these three films. While the three films could be seen to perpetuate what might be called the 'myth of psychopathology' that the genre requires, the murderers in *Peeping Tom*, *The Eyes of Laura Mars*, and *Strange Days* are almost banally evil. In the main they are denied extraordinariness or singularity. Primarily, they are duplicitous in hiding their identity as murderer.

That the identity of the murderer is not revealed in the narrative, and to the spectator, until the final scenes in *The Eyes of Laura Mars* and *Strange Days*, suggests that their murderers could be anyone. And, in merging the view of the murderer with our own, they are always 'everyone', always more than themselves. The frame is also often multiple. It is filled with not a Point of View Shot but with what we might call a 'points of view' shot, one that combines multiple viewpoints, that merges the vision of murderer, victim, and spectator.

The Eyes of Laura Mars and *Strange Days* will finally reveal their monsters. The latter subsequently indulges in a range of other classical codes (like romantic union and equilibrated closure) and yet its self-reflexivity is the most shocking. Its points of view shots of the most gruesome murder are the most difficult to take. Where *Peeping Tom* has the cross hairs of the lens that the murderer is filming through, and *The Eyes of Laura Mars* has a haziness to the image to label the scenes of murder, *Strange Days* offers no such distancing devices. Indeed, it goes all out to make the superimposition of the shared experience seamless. Perhaps it can afford to with its later compromises to convention, but nevertheless its focus is not just the self-reflexive spectacle but the self-reflexive spectator. While I am suggesting that the former breeds the latter, *Strange Days* makes this explicit. As Laura Rascaroli notes of Bigelow's film, 'the screen, barrier between the auditorium and the action, between fiction and reality, disappears. The spectator's eye is *there*, in the film space...' (1998)

Returning to Metz's earlier point about disavowal and the cinematic spectacle, that 'I watch it, but it doesn't watch me watching it' (1982: 94), the thing about the spectacle in *Peeping Tom*, *The Eyes of Laura Mars*, and *Strange Days* is precisely that it *does* watch me watching it. In other words, in these films, visual images are seen to be created, and created to be seen. Not only is the external spectator incorporated into the highly subjective image, but the internal spectator is utterly aware of him or herself as spectator as in those horrendous moments of spectatorial realisation: the victim's face in *Peeping Tom*, Laura's despair in *The Eyes of Laura Mars* and Lenny's contortions in *Strange Days*. Nowhere is the excessive presence of the spectator more evident than in *The Eyes of Laura Mars* in which, ostensibly, we receive two Lauras when her vision merges with that of the murderer who is looking at her. In making the spectator her own spectacle, the dismantling of the spectator-spectacle divide is guaranteed.

Not only do the films incorporate the spectator but the spectator's response. In this way we are presented with very clear guidelines of how to react to these difficult spectacles. Except in *Peeping Tom*. Where watching a murder is a source of trauma for Laura in *The Eyes of Laura Mars* and for Lenny in *Strange Days*, for Mark it is a pleasure, and one that he indulges in over and over again, in his repeat murders and in watching and re-watching the films of his murderous acts. The only witness to Mark's murders is his blind landlady who wanders into his home cinema: his room where he is screening his footage. The spectator is noticeably denied an on-screen set of eyes, a surrogate self who gets to be appalled by Mark's acts, and, as such, the film opens itself to charges that it lacks an ethical framework. It is in a similar vein, that our being encouraged to feel sympathy for Mark courts controversy. It is little wonder that *Peeping Tom* would cause such a storm.

Acceptance and the acceptable

Michael Powell's *Peeping Tom* stands as a landmark film in terms of the controversy that it generated and, consequently, the directorial career that it ruined. As Adam Lowenstein notes, the brouhaha of the time has determined most readings of the film. He argues, instead, for locating it within the British New Wave, and, most importantly, within its reflection of the social crisis of the time. What was so troubling to the critics of the period, he finds, is not the film's horrors but their insinuation, not what was depicted but how the spectator was so successfully implicated within it. The film drew, he notes, 'resistant viewers into a recognition of their own reflection within this mass culture' (2000: 224).

The implicatedness of the spectator has been a popular theme within the critical reception of all the films under discussion. In their study of the self-reflexivity of *The Eyes of Laura Mars*, Lucy Fischer and Marcia Landy see its primary function as the implication of the spectator within the depiction of violence against women; that is within the (male) sadism of cinema:

> The [film's] orchestration of male and female, fictional and 'real' spectators, threatening and random surveillance are concentric, all leading to the same object of regard, the focus on the female and on scenes of violence, creating a bond of complicity between the internal and external spectators to the film [...] The reflexivity not only assimilates the audience into the narrative but also creates a sense in which the audience is implicated vicariously or actively in the act of looking at and of experiencing a world where there is no escape from media manipulation, psychopathology, and aggression.

(1987: 75)

In the perpetuation and inevitability of this violence, self-reflexivity is a coercive force, yet it remains intimately connected to the issue of responsibility – the spectator's complicity in the perpetuation of this violent world. Silverman raises a related issue in her discussion of *Peeping Tom*, a film which also portrays extreme violence towards women whilst emphatically aligning the spectator with the murderer. For Silvermann, as for me, *Peeping Tom*'s self-reflexivity exposes the mythic processes at the heart of classical cinema: the safe distances that characterise (fetishistic) spectatorship. According to Silvermann:

> *[A] recurrent motif in the murder sequences – a series of images seen through the cross hairs of the view finder [...] [–] functions as a powerful metaphor for the barrier Mark tries to erect between himself and his victims so as to dissociate himself from them, and thereby consolidate his own claim to the paternal legacy. Here, too, Mark's project converges with classic cinema, which also turns upon the fiction that an irreducible distance isolates the viewer from the spectacle.*

> (1988: 34)

It is the navigation of these safe distances by these self-reflexive films, that has lain at the heart of this discussion.

Peeping Tom, The Eyes of Laura Mars and *Strange Days* draw their effectiveness (and controversy) precisely from the alignment and merging of the spectator's and the murderer's gaze. This alignment, as the films' critics have suggested, is utterly revealing of the sadism of cinema; indeed it is cinema's sadistic gaze that the spectator is made to share. However, I would like to suggest that it is instead the masochistic economy of cinema in which the spectator is always already implicated, and that these films divulge.

Within her application of Gilles Deleuze's work on masochism to cinema, one of Gaylyn Studlar's projects has been to confirm the masochistic rather than sadistic motivation of spectatorial pleasures (Studlar 1988)[2] She asserts the consensuality of the masochistic relationship, the 'mutual agreement between partners' (23), and thus equates the contractual alliance of the masochist and his or her partner with the contractual alliance between the spectator and the screen:

> *A willing volunteer in cinema's perverse intimacy, the spectator, like the masochist's partner, is not coerced into the alliance [...] Cinema is not a sadistic institution but pre-eminently a contractual one based upon the promise of certain pleasures. The masochist requires an audience to make humiliation and pain meaningful. Similarly, the cinematic apparatus is meaningless without a spectator to its exhibitionistic acting out.*

> (182)

Within the contractual alliance between spectator and film, the spectator cannot be positioned as sadist to the acknowledged masochist. The dynamic is about masochism and not sadism. Notions of masochism require questions of consent, notions of sadism absent them. While the masochist agrees to – both desires and requires – the other party's infliction of pain within a consensual dynamic, the sadist opposes such a relationship. The sadist's source of pleasure, according to Deleuze's reading of Sade, is the very absence of agreement or voluntariness, the exclusion of masochism (Deleuze 1991: 40-1). Thus, cinema (and art in general) is a masochistic experience, and the violent acts on-screen are actually required and agreed upon elements of a masochistic world.

While neither Laura nor Lenny 'ask for it', want to be endangered or to witness the murders, they are heavily implicated in the visions of the pain that they share in rather than inflict. At the same time, however, Laura, the highly successful fashion photographer, propagates violent images of women, and Lenny sponsors the making of the experience-films: the more thrilling or illicit the film, the higher its market value. In other words, on some level they have consented to the awful but logical conclusions to their professional choices. For Mark, the murders are never simply about sadism but rather a reviving of his troubled childhood, and, in particular, his father's endless filming of his reactions. In this way, Mark is always more than identifying with his victims; he is the victim. And, in true masochistic spirit (or so Freud, and the primacy of the Death Drive, would have it) his sadistic acts are always ultimately about self-destructiveness (1920: 275-338). So much so that the obvious conclusion to his actions, his discovery, and the film's narrative, is his suicide by the very mechanism with which he had killed others.

Peeping Tom, *The Eyes of Laura Mars* and *Strange Days* make their protagonists' (masochistic) complicity in watching gruesome murders apparent. It is through the intense self-reflexivity employed by the films, that the (masochistic) complicity of the spectator is also revealed. Self-reflexivity questions the spectator's mythic distance and safety, the irresponsibility of looking on. It performs that radical Brechtian practise of distanciation, drawing attention to the myth of separation, of dissociation, and the necessary fiction of self-coherence.[3] But the line between a representation perpetuating or critiquing conventional myths – merely unfolding or instead shattering them – is a thin one, perhaps based upon the rigour or optimism of certain theorists or the quirkiness of certain writers or film-makers, as the contrary opinions of horror (as misogynist or as parodic) testify. Self-reflexivity appears a major strategy of implication, a deep faultline in the reassurances of spectatorship, and as it becomes all the more frequent and psychodynamically charged, so the viewer's implication becomes that much more apparent.

What I have argued in this chapter is that the self-reflexivity of *Peeping Tom*, *The Eyes of Laura Mars*, and *Strange Days* makes the content of the films difficult to take not just because of what they show us, but because of their insistence that we are more than implicated in what they show us. In addition, the films need to be seen as acknowledging, exposing and exploiting the (masochistic) complicity that lies at the heart of spectatorship, that lubricates the spectacle-real dynamic underlying our engagement with cinema. As the spectacle and, for that matter, the real become increasingly unacceptable – with, for example, the self-conscious sadism of Michael Haneke's work, as J. Hoberman has described it (1998: 59), and the unconscionable acts of 9/11 and George Bush Junior – the question of the spectator's part in these productions becomes ever more pressing.

References

Clover, Carol (1992) *Men, Women, and Chainsaws: Gender in the Modern Horror Film*. Princeton, NJ: Princeton University Press.

Deleuze, Gilles. *Masochism: Coldness and Cruelty* (New York: Zone Books, 1991).

Dyer, Richard (1986) 'Entertainment as Utopia' in Rick Altman (ed.), *Genre: The Musical*. London: BFI, 175-89.

Feuer, Jane (1986) 'The Self-reflective Musical and the Myth of Entertainment' in Rick Altman (ed.), *Genre: The Musical*. London: BFI, 159-74.

Fischer, Lucy and Marcia Landy (1987), '*The Eyes of Laura Mars*: A Binocular Critique' in Gregory A. Walker (ed.), *American Horrors: Essays on the Modern American Horror Film*. Urbana: University of Illinois Press.

Freud, Sigmund (1920) 'Beyond the Pleasure Principle', *On Metapsychology: The Theory of Psychoanalysis*. Trans. James Strachey. Ed. Angela Richards. London: Penguin, 1991

Heath, Stepehn (1974) 'Lessons from Brecht', *Screen* 15.2 (summer 1974)

Hedges Inez (1991) *Breaking the Frame: Film Language and the Experience of Limits*. Bloomington: Indiana University Press.

Hoberman, J. 'Head Trips'. rev. of *Funny Games*, *Village Voice* 17 Mar. 1998

Lowenstein, Adam (2000) '"Under-the-skin Horrors": Social Realism and Classlessness in *Peeping Tom* and the British New Wave', in Justine Ashby and Andrew Higson (eds.), *British Cinema, Past and*. London: Routledge.

Metz, Christian (1975, 1982) *The Imaginary Signifier: Psychoanalysis and the Cinema*. Trans. Celia Britton, Annwyl Williams, Ben Brewster and Alfred Guzzetti. Bloomington: Indiana University Press.

Rascaroli, Laura (1998) 'Strange Visions: Kathryn Bigelow's Metafiction', in *Enculturation*. 2:1 Fall. Accessed on-line at http:www.enculturation.

Silverman, Kaja (1988) *The Acoustic Mirror: The Female Voice in Psychoanalysis and Cinema*. Bloomington: Indiana University Press.

Studlar, Gaylyn (1988) *In the Realm of Pleasure: Von Sternberg, Dietrich, and the Masochistic Aesthetic*. New York: Columbia University Press.

Williams, Linda (1989) *Hard Core: Power, Pleasure and the Frenzy of the Visible*. Berkeley: University of California Press.

Notes

1   In this genre, self-reflexivity operates on two main fronts: through spectacles (the overt artificiality or staged-ness of the musical numbers with their non-diegetic orchestral accompaniments) and through their frequent depiction of putting on a show, most commonly in the Backstage Musical.

2   Linda Williams has made a similar point: 'Like the person engaging in sadomasochism, the viewer has made a kind of contract with the film to undergo a certain uneasy identification with a

character experiencing terror or pain, at the end of which is the great pleasure of its relief' (1989: 207).

3   For the connection between Brecht and psychoanalytic disavowal, see Stephen Heath, 'Lessons from Brecht', *Screen* 15.2 (summer 1974): 103-28.

18. The Enigma of the Real: The Qualifications for Real sex in Contemporary Art Cinema

Tanya Krzywinska

The hard-core film industry has successfully exploited the spectacle of real sex to carve out a market difference from other forms of cinema. Regulation, distribution and generic form have combined to lend hard core its aesthetic and market specificity. But with the recent appearance of erect penises and vaginal penetration in certain films classified in Britain as 18, there appears to be a challenge to clear divisions between what have been previously categorised as 'legitimate' and 'illegitimate' cinemas. European art films such as *The Idiots* [*Idioterne*] (1998 Denmark/Sweden/France/Netherlands/Italy), *Romance* (1999 France), *Intimacy* (2000 UK/France/Germany/Spain) and *The Piano Teacher* [*Le Pianiste*] (2000 France/Austria) each make use of images that have defined hard core. Their inclusion represents a significant gear-change in the representation of sex in the legitimate cinema. In looking to hard core to win audience attention, European art cinema appears to be using the attraction of real sex to compete with the sensation-inducing spectacle of Hollywood's high-octane special effects laden blockbusters. With the increasing liberalism of institutional regulation of cinema, the gradual legitimisation of the hard core industry due in part to its economic success, and with easily accessible sexually explicit images available on the largely unregulated Internet, the stage is set for European art cinema to include the type of explicit sexual imagery that has hitherto been the preserve of hard core. (While hard-core imagery has not been regulated in all countries, the regulatory regimes of Britain and America tend to set the agenda for what is included in films that seek a broad international audience.)

This chapter seeks to demonstrate that the spectacle of 'real' sex in recent art cinema is, nonetheless, subject to a number of textual and contextual qualifications that legitimate its presence and mark such films off from low-brow hard core. The introduction of explicit hard-core imagery is a new addition to legitimate cinema, but when seen in the broader context of cinema history, the appropriation of certain sexually charged images from illegitimate sex-based cinemas is by no means a new phenomenon. The chapter has two main components: to put this gear-change into the broader context of cinema history and to discuss the specific form of 'real' sex in these recent films with a particular focus on the rhetorical ambiguities, aesthetic frameworks and 'art' values that these films put into play.

That cinema trades often on the spectacle of sex is nothing especially new. As Robert Kolker has noted: 'film and the erotic are linked in some of the earliest images we have' (2002 18). From the sanctioned to the forbidden, the subtle to the blatant, evocations of sex have saturated cinema since its inception. What continues to change, however, is the economic environment in which cinema is produced, distributed and consumed as well as the cultural frameworks that shape the way that representations of sex are regarded and regulated. One significant distinction that has had currency across cinema's history is the common practice of dividing, often along generic lines, the psychological and emotional aspects of sex from the physical. Both provide spectacle of different types. The former in many cases places importance on character study, narrative and dramatic tension while the latter places greater emphasis on the sensationalist effect of portraying sexual acts of whatever type. Bringing the two together has often enabled films to adopt the spectacle of sex in a more acceptable context, an occurrence found at various points in cinema's history. The representation of sex in either psychological or physical terms has proved consistently, and marketablely, controversial. Contentions over the representation of sex and the conditions of acceptability provide a barometer for cultural and ideological tensions circulating around the meanings and practice of sex, as Annette Kuhn and Lea Jacobs have argued in the context of censorship (1998, 1997). The film business operates within such contexts, capitalising in some cases on such cultural pressure points for financial gain and cultural valency. Many films dealing with aspects of sexual authenticity as a source of spectacle have tested, and in some cases been instrumental in shifting, regulatory boundaries, something often exploited actively to attract the curiosity of spectators.

Throughout cinema's 'psychosexual' history, various regimes of dialectical exchange between legitimate and illegitimate cinemas are in evidence. Consideration of such dynamic trading provides a key to understanding how the recent inclusion of 'real' sex in legitimate cinema fits into a broader historical, industrial and rhetorical/aesthetic context.

A common strategy found across the history of cinema is the use of an established, sanctioned discourse or generic form with which to frame the inclusion of publicity-garnering risqué sexual imagery. Often such inclusions have been justified under the ethical rubric of the negative example (although this is now rarely used in overt terms it was quite common in early Hollywood and in a more mischievous way in exploitation cinema during the Production Code era). Following in the footsteps of D. W. Griffith's *Intolerance* (1916 US), Cecil B. de Mille, for example, gave expression to erotic spectacle through the iconography of the biblical epic. De Mille's *Sign of the Cross* (1932 US) charts the triumph of Christian ethics over barbarous pagan passions; the latter providing the opportunity for sexual spectacle. Examples include a lesbian seduction performed in the form of an exotic dance, the sight of Claudette Colbert's 'real' breasts and the voluptuous carnal desires that prompt her character to corrupt the good Christian hero, and, mostly perversely even by today's standards, the exhibition of diaphanously clad, bound women being ravaged in unsubtly coded sexual ways by crocodiles and apes in the gladiatorial arena. Although 'banned' under the Production Code the following year (and maybe a contribution to the decision to impose the Code more stringently), the film was a box office success, not unaided by the controversy that it fuelled in the American press (Walsh 78-80; Black 65-69). For many critics and state censors it was the purported biblical context that sanctioned the inclusion of decadent 'pagan' images (pagan being synonymous at that time with unbridled lust and amorality), enabling the film to 'get away with scenes that would be eliminated in secular context' (Walsh 52).

After 1933 the double-dealing technique of the negative example became a staple of exploitation cinema. Luridly titled films such as *Slaves in Bondage* (aka *Crusade Against the Rackets* 1937 US) and *The Wages of Sin* (1938 US) focused on issues such as white slavery, sexual disease, birth-control and drug use to facilitate salacious content. American exploitation cinema of the 1930s through to the early 1950s afforded a forum for the type of sensationalist sexual images excised by the Production Code, occupying a place between legitimate and illegitimate/hard-core cinemas. Films made under the banner of exploitation often promised more than they delivered but evaded state obscenity rulings by eschewing the explicit imagery found in hard-core stag films (see Eric Shaefer 1999 on exploitation cinema and Linda Williams for a discussion of early stag films, 1990: 58-92).

Sign of the Cross used an established genre (the biblical drama) through which to frame and justify the presence of its outré sexual themes and images. This type of formal hybridisation is also evidenced at several critical junctures in cinema history, occurring often when regulatory bodies were under pressure to change in accordance with shifting cultural values and the industry was in the throes of economic crisis. 1950s 'adult' melodrama and 1970s softcore art and comedy films, for example, adopted a strategy of marrying risqué sexual imagery to an industrially recognised genre (Hunt 1998: 114). With the weakening of the Production Code in the 1950s, American mainstream cinema reintroduced psychosexually inclined 'adult' themes. These were in part a response to the box office success of foreign 'sex' imports in America (such as ...*And God Created Woman* [*Et Dieu... Créa la Femme*] [1956 France]), some of which were immune from MPAA regulation, as well as responding to the threat posed to cinema by television. More explicitly oriented images and topics were reintroduced to the mainstream screen through the established generic framework of melodrama, a factor that is important to the general acceptance of racier themes (as in *A Streetcar Named Desire* [1951 US], *Cat on a Hot Tin Roof* [1958 US], *Baby Doll* [1956 US], and *Written on the Wind* [1958 US]). The focus on the perceived realities of psychosexual problems, rather than anodyne romance, was intended to attract potential adult audiences by offering topics that would not be permitted on family-oriented television.

The sexual health of the America was high on the agenda during this period, sparked in part by the publication and mass consumption of sexological studies such as Alfred Kinsey's work in 1952 and 1958. While these dramas of desire had little in the way of overt sexual imagery, they nonetheless touched base with real sexual issues that were taboo for mainstream American cinema since the introduction of the Production Code and only found previously in the particular, and lurid, context of non-MPPAA-regulated exploitation cinema. Extra-marital affairs, conflicts between personal desire and family values, rape, nymphomania and impotency were therefore groundbreaking and exciting topics in the context of 1950s legitimate American cinema. The psychological emphasis as well as the high-gloss style of such films set them apart from exploitation and hard-core cinemas. 'Adult' melodramas had a connection nonetheless to exploitation cinema, which regularly took sexual problems as an ostensibly socially relevant mask for bringing titillating images to the screen. The strongly marked psychosexual focus of such films, couched in the generic rhetorics of melodrama, bears considerable similarity to the way in which images of real sex have been contextualised and legitimised in later 'art' films. These include those that appeared in the 1970s, such as *Emmanuelle* (1974 France), *Last Tango in Paris* (1972 Italy/France), as well as the more recent flush of art cinema films, such as *Intimacy*, *The Piano Teacher* and *Romance* that bear images only found hitherto in hard core.

Emmanuelle and *Last Tango in Paris* marry the psychological and the physical to construct narratives that place sex within the artfully existentialist context of identity formation and the meaning (or its lack) of being. In *Emmanuelle* sex is rendered as a means of coming to power and achieving an authentic, fulfilled state of being. *Last Tango* focuses on a character who regards sex as a means of achieving existential authenticity but ultimately fails to find it. Both films contemplate the notion that shame and repression are bourgeois affectations that impinge on personal freedom and expression. These thematic and narrative components, borrowed in part from melodrama and in part from French philosophy and pop-radicalism, help to distinguish the films from the episodic, what-you-see-is-what-you-get, form of hard core. Combining dramas of desire with artful cinematography furnishes the spectacle of sex with the rhetoric of high cultural value. This marriage places the films within the culturally sanctioned domain of 'art': an argument that also applies to the more recent flush of art cinema films (although *Baise-moi* [2000, France], with its exploitation/New York underground colouring, is arguably an exception).

The sexual initiation narrative of *Emmanuelle* sets it apart from hard core. Its soft-focus aesthetic, exotic eastern location and psychological framework locate the 'real' elements of the actors' sexual performance in a fantasy and melodramatic context. Alongside its bondage/domination oriented stable-mate *The Story of O* [*Histoire d'O*, 1975 France], *Emmanuelle* is a sexual fairy tale. Both films are couched as erotic fantasy, laced with improbable scenarios and a lot of dressing up. These velvety coming-to-sexual-womanhood tales of sexual adventuring were designed to maximise their market potential by capturing the attention of the *Cosmopolitan*-reading 'where's your G-spot' female audience. The slick photography and semi-mystical approach to female sexuality set them apart from the starkly edgy *verite* style of the New York underground and hard core; the spectacle of 'real' sex is thus located in two very different aesthetic registers.

While *Emmanuelle* posits sexual authenticity within the modal context of languorous fantasy, *Last Tango in Paris* makes its claims on sexual authenticity through a combination of philosophical pretension, pessimism and realism. Bertolucci explains the film as a cinematic exploration of the 'present of fucking' (Bertolucci cited in Mellen: 131), and, with Brando's improvisations and method acting, it is very much a 'performer' film. By virtue of such self-reflexive frames, sexual performance is deeply over-determined and laden with ambiguous coding and resonance; requisite values to claim the film as art-cinema. *Last Tango* actively keeps the viewer at a distance from the proceedings: there is no invitation to regard events as erotic fantasy, as with opening narrated section of *The Story of O* (indicated by the fairy-tale timelessness of the opening words 'One day O's lover ...'). *Last Tango* sells its sex as spectacle, but this comes with efforts to keep the spectator at one remove from the 'present of fucking', a coldness echoed by its soft version of a realist aesthetic and the thematic focus on alienation and the insularity of human relationships. Physical sex provides a temporary escape for two main characters and is couched in a matrix of interlaced yet conflicting psychological investments. The meaning of sex is obscured for the characters: the physical and the psychological slide past each other without much interaction, creating a sense of fragmentation rather than symbiotic plenitude.

As the narrative of *Last Tango* develops, temporary sexual satisfactions give way to a deep pessimism about the viability of what Jacques Lacan has called the sexual (un)relation. As Lacan puts it: 'There is no such thing as a sexual relationship' [*Il n'y a pas de rapport sexuel*] (1991 134). These are precisely the same pessimistic themes that frame and sanction the use of real sex in *Intimacy*, *The Piano Teacher* and *Romance*. By being placed in a psychosexual context, the spectacle of 'real' sex is given an emotional and philosophical colouring very different from the more superficial and immediate spectacle of the real found in hard-core cinema. The inclusion of a psychosexual dimension, borrowed in part from melodrama, makes the designation of the 'real' a relative and complex affair, an aspect that is underlined in the way such films play reflexively at the interface between the body-mechanics of sexual performance and its staging for cinema.

The recent representation of real sex in legitimate cinema trades in a qualified way on a transgressive kudos, albeit that the nature of transgression differs within individual cases and depending in part on their cinematic heritage. With the home video success of sex-based art films such as *Last Tango in Paris* or *Betty Blue* (*37°2 le matin* 1986 France), it is not surprising that studios such as Studio-Canal (which began as hard-core production house) looked to real sex as way of increasingly the relatively small market for its art cinema products. The hard-core video industry had an estimated global annual turnover of 4 billion dollars in the mid 1990s, testifying to widespread interest in explicit sexual material that cinema could potentially exploit (O'Toole 1999: 351). While *Intimacy* and *The Piano Teacher* took quite small returns at the box office in Britain, they nonetheless attracted a great deal of press coverage, mainly because they contained sexual images that had not previously been seen in legitimate cinema in Britain. Although there are national differences in the way sex and its representation are regarded, the inclusion of real sex in legitimate cinema pushes at regulatory and generic boundaries.

While simulated sex acknowledges normative 'appropriateness' of purpose, the act of putting real sex on camera disturbs normative rhetorics of sex as an intimate and private affair. When characters have 'real' sex on screen, spectators are to some extent taken out of the frame of fictional representation, focus shifting perhaps from character to actor. A modal ambiguity is created between the real and fiction. In *Intimacy* it is Mark Rylance, the actor, as well as Jay, the character, that has an erection. Actively exploiting such disruptions to the distinction between fact and fiction further allows narrative-based films such as *The Idiots*, *The Piano Player* and *Intimacy* to explore the complex role that performance plays in the protagonists' lives, as well as sexuality and sexual relationships in general. As with *Last Tango in Paris*, what each have in common is that these fictions are conducted through real (sexual) bodies, underlined by the centralisation of 'real' sexual activity and nakedness as well as the aesthetic context of realism and the quest by director and performers for authentic performance. With the attenuation of devices that might help to mark performance off from the real, the modal positioning of these texts becomes unstable. The inherent ambiguity of staging real sex for the screen becomes an overt thematic impetus that focuses on the convolutions of existential matters. The use of psychologically based narratives within which to frame 'real' sex in such films also works against the way that hard core isolates sexual sensation from the wider and messy ramifications of inter-personal relationships. *Last Tango in Paris*, *Intimacy*, *The Piano Teacher* and *Romance*, for example, place real sex in a thematic psychological minefield of reflections, refractions, mis-connections, social, personal and inter-personal contradictions and transgressions, that are rarely present in the comparably untroubled sexual spaces of hard core (Michael Ninn's artful hard core excepted).

With such historical, contextual, aesthetic and performative factors in mind, we can move on to a closer analysis of the specific attributes and ambiguities of the use of 'real' sex in recent art cinema films, focusing specifically on *The Piano Teacher* and *Intimacy*. Both films acknowledge, in different ways, the place hard-core film has in contemporary culture and the way its particular formal devices have played a role in shaping the mediated coding of 'real' sex. The films address this thematically, as well as borrowing and reframing formal elements from hard core.

Intimacy opens with a scene that bears some formal comparison to hard core, but with some significant differences. The scene borrows from the 'stranger sex' format: a narrative device that has often been deployed in hard core because it tends to sideline complex emotional connections in favour of no-obligation carnal pleasure. The context is an unkempt London flat inhabited by a thirty-something man, who we first see stretched out sleeping on a sofa, mimicking and gender inverting the languid female nude odalisques of nineteenth- and early twentieth-century painting. A hand-held camera follows as he opens the door onto a thirty-something woman. Cursory greetings are exchanged, with no courtly flirtation, emphasising self-consciousness and establishing that they do not appear to know each other well. Clothes are discarded awkwardly, without recourse to the mannered style of striptease, and they fuck urgently on the debris-strewn floor. The pace of editing speeds up, fragmenting the coupling and isolating each of the protagonists. Hand-held camerawork and a short depth of field without skin-enhancing lighting effects intensify the impression of immediacy and presence given to this explicit brief encounter. These are the types of devices we might expect from hard core or from *verite*: the two styles coming together under the illusion of unmediated realism. Unlike hard core, the sexual encounter is not staged rhythmically through various 'acts' or positions and there is no cum-shot, although the spectator is left in little doubt that penetration has occurred. As with hard core, the sexual performance of the actors is highlighted in this scene, with all other aspects in abeyance. There is no non-diegetic music and ambient close-miking is used to enhance the intimate presence and texture of the couple's breathing and the sounds of skin moving across skin.

The sum of these strategies gives the sense that the camera is following, rather than orchestrating, a real rather than fabricated and choreographed event; going, as it were, with the action. These are techniques often used in hard core to encode sex as authentic in audio-visual and performative terms, particularly in the low-budget 'authentic' end of hard core rather than silicone-enhanced spectacle of higher-budget offerings. Even if some of the typical shot patternings of hard core are missing (there are no close-ups of genitals for example), the whole emphasis of this episodic scene is focused on fleshly connection and sexual performance. But such a comparison with hard core must also be considered against the broader structure of the film's narrative.

The opening scene acts as a kind of enigma posed to the viewer about the nature of the connection between the couple: Who are they? How are they connected? What repercussions might this sexual encounter have? These are questions that are unlikely to arise with any insistence in a hard-core film. The scene compares with the stylistic resonances of on-the-fly techniques used in some forms of art cinema (*verite* and Dogma 95 for example) but resonates equally with the style of raw low-budget hard-core European films, as opposed to the slicker, suntanned, more continuity-shot style of 'mom and pop' American hard core. However, as the film progresses, the performance of real sex is placed within the narrative frame of emotional ramification, which lends the film's real-sex thematic an artful and melodramatic justification. This is a strategy present in most of the sex-focused art films I have mentioned. The spectacular pleasure of watching real sex in this context comes at a price: the spectator is narratively cued and cajoled into making an emotional, empathic and speculative investment in the two characters. In hard core the spectator is rarely interpolated in such ways: it is the pleasure and sensation of the actors that we are invited to identify with rather than the psychological complexities and conflicts of a central character.

With its smooth unobtrusive camerawork and seamless editing, *The Piano Teacher* differs from the circumstantial style of hard core. But there is one particular formal device in common with hard core: the use of real time in a number of key scenes. The first of these is a 10-minute sex scene, the one scene in the film which operates most like that which might be expected of a hard-core production. Unlike hard core, the scene has no orgasmic climax, however. The withholding of orgasm, a condition for sex insisted on by the title character Erika Kohut (Isabelle Hubert), as well as the partially out-of-frame act of fellatio, plays with both spectators' and the male character's expectation of a climatic resolution to earlier sexual tension between the pair. Real sex lurks at the margins of the scene thematically and literally. This is in keeping with the film's focus on the lead character's pathologised confusion between sexual fantasy and reality (reiterating that outworn spectacle of the sexually repressed, hysterical woman that is given a more refreshing and reflexive treatment in *Romance*). Like *Last Tango* and *Intimacy*, the film addresses sex in a psychosexual context, and each centralises the failure of inter-personal communication. In *The Piano Teacher*, however, the failed communication involves a misunderstanding about the status of the central character's masochistic fantasies, which she and her pupil take in different ways all too literally.

A central contention of this chapter is that hard-core conventions provide a benchmark coding for 'real' sex in art cinema. Such films treat these conventions in self-reflective ways, however, to raise questions about the status of fantasy, spectacle and the real. The direct representation of real sex in *The Piano Teacher* comes not in the central character's performance, as it does in *Intimacy*, but through the inclusion of a short section of a hard-core video that Erika views in a porn shop. The video includes many of the audio-visual codes of authenticity that are regularly seen in such films. The graininess of the video image, the jerky camerawork and the close-up of a woman fellating a man – intensified by being blown up to fit the widescreen cinematic frame – are juxtaposed against the rich celluloid texture of the rest of the film. This may appear to make the video seem more 'real' in conventional audio-visual terms, but when viewed in the context of the diegetic real difficulties that Erika experiences in her own sexual encounters, it comes to represent something ideal, unattainable, enigmatic and very unreal. This is best illustrated by the fact that an attempt at fellatio, seen previously as the source of pleasure in the hard-core video, ends with Erika throwing up. Not what might be expected to happen in the choreographed, unimpeded ecstasies of hard core's pornotopian world.

The real of sex means, therefore, something very different in the diegesis of *The Piano Teacher*, as is also the case with *Romance* and *Intimacy*. The spectacle of hard core's unconditional 'real' sex that Erika views in the pay-per-view booth at the video shop is juxtaposed with the painful reality of Erika's fraught relationship with her pupil. The spectator is left with the question as to what exactly constitutes real sex: Erika's excruciating attempts to act out her masochistic fantasies, misunderstood by the object of her desire, or the pornutopian hard-core sex she sees in the booth. As in *Last Tango, Intimacy* and *Romance,* real sex between real people is a messy alienating business, worlds away from the formalised images of sexual ecstasy found in hard core. In *The Piano Teacher*, the inherent spectacle of hard-core sex is drained of its power to signify the real.

Following a path instituted by Max Ophüls in melodramas such *La Ronde* (1950 France) and *Letter From An Unknown Woman* (1948 US), recent 'sex'-focused art films such as *Intimacy, Romance, Eyes Wide Shut* (1999 US/UK) and *The Piano Teacher* are intently focused on the convoluted circuitry of sexual desire and the interlacing of performance, fantasy and the real. This provides a narrative context within which explicit imagery occurs, constituting an important modal difference from hard core and having a significant impact on the meaning of the spectacle of real sex. Sexual sensationalism is shifted into the melodramatic register of psychological conflict and tension. Hard core emphasises the physical mechanics and rhythms of sexual performance. Psychological dimensions are only present when they add something to the spectacular and sensational intent of representing 'real' sex (although psychological aspects are more common in softcore and the few examples of hard core that have 'artistic' pretensions). Unlike hard core, explicit art cinema is centred on complex characterisation, and in some senses this distinction reiterates well-established rhetorical differences between pornography and eroticism that have often been deployed to demarcate boundaries between legitimate and illegitimate texts (see Sontag 1982).

In different ways, the more recent examples frame sex in terms of established art values. The cinematic representation of real sex, it seems, is sanctioned only if certain signifiers of 'art' are present. The excision of the penetration scene in *Baise-moi* by British censors appears to be related to the fact that the film has far fewer conventional signifiers of 'art' than others of the current trend. Both *Intimacy* and *The Piano Teacher* make very direct appeals to 'art' within their storylines: drama in the former and classical music in the later. *The Piano Teacher* for example, sandwiches the hard-core film that Erika Kohut sees at a porn store between two pieces of high-brow classical music. The music that is part of Erika's mental furniture becomes temporarily masked out by the overwhelming effect of watching the video. A tension between high and low culture becomes apparent. The use of classical music contributes to the way the film constructs high-cultural context for the inclusion of low-culture hard core.

The presence of explicit imagery in these sex-based art films has a resonantly ambiguous – and therefore 'artful' – status; titillation is rendered more complex that it is in hard-core. Through the rhetorical frame of psychological realism, sex and desire becomes a source of dramatic and existential enigma. This reaches beyond the frame to the spectator, who is not left in the dark simply to enjoy at the level of spectacle and sensation. In hard core the presence of a diegetic spectator often works to make spectators more comfortable in their voyeurism, implying that they are not alone in their voyeuristic pleasure. This is not the case in recent art cinema films such as *Requiem for a Dream* (2000 US) and *The Piano Teacher*. In *Requiem*, Marion Silver (Jennifer Connelly) trades sex for heroin, culminating in a scene in which she has sex with another woman surrounded by well-dressed men. This is the type of scene that might be found in any number of hard-core movies, but here it is contextualised by binding the scene into the wider narrative arc that focuses on the effects of addiction. *Romance*, too, seeks to destabilise untroubled titillation through its focus on Marie's sexual experiences, from which she learns that 'you can't have a face when a cunt tags along'. The film stages graphically the Madonna/whore binary in one fantasy scene. A number of women lie on benches and are bisected by a barrier that prevents visual access from either side. On one side of the barrier – a clean, clinical-looking area – their faces are stroked by men; on the other – sleazy and dark – men fuck the women's lower halves. As with the decadent sex-party scene in *Eyes Wide Shut* (which would not look amiss in *The Story of O*), the scenario could be lifted from one of the more elaborate hard-core films. But, rather than being presented simply as erotic spectacles, both scenes invite the spectator to contemplate the muddled relationships between sex, desire and power. When we watch Erika watching the hard-core action, watch her delve into a bin to fish out and sniff 'used' tissues, we are not invited to immerse ourselves in the hard-core images. Their presence is fractured and interrupted by the protracted reaction shots and the narrative context. As explained above, within the frame of the narrative, *The Piano Teacher* positions hard-core sex as an unattainable manufactured fantasy. Unlike hard core, these films foreground the cultural construction of sex, desire and gender; their conflicts, contradictions and pressures. Images of real sex are intentionally titillating, yet spectators are also invited to consider the nature of such excitement, a claim to the type of artistic value also likely to placate censors.

Films such as *Intimacy, Romance* and *The Piano Teacher* invoke the immersive sensationalism of hard core; but, unlike hard core, these films frame 'real' sex in terms of issues such as identity politics, power, and the blurred relationships between reality and fantasy, the ideal and the actual. Often striking chords with the psychological realism of melodrama, which locates the physical within the psychical, these films contemplate the complexity of sex and sexual desire in a way that differs substantially from hard core. Rather than buying into overly simplified distinctions between authenticity and performance, it is the awkward slippage between the two that provides these films with their major thematic and philosophical focus. In framing sex this way, such films are sanctioned as more culturally and artfully valuable than the low culture bump-and-grind, one-purpose goal of hard core. They provide commentaries on the spectacle-based commodification of sexual performance in contemporary culture and, unlike exploitation and hard core, treat sex within the familiar and culturally established generic context of the well-made drama. What they also demonstrate is that established hierarchal regimes of 'good' taste are still in operation in the circuit between production and regulation.

References

Doherty, Thomas (1999) *Pre-Code Hollywood: Sex, Immorality and Insurrection in American Cinema 1930-1934*. New York: Columbia University Press.

Hunt, Leon (1998) *British Low Culture: from safari suits to sexploitation*. London and New York: Routledge.

Jacobs, Lea (1997) *The Wages of Sin: Censorship and the Fallen Woman Film, 1928-1942*. Berkeley, Los Angeles and London: University of California Press.

Kolker, Robert (2002) *Film, Form and Culture*. Boston and London: McGraw Hill.

Kuhn, Annette (1988) *Cinema, Censorship and Sexuality, 1909-1925*. London: Routledge.

Lacan, Jacques (1991) *Le Seminaire. Livre XVII. L'envres de la psychanalyse. 1969-1970*. Jacques-Alain Miller (ed.). Paris: Seuil.

Mellen, Joan (1974) *Women and their Sexuality in the New Film*. London: Davis-Poynter.

O'Toole, Laurence (1999 2nd edition) *Pornocopia: Porn, Sex Technology and Desire*. London: Serpent's Tail.

Schaefer, Eric (1999) *"Bold! Shocking! Daring! True!": A History of Exploitation Films, 1919-1959*. Durham and London: Duke University Press.

Sontag, Susan (1982) 'The Pornographic Imagination' in *A Susan Sontag Reader*. Harmondsworth: Pengiun.

Walsh, Frank (1996) *Sin and Censorship: The Catholic Church and the Motion Picture Industry*. New Haven and New York: Yale University Press.

Williams, Linda R. (2001) 'Sick Sisters' *Sight and Sound* July 2001.